THE WOLVES AT MY SHADOW

The Story of

INGELORE ROTHSCHILD

Our Lives: Diary, Memoir, and Letters

Social history contests the construction of the past as the story of elites—a grand narrative dedicated to the actions of those in power. Our Lives seeks instead to make available voices from the past that might otherwise remain unheard. By foregrounding the experience of ordinary individuals, the series aims to demonstrate that history is ultimately the story of our lives, lives constituted in part by our response to the issues and events of the era into which we are born. Many of the voices in the series thus speak in the context of political and social events of the sort about which historians have traditionally written. What they have to say fills in the details, creating a richly varied portrait that celebrates the concrete, allowing broader historical settings to emerge between the lines. The series invites materials that are engagingly written and that contribute in some way to our understanding of the relationship between the individual and the collective.

Series Titles

A Very Capable Life: The Autobiography of Zarah Petri
John Leigh Walters

Letters from the Lost: A Memoir of Discovery
Helen Waldstein Wilkes

A Woman of Valour: The Biography of Marie-Louise Bouchard Labelle
Claire Trépanier

Man Proposes, God Disposes: Recollections of a French Pioneer
Pierre Maturié, translated by Vivien Bosley

Xwelíqwiya: The Life of a Stó:lō Matriarch
Rena Point Bolton and Richard Daly

Mission Life in Cree-Ojibwe Country: Memories of a Mother and Son
Elizabeth Bingham Young and E. Ryerson Young,
edited and with introductions by Jennifer S.H. Brown

Rocks in the Water, Rocks in the Sun
Vilmond Joegodson Déralciné and Paul Jackson

The Teacher and the Superintendent: Native Schooling in the Alaskan Interior, 1904–1918
Compiled and annotated by George E. Boulter II and Barbara Grigor-Taylor

Leaving Iran: Between Migration and Exile
Farideh Goldin

My Decade at Old Sun, My Lifetime of Hell
Arthur Bear Chief

The Wolves at My Shadow: The Story of Ingelore Rothschild
Ingelore Rothschild, edited by Darilyn Stahl Listort and Dennis Listort

THE WOLVES AT MY SHADOW

The Story of
INGELORE ROTHSCHILD

edited by DARILYN STAHL LISTORT *and* DENNIS LISTORT

Published by AU Press, Athabasca University
1200, 10011 - 109 Street, Edmonton, AB T5J 3S8

ISBN 978-1-77199-061-5 (pbk.) ISBN 978-1-77199-063-9 (PDF)
ISBN 978-1-77199-064-6 (epub) DOI: 10.15215/aupress/9781771990615.01

Cover design by Natalie Olsen, kisscutdesign.com
Interior design by Sergiy Kozakov
Printed and bound in Canada by Marquis Book Printers

Library and Archives Canada Cataloguing in Publication

Rothschild, Ingelore, 1924-2006, author

The wolves at my shadow: the story of Ingelore Rothschild / Ingelore Rothschild; edited by Darilyn Stahl Listort and Dennis Listort.

(Our lives : diary, memoir, and letters)
Issued in print and electronic formats.

1. Rothschild, Ingelore, 1924-2006—Diaries. 2. Rothschild, Ingelore, 1924-2006—Childhood and youth. 3. Jews—Germany—Diaries. 4. Jews—Japan—Diaries. 5. Jews, German—Japan—Diaries. 6. Jewish refugees—Japan—Diaries. 7. Japan—History—Allied occupation, 1945-1952—Personal narratives, Jewish. 8. Holocaust, Jewish (1939-1945)—Biography. I. Listort, Darilyn Stahl, 1949-, editor II. Listort, Dennis, 1946-, editor III. Title.

DS134.42.R68A3 2017 943'.0049240092 C2017-900948-6
C2017-900949-4

The photograph in the background of the Part Two opening pages was taken by I. R. Tomaskiewicz and appeared in a 1899 publication under a Russian title that can be translated to *Great Path: Views of Siberia and Great Siberian Railway*.

Assistance provided by the Government of Alberta, Alberta Media Fund.

In loving memory of my mother.

I miss you.

~Dari

Acknowledgements

We extend our sincere thanks to all those who assisted. Readers and reviewers at various stages of the book's planning, development, transcription, research, and editing were of tremendous help to us. We appreciate the efforts of Linda Carlucci, Stephen Duffie, Allison Duffie, Teresa Listort, Cynthia Listort, and Ray Engineer. Additional support and guidance came from Tom DeAngelo, Therese Paff, Amiel Tokayer, M.D., Gail Campato, Mark and Louise Stahl, and Steven Silverman, M.D. Thank you to George Nicholson at Sterling Lord Literistic and to John Brenner at the State Historical Society of Missouri for their encouragement. We appreciate permission granted by Cole Smith from Atlantic Fleet Sales for the photograph of the Marine Falcon. The entirety of special regard, gratitude, and recognition is conveyed to Marjory Allen Perez, genealogist, for her painstaking and tireless labour.

To my sweet sister-in-law, Chery Duffie, who unexpectedly passed away at the age of fifty-eight, thank you for being our most passionate cheerleader.

At Athabasca University Press in Alberta, Canada, we thank Megan Hall and Karyn Wisselink for their editorial work. Also, we would like to extend our gratitude to Pamela Holway, senior editor at Athabasca University Press, for all her efforts, for believing in the manuscript from the first time she read it, and for her constant encouragement. We could not have done this without her.

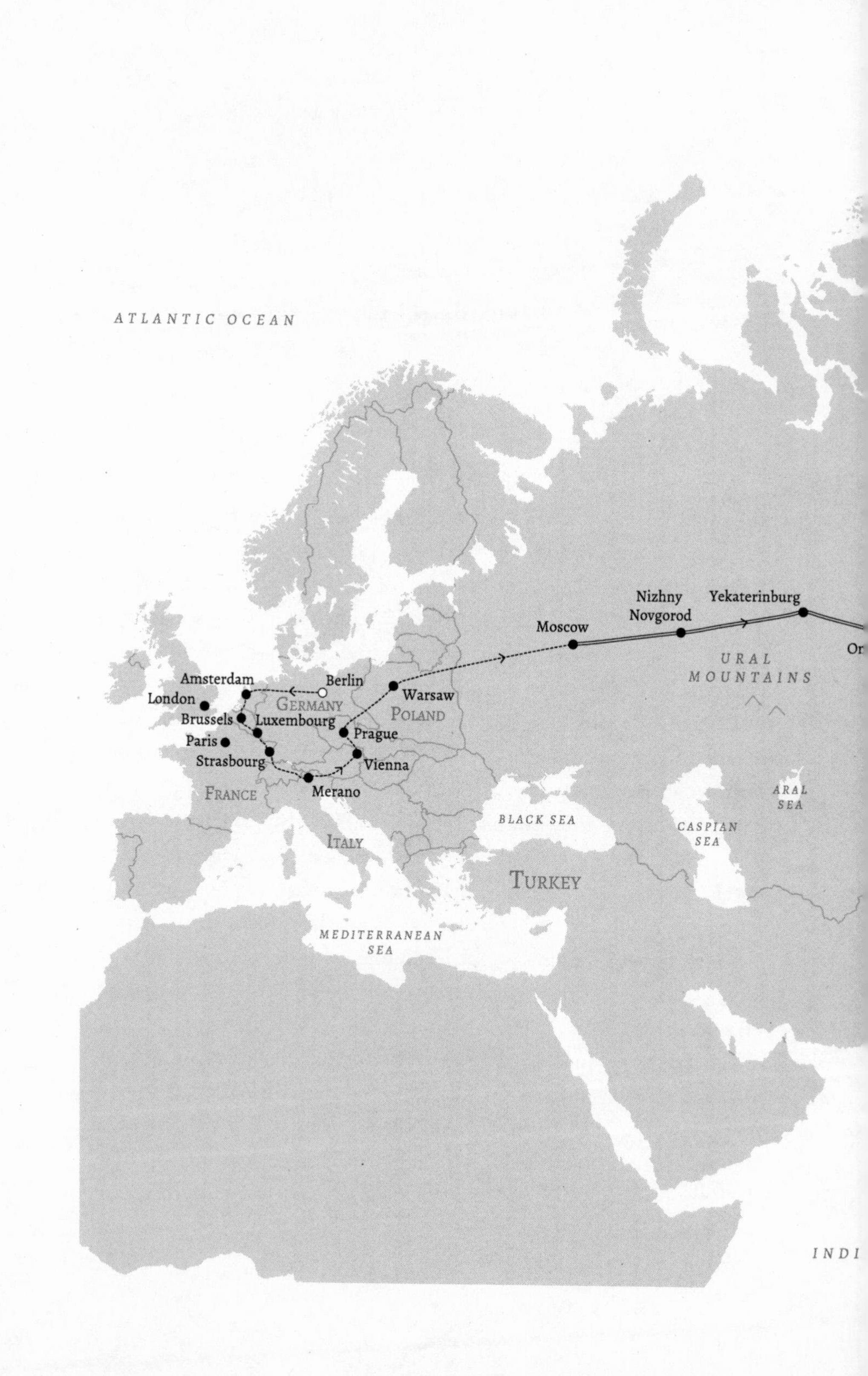
ATLANTIC OCEAN
Nizhny
Novgorod
Yekaterinburg
Moscow
Or
URAL
MOUNTAINS
Amsterdam
Berlin
London
Warsaw
Germany
Poland
Brussels
Luxembourg
Paris
Prague
Strasbourg
Vienna
Merano
France
Aral
Sea
Black Sea
Caspian
Sea
Italy
Turkey
Mediterranean
Sea
INDI

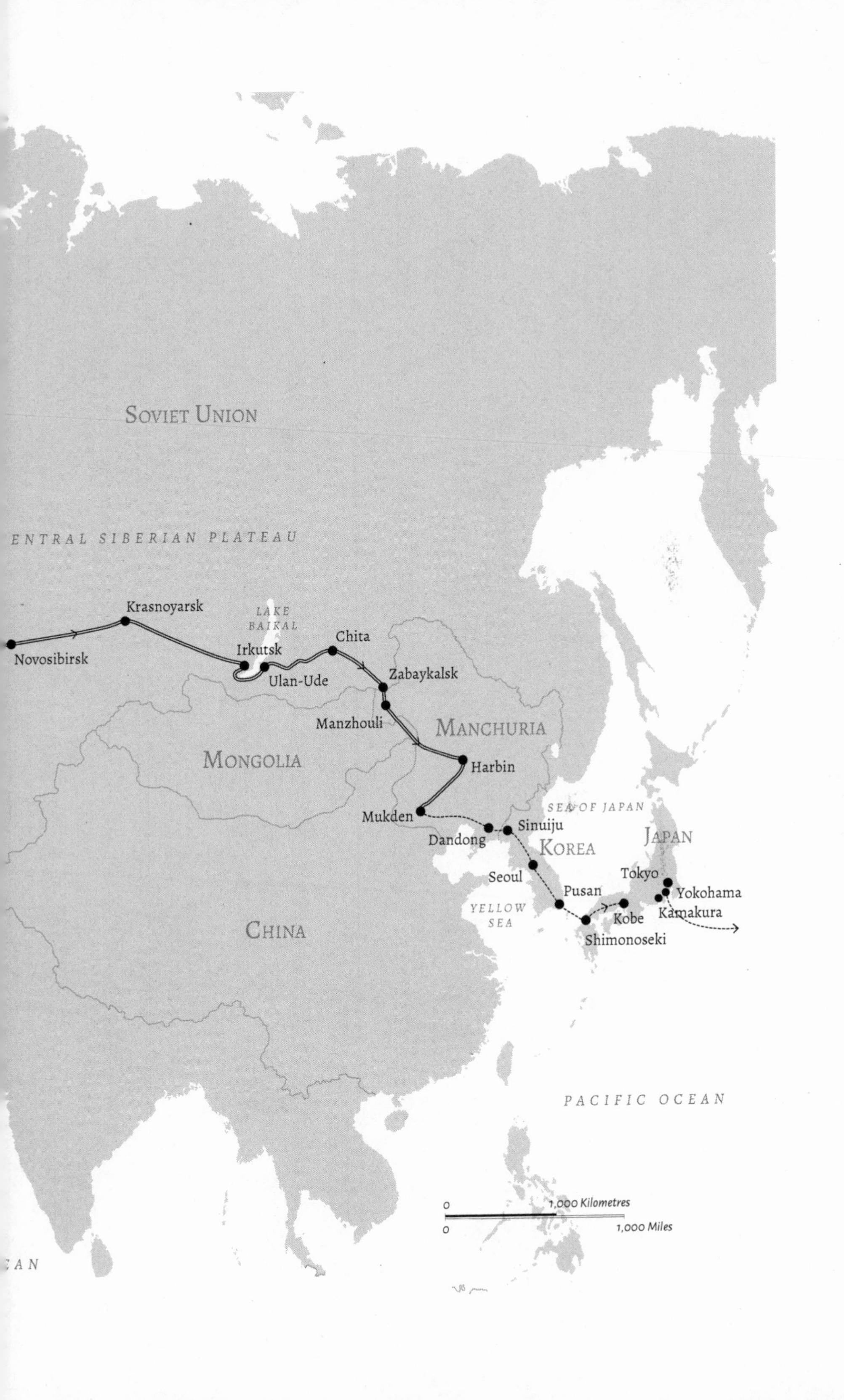

Soviet Union
ENTRAL SIBERIAN PLATEAU
Krasnoyarsk
Novosibirsk
LAKE
BAIKAL
Irkutsk
Ulan-Ude
Chita
Zabaykalsk
Manzhouli
Manchuria
Mongolia
Harbin
Mukden
Dandong
Sinuiju
SEA OF JAPAN
Korea
Japan
Seoul
Tokyo
Yokohama
Kamakura
Pusan
Kobe
Shimonoseki
YELLOW
SEA
China
PACIFIC OCEAN
0
1,000 Kilometres
0
1,000 Miles
AN

Contents

Part Three

Preface

On Monday, 8 June 1936, the day before her twelfth birthday, my mother, Ingelore Erna Rothschild, received a diary as a gift from her parents. They were in a café at an impromptu party in the Siberian city of Irkutsk in Eastern Russia. Over the next two years, my mother regularly recorded her memories and reminiscences of her remarkable journey from Berlin, Germany, across half the world to Kobe, Japan. In April 1938, during a severe rainy season, which caused one of the deadliest floods on record in Japan, a mudslide tore through Ingelore's family home in Kobe and destroyed her diary. Eight years later, while sailing from Japan to America she began to record her story once again, on a pad of paper given to her by her father.

In 1948, after settling in Queens, New York, Ingelore enrolled in a summer secretarial course. To practice her dexterity and her English she translated and transcribed all her handwritten recollections, typing them onto onionskin pages. Although her handwritten remembrances are lost, what remains are the dozens of memories she typed, single-spaced on the backs of scrap paper.

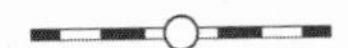

In 1999, my mother gave me a box. "Here," she said, "is a part of my life." It was not until years later, after her death in 2006, that I opened it. Inside were three hundred and forty-two unbound typewritten pages. I wish she had told me at the time that that box would reveal a fascinating, heartbreaking, and at times joyous and humourous story of her experiences and travels as a child and as a young woman. Had I known, I would have gathered those pages up immediately, carefully read every word, and then sat down with her to hear more of her story.

After her death, I pored over those delicate sheets. What I learned from those pages about the first quarter-century of her life is something I cherish. But I also feel a vague sense of nagging emptiness. I feel foolish that her account was there for the reading while she was still alive. Although I had missed her since the day she died these pages made me miss her even more.

My mother kept a fairly detailed record of her journey. Like many of her generation, those who lived through the Great Depression and World War II, she chose not to talk much about the times, strange places, and difficult learning experiences that, for better or worse, shaped her values and outlook. Through her writing, I was able to see her as a child blossoming into a young woman. I know so much more of my mother now. Suddenly I could picture my mother's father, Kurt Rothschild, my grandfather, a man who died the month after I was born. He had come to life for me and I sensed a bond with him in a deeply personal way.

My grandfather spent his entire adult life working for the J. Gerber Company. The company supplied textiles, raw materials, high quality processed fruits, vegetables and other foodstuffs, and ingredients for the food processing industry, as well as protective clothing and safety items for use in industrial environments to international markets, governments, institutions, and corporations. My grandfather served in many capacities at Gerber, as salesman, as an office manager, as company manager in Kobe, and as an assistant and resource person to several other management teams and personnel.

My earliest recollection of Doris Chasanowicz Rothschild, my grandmother, endearingly called "Omi," is of her holding me in her apartment in Queens, New York. She was often called upon to babysit me as a child and as a result I spent a good deal of quality time with her. Eventually, she moved to Jersey City, New Jersey where she died in 1982.

Using my mother's writings of her early years in Berlin as a point of reference, I understand now something of the time and place of her youth. During the 1920s, most German Jews were accepted as German citizens. At that time, Berlin's Jewish community was the largest in Germany—there were more than a dozen synagogues in the city. Even as late as 1933, German Jews were largely urban, professional, prosperous in business, and socially integrated. My grandfather, a respected businessman, and his family enjoyed both affluence and social standing. They often attended the philharmonic and the opera, and their home was filled with books, Oriental rugs, interesting curios, art, and strains of music. However, with Hitler's ascendency, my grandfather knew things would change rapidly. His first concern, of course, was for his wife and child, and he devoted himself to planning their escape to Japan.

After my husband, Dennis Listort, and I dusted off my mother's box of typewritten sheets and began raking through and then reading the pages haphazardly contained inside, we understood instinctively that Ingelore's story was remarkable. The flight from Nazi Germany, their journey through the Soviet Union and China to Japan as seen through the eyes of an exceptionally perceptive and thoughtful young girl was unique. We also realized that others would also find her story compelling.

We knew, of course, that Ingelore's native language was German, but we discovered that she had been tutored for several years in both French and English while still in Germany. During her decade in Japan, she was tutored again in English and she also learned Japanese. When she set down her memoir after arriving in America, she was enrolled in a secretarial course and so she typed her memories, translating them from German into English. In many places, however, it was obvious that English was not her first language. Sometimes the syntax of her sentences grew tangled, perhaps reflecting the sentence structure of her native tongue, and it became hard to sort out the meaning. We can only imagine how difficult it must have been for her to keep the grammar and vocabulary of four languages straight. In cases where clarity was compromised, we edited her original as we thought best and where revisions increased effectiveness or enhanced meaning we did only what was necessary.

Ingelore was reluctant to talk about her childhood. On occasion, and with gentle prodding, she would share some of her story, at times providing information that her journal did not. It is regrettable that she did not speak more often of her fascinating life. My grandmother however would sometimes relate bits and pieces of their lives over dinners and at family get-togethers. And, on at least two occasions, my great uncle, Sieke Chasanowicz, when visiting with my mother and our family in Ossining, New York, also spoke of those times. So as not to lose this oral history, we have incorporated their stories into Ingelore's written account, as my husband and I recollect them and in our own words. Thus, the story that follows is a blend of Ingelore's written account, her oral recollections, and those of her mother and her uncle.

Ingelore's writings also contained a number of vignettes that we felt would only be of interest to immediate family members and to those who knew Ingelore and my grandparents personally. Although to us these tales form an integral part of the intriguing embroidery of Ingelore's life, we chose not to include them because they strayed too far from the central line of her story: the trials and tribulations of the Rothschilds struggling to stay ahead of the Nazi wolves who were, for so long, at their shadow.

Part I of this book describes the hunt and the chase, as Ingelore and her parents flee the escalating Nazi juggernaut in Germany just prior to the outbreak of World War II. Part II contains her recollections of their journey of escape. Part III recounts the decade that Ingelore spent on the island of Honshu, from her arrival in 1936, through the war years, and during the occupation of Japan by Allied forces.

Every minute of organizing and editing my mother's journal has been an act of love. I consider her story a revelation, a discovery, and a legacy. I am very thankful it has survived, not only for me, but also for my grandson, Aidan Steinberg, my brother, my husband, and my children. Now they will have the same opportunity I did to learn more about her. It is my sincere hope that other readers will find in her story some measure of inspiration.

Darilyn Stahl Listort
Boynton Beach, Florida
February 2017

PART ONE

The *Marine Falcon* was a freighter ship with accommodations for 550 passengers.

We Sail to America

October 1946

I itch all over.

If it wasn't for Lena, the girl confined to the ship's infirmary in the bed next to mine, I do not know what I would do. Her mother, a fellow passenger on the *Marine Falcon*, has knitting as a hobby. Earlier, at my urging, Lena persuaded her to lend me a set of needles. When Dr. Hoke and Nurse Pat aren't watching, I slide them down as far as I can between my skin and the plaster cast that girdles my midsection from the top of my rib cage to my tailbone to scratch the most persistent itch. But it provides only momentary relief.

My father is at my bedside. "Here, darling, the pad I promised you." I flip through it. Each sheet is unlined and without margins. "It's just like the diary we gave you for your twelfth birthday. You wrote in it almost every day." That diary, full of my writings, had been ruined in a mudslide that nearly destroyed our home in Japan. "It's time to start writing again," father says. "You've a fascinating story to tell."

"I'm not so sure I do," I say.

He smiles. "Nonsense! Think about it! You lived in Berlin for twelve years. You travelled through, how many were there, thirteen, fourteen countries? You lived in Japan for a decade. Now, you're on your way to America! Who can say they've experienced what you have in their first twenty-two years?"

Lena looks at me. "Is all that true?"

"Yes," I moan. "I'll think about it," I tell my father.

"We won't arrive in Seattle for another week. You're bedridden. What else is there for you to do while you wait?" he teased.

As usual he's right.

And so, I write. Each page is blank, no boundaries or constraints. I decide to write whatever is of interest that I can recall. Some memories are clear and precise. Others are like objects in the fading light of dusk, certainly there, but indistinct and out of focus. I'll do my best to tell the story as it occurred, giving names and places when I'm sure of them. I may wander in and out of time and place, and if I do, then I'll go back at a later date to remedy what I can.

This is what I remember.

I Begin

I was born on 9 June 1924, and the story of my birth has been a subject of conversation on all my birthdays since. Usually, the story is recited just before I open gifts, cut a cake, or slather butter on a pastry. Even now, after almost a quarter of a century, my parents still find the account endearing. Throughout the years, both family and friends at my birthday parties in Germany and at several of my galas in Japan have regarded it as amusing, while I consider it an irksome yet necessary anecdote. The retelling of the events of that day commemorate what my parents have sworn to me and to all others to be the moment of their greatest joy.

For me, it's unnecessary, almost jejune. I always feel a sense of embarrassment when my father begins.

"At dawn, there was a slight mist of rain which quickly gave way to sunshine," he says. "Soon after we had risen from bed, mother and I began to prepare a small meal."

"My term was uneventful, almost routine, with only slight discomfort during the third and fourth months," my mother interjects. Then, impatiently, "But by that first week of June, all I wanted was for my baby to be out of me!"

Here, the audience always laughs.

"Was the birth straightforward?" someone invariably asks.

Ingelore and her father at Tiergarten Park, circa 1926.

Predictably, my father stands at this juncture, comes to where I am seated, positions himself behind me, and places his hands on my shoulders.

"If it wasn't for the trolley, this birthday would've been in July!"

There are more hysterics since everyone knows what's coming.

"After our meal," my father relates, "*mein Liebste* and I went outside. I thought we'd walk about the street in the bright, warm sunshine. But she wanted to ride the trolley!"

At this point, the audience is convulsed with laughter. My friends are bored and impatiently waiting to eat!

My mother says, "I wanted my baby out of me! I thought if I moved a little bit–"

Father interrupts, "Move? A little, you say? First it was hopping up to enter the car! Then you wouldn't sit! Then the hopping on one foot, then the other, back and forth, all the while as the trolley jolted along!"

"I thought it might begin the process," mother continues. "And then, not long after we returned home, the pains began. Quickly, our little *Schmetterling* arrived to our shouts of joy and thankfulness."

A short while after my birth, my father gently examined me to make sure I had ten fingers and ten toes and then he swaddled me securely. He caressed me and then placed me at my mother's breast, my voyage just begun.

I have often looked back on our long and frightful journey away from the fascism that engulfed half the world and have contemplated my mother's need to ride that trolley that day. My father and I joining her on the trolley's route–an eerie foreshadowing of our harrowing flight and the subsequent fear of pursuit which tormented us for so long.

I know I was born in Charlottenburg, a middle-class *Bezirk* west of Berlin proper. My parents spoke of the suburb in nostalgic terms describing its broad avenues, the majestic steeples and spires of its synagogues and churches, the trolleys that lumbered along wide, clean streets, its theatres and cafés, the breathtaking architecture of the area, and its well-kept storefronts and modest apartment houses. When I was two years old we moved from there to Wilmersdorf, another *Bezirk* of Berlin that I believe was slightly southwest of Charlottenburg. Sadly, my first home has disappeared totally from my memory. Although it must have been near Tiergarten Park because my father would reminisce about long tranquil days when he would take his infant daughter on leisurely outings through the lush greenery there.

I remember nothing about the move or the old place but our enormous apartment in a brand new building in Wilmersdorf is still clear and distinct to me. Even now, after more than a decade, it is as though we had just moved out yesterday.

My room was the first one off the large foyer. It was light and airy and filled with all those things little girls cherish including a large metal cage with my lovely canary, Hansi, who sang all day long.

There were shelves and wooden chests that held a myriad of books and toys. I was fortunate because my mother's older brother, my Uncle Sieke,[1] travelled to the Leipzig Toy Fair four times a year. Since I was his only niece, Sieke would secretly fill my room with the latest playthings upon his return so that when I awoke in the morning or came home from school in the afternoon I was witness to his clandestine magic. This always prompted me to fantasize that I was a revered monarch in a wondrous fairyland realm. There were dolls that cried, ornate carriages fit for princesses, wooden blocks, stacks of books and colouring pencils, an easel and paints, marionettes, stuffed animals, music boxes, and so on. How I loved my Uncle Sieke! My beloved Gerta's room was also nearby. Gerta Klaus was our housekeeper and cook and for many years my nursemaid and best friend.

A few steps away from my bedroom, on the same side, was the entrance to the library, my favourite place in the apartment. Next came the dining room and the kitchen across the hall. Next to the dining room was the living room of which I remember little, and finally, what felt like miles

---

1 Siegbert "Sieke" Chasanowicz owned and operated a key and lock factory in Berlin. As mechanical toys became more popular, his business expanded to include the manufacture of spring mechanisms and gears for playthings that required them, in addition to hinges and clasps for boxes and containers.

away, was my parents' bedroom which was restricted to me until I was much older.

It was in the great distance between their room and mine that lay my terror.

On one of the first nights in that house I had a nightmare, one that came back to me again and again and terrified me for much of my youth. A nightmare that I can still recall in all its gory detail, *mein böser Traum.*

I dream of being nestled under a cozy blanket in the library late at night as I thumb through an atlas by candlelight. While my parents sleep in their bedroom, I imagine travelling to cities near and storied places far away.

Suddenly, a knocking summons me to the front door. I tiptoe there. Eagerly, I reach for the handle but, remembering the cautions my parents drummed into me, I first peek through the keyhole.

There, to my horror, stands an old man draped in tattered, mud-stained clothes. He leans on a cane, his right leg is missing below the knee. One eye is bright with fire, yet cold, a muddy steel blue. His other eye is sutured shut. His long white beard is dripping with blood.

"Go away!" I shout. "I won't open the door!"

"Open up, little girl," he barks in a breathy baritone as he continues knocking on the door.

"No! I won't! My father wouldn't want me to let you in."

"If you don't open the door immediately, I'll come through it!"

I tremble with fear while hastily checking the bolt to make certain it is latched securely.

He is screaming at me. "This is your last chance! If you don't open the door at once, I'll break it down!"

Through the keyhole I can see that the man is vapourizing into swirls of angry black smoke. In a moment the sinister cloud drifts through the keyhole, entering my home. The cloud quickly gathers and returns to its grotesque physical form and the ogre stands in front of me laughing hideously, the drool from his distended mouth oozing onto his bloodied beard. He reaches out and tries to touch me. Screaming, I run toward my parents' bedroom. I hear his heavy footsteps and the hollow sound of his cane slamming onto the floor as he follows me down the hall. Thrump! Smack! Thrump! Smack! He's chasing me, coming closer and closer!

I burst into my parents' bedroom. Reaching the foot of their bed, I'm horrified to find the bedclothes undisturbed, my parents absent. The monster is now behind me ready to capture me, his palms opened wide, his gnarled fingers outstretched. He's reaching to grab me! I see a raging inferno in his eye!

Closer! He's no more than an arm's length from me now!

Invariably that's when I wake, breathing rapidly, sweating fulsomely, my heart fluttering faster than all the wings of a flock of birds frightened by a skulk of foxes.

Although I dreamt it often during my adolescence, sometimes with eerie variations, my nightmare didn't interfere with the rest of my life other than as a recurring premonition. I understand it now as a wretched metaphor for the chase and the hunt, the fear and the panic, and the agony and the dread of all that was soon to follow.

Throughout my younger years, my father was warm and gentle, though firm, with an iron will. A tall and distinguished man with long legs, a trim waist, muscular thighs, chest, and arms, and pencil-thin fingers. With a nearly square chin, pronounced cheekbones, full, dark hair and deep-set eyes the colour of amethysts, I imagine him as a famous motion picture actor—a handsome leading man of ultimate refinement and gallantry capable of saving all damsels in distress.

How I wished he could have saved me from my nightmare!

All who knew my mother considered her a saint. She rarely denied me or anyone else anything. A kind and giving person with ready praise for everyone, she was incapable of a mean word or petty thought. I admired her radiant beauty: her pleasant eastern European facial features, her loving smile, and her snow-white teeth. As with the eyes of a lynx, her amber irises glowed both in sunlight and in darkness. The crown of her head was a majestic field of windswept hair, the colour of autumn wheat, waves of undulating curls and ringlets. She always smelled as fresh as wildflowers in a meadow. My friends often told me my mother was beautiful. They noticed her bearing, the way she carried herself with

Kurt and Doris with Ingelore in their home in Wilmersdorf, circa 1927.

poise and grace, and her innate glow of understated comeliness. That made me proud. I felt so special to be her daughter.

Even as a child it wasn't difficult to see that my parents were best friends. After all, it was the two of them at the helm of the family, with their two subordinates, Gerta and me. Gerta was my parents' respected assistant and she was in control some of the time. I, on the other hand, was an inquisitive and well-mannered child bursting at the seams to be grown up. Gerta and I would sometimes battle for the upper hand, both reaching for a position in the upper ranks of the household.

I could see then, as I do now, how Paps and Mutsch managed a magical relationship. My parents are more than friends. There's something between them that has endured ever since I came to understand what it is when two people are deeply in love.

When we lived in Germany, there were many times when Paps returned from work with armloads of fresh-cut flowers for Mutsch. On other occasions he brought her chocolates, sometimes a curio or a culinary treat, perhaps a fountain pen from a local shop or a torte from a café. When business permitted he would shower Mutsch with magnificent pieces of jewellery. She still wears an immense diamond ring that sparkles like fire. Over the years he's picked out necklaces, most with matching earrings, watches, gem-filled brooches and pins, and silver and gold bracelets and rings.

I recall Mutsch's wondrous wardrobe of silks and wools, cashmere and linen, her fur coats, sateen shawls, and all her beautiful shoes of various colours and styles. All these gifts from Paps were not meant to placate but were given out of love and adoration with a genuine selflessness. I know this because I don't recall my father ever coming home with anything for himself. To be fair, Mutsch often would counter and present him with a box of the cigars he enjoyed so much. I, too, sometimes showered him with collections of my exquisite artwork or I'd present to him a short play or recital.

There were times of silliness between them. They secretly, or so they thought, called each other by pet names. I overheard them whispering darling and sweetie or endearing phrases such as *mein Retter in der Not* and *meine schöne Kürbis*.[2] I understand now that there's something to be said for such frivolity.

Wednesday nights were often festive for them. After an early dinner Paps would escort Mutsch to a theatre, walk with her through the streets of Wilmersdorf to see the shops or attend an opera, visit a museum, or go to a café just for tea. I never minded. I loved seeing them so happy, preparing for their night out. It also meant that I remained behind with Gerta and she and I would do whatever we wanted.

I can see in my mind's eye evenings at the supper table when Paps would begin with a prayer for continued sustenance and freedom from oppression. Then he would relate his business issues and concerns. He valued Mutsch's opinion and he would often seek her insights on business matters. He understood that she was an intelligent woman who often saw things in different, unexpected, and intriguing ways.

My parents had many shared interests. They were excellent bridge players, they could communicate without words, an extension of the understanding they shared. They had the same taste in music, literature, and art. Usually, both of them were amused by the same witticisms.

I have always felt that a certain fable of love from Greek mythology bore a strong resemblance to the love between my parents. In the fable, a loving couple is rewarded by the gods for their generosity, piety, and for their adoration of one another. When asked what they would treasure in return, the couple tells the gods that they would prefer to die at the same instant—to spare the other any suffering or grief. I imagined Paps and Mutsch feeling the same way.[3]

I remember Mutsch reaching out to touch Paps' arm no matter where they were or who was present at the time. It seems they were always connected that way. She would rest her palm on the top of his wrist, lacing her fingers there, gliding her thumb back and forth on his lower

2 "My knight in shining armour" and "my lovely pumpkin."

3 *Baucis and Philemon* is the tale of an elderly couple. According to Greek mythology, Zeus granted the couple their wish to die at the same time and he transformed them into a pair of intertwining trees, one oak and one linden.

arm. When Paps suffered one of his severe headaches she would not let go of him. It was her way of showing her deep and abiding love for him.

In return, Paps would often lean down to tenderly kiss her brow.

The Calm Before the Storm

As a little girl I considered the library a sanctuary for enjoyment and learning. Every Saturday afternoon after Paps returned from work, he would present gifts to my mother and me, a bunch of flowers for Mustch and a pineapple or a coconut for me—both rare in Germany in those days. Then, he and I would rush to the library to spend the rest of the afternoon there. The panelled walls were lined on three sides with books, mostly classics in German, French, and English. Some volumes were leather bound, their titles embossed on the cover in gold. There were books of poetry, history, science, art, philosophy, and biography. Who could ever read all of them I often wondered!

Spaces on the shelves were filled with Meissen porcelain figurines and crystal vases as well as hand-carved wooden sculptures from Africa brought to us from the Congo by my Uncle Hans.[4] Two large couches in soft velvet, several deeply cushioned armchairs, Paps' enormous wooden desk, a few straight-back chairs, and a coffee table completed the furniture. Underfoot, oriental carpets in patterns of blue, red, and beige lay over the polished parquet flooring. Bunches of lilacs, tulips, chrysanthemums, and other varieties of seasonal flowers stood in vases. But the

4 Hans Rothschild, Kurt's brother, worked for the J. Gerber Company based in Cape Town, South Africa. His travels from there to Berlin and back necessitated stops in the Congo and in other African countries as well.

highlight of our Saturday afternoons together was when Paps would play with me or read to me.

"What would you like to do, *Lorechen*?[5] Whatever you say, that's what we'll do."

Usually I wanted Paps to read to me. We would cuddle in one of the chairs and begin with Schiller's *Der Erlkönig* as it was my favourite. I would ask him to read it over and over again even though it never failed to frighten me.[6] I felt safe on his lap, his strong arms around me, but I still shivered with apprehension every time he read that story.

Sometimes I wanted him to recite poetry, other times I asked for the fascinating Greek myths of gods and mortals, the enchanting Arthurian legends, or a Shakespearean play with Paps speaking the different parts in different voices. Fairy tales and children's stories I saved for Mutsch to read to me. Other times we would play games, such as checkers and chess.

Best of all were the late autumn afternoons when the sun set early. The whole room glowed red, purple, and mauve as the sun's rays crept back along the carpets. Then Paps would sing our favourite tune, *Guten Abend, gute Nacht,* in his mellow tenor voice as we stood in front of the window watching the sun go down.

During one of those afternoons a thunderstorm developed quickly. The morning had been dark. And the wind had gradually picked up. Bolts of lightning zigzagged across the black sky and roars of thunder bellowed from the firmament. Like galloping horses, the clouds feverishly charged by. As we watched in awe, sheets of rain crashed into the windowpanes.

"Amazing, isn't it?" Paps mused. "It's nature's show of unforgiving force. Nothing man can create will ever be as potent or as sinister."

---

5 *Lorechen* means *little Ingelore*. It also may be a synthesis of the last syllable of *Ingelore* and the last syllable of *Mädchen*, the German word for girl.

6 Ingelore's recall here is faulty. The poem she mentions is by Goethe, not Schiller. For most young children, *Der Erlkönig* (*The Elf King*, or sometimes *The Alder King*) is a terrifying tale of a fantastical apparition trying to lure a young boy from his father's embrace as they ride home on horseback in storm and in darkness. When they do arrive, the boy is dead in his father's arms.

"Really, Paps?" I asked, attempting to hide my fearfulness.

"Yes, nothing ever will compare."

A few years later I realized that was one of the few times when my father was wrong. How unaware we were then! How did we not see the parallels? Yet, how could we have known? Like a freight train hurtling across the country at full-speed, the National Socialist German Workers' Party was stampeding through Germany, gaining supporters and converts and becoming more powerful and influential by the day.[7]

A human storm of unimaginable might and terror was brewing.

It was in our cherished library in the year 1928 or 1929 that my father sat me down, gathered his breath, and explained how the terror, later to be called the Holocaust, began. "As it is with many things, the actions of the few profoundly influence the lives of the many. This is true both of virtue and of evil."

"You'll tell me of the genesis?" I asked.

He snapped. "Don't use that word! This evil can't be chronicled with words from Scripture! It's better to . . ." he thought for a moment, ". . . to say pestilence."

"Yes, father."

"Remember there's so much good in people. Think of the battlefield medics and nurses who tended to the legions of wounded during the Great War. Their courageous actions affected scores of people."

Then he became visibly shaken. "I'm grateful for the numbers of caring, civil and righteous people, those who've helped us and who've concealed us from the Nazi wolves whose prey will surely total thousands, perhaps tens of thousands. And I fear this is only the beginning! We must also

7 The Nazi party or *Nationalsozialistische Deutsche Arbeiterpartei* (NSDAP) had only 17,000 members in 1926, but by March 1930 membership had grown to 210,000 (Friedrich, 355). Their legislative membership had also increased from 12 members in 1928 to 107 in 1930 (Vogt, 94).

acknowledge the prayers and consolation offered by rabbis and priests to the multitudes of grieving families. In those ways," he whispered, "the good of the few eases the sorrow of the many."

He was quiet. "It was about eight months after you were born. It was cold outside. On my way home from work I stopped to rest at a street corner. On the curb was a pile of newspapers just for the taking. They were issues of the *Völkischer Beobachter*, the newspaper of the Nazi Party. Stacks of them were everywhere in Berlin. I read it to keep abreast of the events of the day. The featured article that day concerned a rally to be held in Munich. I understand now that few realized, save perhaps the dozen or so founders themselves, that the meeting would mark the onset of the plague that would ravage most of Europe.[8] It was then that the political, social, religious, and racial contagion commenced."

Against these insidious developments just outside our door, there were also times of calm and cheerful expectation. Birthday celebrations have always been important to us and my father's birthday on the twenty-fifth of May was always a happy day.

I remember as a young child drawing pictures with my colouring pencils and struggling even with Mutsch's help to write a birthday message of *Alles Gute zum Geburtstag* in script on a piece of tag board. My poster looked wonderful to me but Mutsch said to do it again to make it more presentable for Paps. And so I did, dozens of times.

I remember that in the weeks prior to my father's birthdays, Mutsch and I would sometimes reserve one or two days to shop for gifts. We would pick a book or two and one time we chose a piece of sculpture for Paps' desk.

All during these preparatory phases Mutsch would swear me to secrecy. I would be bursting to tell Paps every time we sat for supper or cuddled in the library. To keep silent was the hardest thing for me!

After all these years I still can smell the sweet aroma of the *Bienenstock* cake baking in the oven on my father's birthday and the culinary perfume

8 On 27 February 1925, a rally was held in Munich to mark the occasion of the re-founding of the Nazi Party. Over 5,000 people attended (Benz, *A Concise History of the Third Reich*, 15–16).

of *sauerbraten* cooking on the stove wafting all around. Mutsch would prepare green beans and spaetzle along with trays of cheeses and garden vegetables. I would present rafts of Roggenbrot, delicious rye bread, and butter to the table. Under Mutsch's direction Gerta arranged crystal wine glasses for the adults.

Soon, Omi and Opa, Uncle Alfred and Aunt Hilde with their daughter, my little cousin Gert, Uncle Hans and Aunt Lotte, my other Uncle Hans and his wife, Aunt Evchen, or, as we always call her, Eva, and Aunt Jenny, Paps' oldest sibling, all arrived to wish him happy birthday, spend time with him, and celebrate the precious gift of family.[9]

On his fortieth birthday, I saw Paps, who was standing by the window talking with Omi and Gerta, lose his balance as he drank from his glass. Omi reached to steady him. The wine splashed onto his shirt cuff and the glass nearly fell from his hand. Uncle Alfred saw this and went to Paps. Gerta ran to the kitchen to get some cloths and cleanser.

"I'm fine. I just feel a little dizzy. I think a headache is on its way. Don't worry. I'm fine."

And so, we lolled about gabbing while Aunt Jenny finished setting the dessert plates as Mutsch readied to bring the *Bienenstock* to the table. Paps was already sitting down, his elbows on the table edge, his forehead resting in the cup of his palm. Suddenly, he sat up straight, thanked everyone for celebrating his day, and proceeded to cut the cake. What a happy day that was!

None of us knew at the time that Paps was already suffering from debilitating headaches and that he would continue to suffer from them for many years to come. Had we known perhaps something could have been done for him.

9 *Omi* and *Opa* refer to Ingelore's paternal grandmother and grandfather, Hedwig and Leopold Rothschild. Alfred and (the first-mentioned) Uncle Hans are Kurt's brothers. The second "Uncle" Hans, and his wife, "Aunt" Evchen (the Mendelsohns) were long-time family friends of Ingelore's parents, but not blood relatives.

Deception and Dismay

1929

One day early in November of 1929, Gerta and I were playing on the sidewalk in front of my house. Gerta was looking after me because Mutsch had gone to the grocery store. We decided to walk up the street to look at the stately trees. Gerta reviewed them with me: some oaks, a maple, a chestnut, and two magnificent lindens with intricate webs of branches.

At one point Gerta stopped to look at a poster tacked to the trunk of one of the linden trees.

"What's that?" I asked her.

She explained to me that it was a notification for a rally held in Nuremburg several months before. She told me that she'd heard gossip and rumours about it and that most of her family and friends had considered the rally an omen of a strange villainy looming.

On the poster I saw a black cross emblem in a circle of white which for some reason I perceived as a bird with broken wings struggling to fly. It was the first time I had come to recognize the *Hakenkreuz*, the swastika. The symbol appeared to be moving, rotating slowly near the top border.

I saw the words "Freedom and Bread!" and "Our Fateful Hour!" At once the poster frightened me.

Gerta assured me. "Don't worry, the meeting was quite a distance from Berlin and from us, far beyond the shadows of these trees."[10]

I would often stare at Gerta. She was in her late teens then, tall, blonde, with enormous green eyes, exquisitely beautiful. Her father, a German Army officer, had died in Belgium during the Great War. She lived several kilometres from us. To earn money for her mother and her two younger siblings she came to us as a housekeeper shortly after I was born. Paps worked long hours and was away often on business and Mutsch needed a helping hand to maintain our home and to assist with my care. Gerta arrived late on Sunday night and stayed with us until late Friday afternoon at which time she returned to her mother and brothers for the weekend. Paps paid her well and she earned every *pfennig* since our home was large and needed a great deal of attention.

And, I'm told I was quite a handful.

We'd been playing for an hour or so oblivious to passersby while we sat and chatted, about nothing really, just silly things, enjoying the crisp air and sunshine.

Suddenly I noticed surprise in Gerta's eyes. I turned to follow her line of sight. A short and overweight man was standing near us. His thin-framed spectacles rested on the tip of his stubby nose, enlarging his beady eyes. Well dressed with shiny shoes, he appeared to be a professional, maybe a doctor or a banker.

He spoke to Gerta in a gruff voice.

"Are you Fraülein Rothschild?"

Gerta looked afraid. "No, I'm not. Who are you? Why do you ask?"

He turned to me.

---

10 Presumably, the poster that Gerta saw was for the rally of 2 August 1929, when factions of the Nazi Party gathered in Nuremberg for what was called the "Day of Composure." Events like the rallies held in Nuremberg eventually moved to Berlin as well. Spectacles such as these allowed the Nazi Party to show the German populace its power and influence and to declare the inevitability of Hitler's rise to power (Burden, *The Nuremberg Party Rallies*, 49).

"And you?"

"My name is Ingelore."

As he reached into his pocket, Gerta edged closer, putting her arm around me. She barked at him, "Go away. We're not interested in anything. Leave us alone."

From inside his suit he retrieved a paper, its folded edge secured with a wax seal. He extended it to me.

"I'm Wilhelm Bayern. Herr Rothschild and I have been in touch over the past few days." He cleared his throat with a raspy gurgle and then pointing to the paper he said, "It's imperative your father receive this."

He shook the paper in front of my face making sure I focused on it. "This is very important. See to it that he is given this document as soon as possible. Do you understand?"

Gerta snatched it from his hand. "I am the housekeeper. I'll see that Herr Rothschild receives this."

With that, Herr Bayern tipped his bowler and hastily waddled down the street.

"Can we open it?" I asked.

Gerta snapped, "No, of course not. This isn't for you, nor is it for me. It's for your father."

She dragged me into the house. Inside, she ordered me to the kitchen table. She placed the sealed paper on the countertop. She looked nervous, pacing back and forth, wringing her hands. Worry draped her face like a leaden veil.

"What's wrong?" I asked her.

"Be quiet!" she growled. "It's not your concern. Go to the library. Use your easel. Draw for me."

Quickly, I went to the library. I busied myself with colouring pencils trying to make pleasant pictures for Gerta.

Not long after Mutsch came home. She walked past the library without looking in and then went into the kitchen. As she was putting the shopping bags down on the table I heard her ask Gerta about me.

Gerta spoke so softly I couldn't hear her words. I remained motionless and I began to wonder if the incident with Herr Bayern had something to do with me. I was searching my memory for any misdeed or misconduct I may have committed. What was in the document for Paps? Was it a report of my misbehaviour? What had I done? What had I failed to do?

Mutsch and Gerta continued whispering. There was anxiety in my mother's voice and I was scared witless when she became short of breath. I heard her gasp, "Is it an eviction notice?"

I didn't know what eviction meant.

Soon, Gerta went to her room. Mutsch unpacked her bags and placed the items in the cupboard.

Doom huddled around me. I knew father would be home soon.

I don't know how long it was before I heard Paps come in the door. I looked at my easel. I'd completed dozens of drawings for Gerta. Now I waited. I felt an anguished despondency for whatever wrongdoings I had committed.

Paps and Mutsch whispered to each other for a few moments and then I heard Mutsch say, "If it is, then what are we to do?"

Paps was not upset. In a calm but stern voice, he said, "It's not a question of heritage or honour. It's a question of survival."

I didn't wait any longer. I ran into the kitchen pleading. "I'm sorry! I don't know what I did but I am truly sorry! Whatever the paper says, I'm sorry!"

Paps reached down, grabbed me, and lifted me high into the air. He burrowed his nose into my stomach making me laugh uncontrollably.

"No, Lorechen! It's not you! Did Herr Bayern frighten you today? No, it's all right. He's our friend. Don't worry. Everything will be fine."

Mutsch went to the cupboard. She handed me a few *pfeffernüsse*, a luscious nut-filled cinnamon cookie that Gerta made.

My dread had passed. I was relieved. I no longer felt guilt and shame.

Paps continued to hold me. "How would you like to play a game, Lorechen?"

"Yes!" I beamed. "What kind of game?"

"It's a name game. We'll play it only when people we don't know come to the house." This sounded so mysterious to me! I wanted to play so badly!

Paps explained, "When a stranger asks we'll tell them our surname is Völker and we'll use the given names of our ancestors, too! I'll be Leopold Völker, named for my father, Mutsch will be Ernestine Völker, named for her mother, and you, my angel, will be special. You will use your middle name Erna, to be Erna Völker. It's like a trick. We'll pretend we're someone else. Won't that be fun?"

"Yes! We're all Völker!" I thought for a moment. "Will Gerta be Völker, too?"

"No dear, Gerta will be who she is. She needn't play the game, do you understand?"

Years later I learned that the purpose of Herr Bayern's visit that day was to let father know he had officially changed our names on our apartment's lease. He had conferred with Paps on several occasions, warning him of the rising Nazi influence. "The black horde is defiantly and overtly anti-Semitic," he explained.

A full-blooded German and a Christian, Herr Bayern sympathized with us because his younger brother had married a Jew. He destroyed the original lease and created a new one, delivering a copy to us and a copy to the Records Hall so that in the event of law enforcement inquiries or a governmental review of real estate records we wouldn't attract attention. It'd be dangerous going about with the surname Rothschild. That day, I pledged I'd be ready to play Paps' game whenever necessary. Later, at one time or another, all of us needed to so that our true identity wouldn't betray us. For years I was frightened even to say the name Rothschild.

The night after Herr Bayern's visit, I woke in darkness. I could hear foggy voices coming from my parents' bedroom. I recognized Paps' voice, then Mutsch's, and I thought I heard Uncle Sieke's voice too. But there was also a fourth voice, a man's, one I didn't recognize. It was nasally and scratchy. Whoever this man was he was rude. He didn't stop talking when Paps was speaking. He spoke over my mother's words, too.

Hoping to hear better, I sat up. At the foot of my bed was a pinwheel and a package laced with ribbons. It must be Uncle Sieke! He always brings me toys! I was about to open it when instead I got up and tiptoed into the hallway gradually making my way to a corner in the kitchen. I could hear the conversation clearly now.

"It continues to be bad, Sieke," my father said. "Unemployment will worsen. Many of the factories are already closed. Farmers are unable to make a living in spite of their hard work. The people have nothing and now they'll have less!" He implored, "Even in America, they're drowning in destitution! Everyone wants for bread!"[11]

Sieke said, "It all stems from the Treaty. No wonder the Nazi ranks are swelling. It's the martyrdom they play on, revenge for the economic edicts from Versailles against our people." He went on trying to reassure them, "But we'll be all right. My business has been good even through these hard times. Kurt, you continue to do well. If not, then I'll help you all I can."

"I'll do my part as well," Mutsch added, "in regard to our expenses. We'll tighten our belts just in case."

I feared this meant Gerta would be dismissed. I was being selfish but I couldn't help it. I loved Gerta as a sister. A part of my heart and a part of my life would be missing without her.

The man's voice, which I still didn't recognize, kept on speaking without regard to my family's conversations. It was bizarre not only because he remained ill-mannered but also because he now was talking about the Buddha! I was so confused!

"That's something we'll maintain," said Paps. "Gerta will stay."

A flare of static startled me. Then it dawned on me! The reason my parents' bedroom was off limits was because Paps' radio was in there on a nightstand. I was told never to touch it. He told me it was a lifeline for us to hear news affecting our family and our daily lives. I remember calling it *der sprechen Kasten*, the talking box.

The nasally voice coming through the static was reporting on the situation in America which had recently worsened. The voice described the

11 From the end of the Great War until the mid-1930s, the German economy was in shambles. However, it was the Great Crash of October 1929 that dealt the final crushing blow and sent the country reeling (Fischer, *Nazi Germany: A New History*, 214–15).

stock market collapse: businesses failing, banks closing, nonexistent credit, and families leaving their homes to live on the streets. Soup kitchens and long bread lines were everywhere. It sounded like chaos.

Paps said, "It's horrible everywhere."

Sieke exhaled. "This is more fodder for the Nazis. The newsman was right when he quoted Buddha. We'll rue these hard times and not just for economic reasons. What was it he said? *When the student is ready, the teacher appears*! We must be careful and vigilant in all things."

My Birthday

1930

In anticipation of my sixth birthday, which was only two weeks away, I planned to mind my manners, pick up after myself, be polite to a fault, and to be as helpful as I could with regard to duties around the house. Of course my parents noticed.

"You're perfect," my mother said. "It's not necessary for you to try so hard."

Father teased, "We're satisfied with you. There's no reason to call the stork to take you back!" And then, after a few moments, "Your mother and I have decided that you can invite several friends to our home for a party!"

"Thank you!" I answered with excitement. A party with my friends!

That year my birthday fell on Monday so my parents arranged for a party the previous Sunday. Gerta was alerted as were Omi and Opa and our relatives who lived nearby. Alas, on that Thursday, Paps told me that my grandparents, along with Aunt Jenny, Uncle Hans, Uncle Alfred, and Uncle Erich were all unable to come.

"They have matters to attend to, nothing that's an emergency, but things that require their immediate attention. Uncle Sieke, too, is away on business. They have sent regrets and have promised gifts for you."

I was saddened my grandparents and relatives wouldn't be joining me but I also was overjoyed with the prospect of belated presents! My relatives, especially Uncle Sieke, were generous and I always appreciated their largesse.

Although my parents allowed me to invite ten friends to the party my father told me that the invitations should indicate that gifts were not necessary.

I was taken aback. "But why? It's my birthday!"

"You know many families are trying to persevere through difficult times now, Lorechen," Paps explained. "They're not as fortunate as we are. It may be a hardship for them to spend what little they have on anything other than food and necessities."

Mutsch said, "You'll tell everyone to bring a flower. We'll place the sprigs in a vase as the centrepiece."

Part of me understood completely. Yet a part of me, well perhaps it's best I don't say.

Gerta chimed in. "We can have a treat for them. I'll bake cookies. When your guests arrive we'll trade their flowers for cookies!"

"Besides," Mutsch added, "there'll be gifts enough from your relatives. Paps and I will have something for you, too."

Plans were finalized. Mutsch and Gerta arranged for food and activities and I was watched very carefully as I wrote invitations.

The day of the party was warm with bright sunshine. Though some friends could not come, many did. First to arrive was Adah Metzger, a gorgeous little girl from synagogue, bright-eyed with jet-black hair. Then, Inga Goldman came. She lived a few houses down. She was plump but so pretty with hair the colour of the sun. After she entered the foyer, Gerta said, "Thank you for visiting this afternoon, Inga." Mutsch then asked her, "How are you today?" Inga was so flustered all she could do was hand Gerta her flower, accept a cookie in return, crane her neck downward, and bury her face in her hands, the force of which caused the cookie to crumble in her palms. When Gerta handed her another cookie, she grasped it tightly and Gerta advised her to keep her arms at her sides for now.

The three of us played in my room. Later, other classmates came by. There was Dieter, a boy somewhat meek as I recall, but who excelled in our recess games, and Levi, a tall boy, very smart but so unkempt with his shirt too small and his shorts too big. To me he looked like a scarecrow. But for some reason I fancied him.

Everyone brought a flower. I've always adored the magnificence of flowers, especially orchids, but I can't remember by name the flowers the children brought that day. I do recall how when Mutsch brought the vase of blooms to the table everyone remarked that the spray was splendid in colour and texture.

Before I served the cake Gerta took us outside. We played games, sang songs, and then she sat us down on the grass. From her pocket she retrieved a book with a tattered cover. I knew right away which one it was. She began with my favourite tale, the one father had read to me a thousand times, *Der Erlkönig*, and, as I knew it would, the story frightened all of us but in such an exciting and intoxicating way.

My memories of that day are fairly clear since it's the only birthday party in Germany that my friends were permitted to attend.

That was sixteen years ago. Of the children there that day, one in particular presently comes to mind. I haven't thought of Inga Goldman lately but suddenly I see her before me, and a flood of remembrances overtakes me and I'm overwhelmed with thoughts of her.

She and I grew up in Berlin, each of us an only child. Inga's parents, Jules and Naomi Goldman, and my parents met at a bridge class and became close friends. My father and her father were in the export-import business and though they didn't work for the same company they both travelled through Europe, occasionally crossing paths in a foreign city where they would play tennis or just sit and talk for hours over coffee.

I remember going to the *Staatliche Museen* with Inga, her parents, and my parents. At the time there was a new collection of Egyptian artifacts there. Our parents also had season tickets to the *Berliner Philharmoniker*

Gerta leads the birthday guests in games and songs (above).
The children gather for a photograph (below). Ingelore, on the far right, embraces her friend, Adah Metzger.

and the *Staatsoper*. On a few occasions they took us with them. The performance halls were beautiful with their gleaming chandeliers and gilded busts of famous musicians. We sat in red velvet chairs overlooking the stage. We saw bows of a dozen violins, every one moving in unison. When ballerinas appeared their costumes created a magical world of billowy filmy pastels when they leaped through the air.

I didn't appreciate Naomi's nickname for her husband. She called him *Dickerchen*, which means *little Fatty*. He walked in an odd way, balancing his protruding stomach by leaning slightly backward, his large head swaying to and fro. His gait faintly reminded me of a rooster. I called him gentle Uncle Jules because he smiled so easily. I still can smell the minty cologne he generously splashed on his face after shaving.

With no other siblings Inga and I often felt lonely. She said many times, "A large family! I want lots of children when I grow up!"

I once told Inga that when I was three years old I asked my mother for a brother or sister. Mother later confided that although she and Paps had wanted another child the times were so unsettled that they were afraid to have two little ones to care for.

I know I don't want to have a lot of children but I know I'll never have just one.

Inga was a very sensitive child. One day, out of nowhere, she shouted, "Remember last year? That was the best summer!" That year, I believe it was 1933 or 1934, we enjoyed a wonderful summer with our families taking frequent visits to the lake. We rowed in our kayak, swam in the crisp water, and snatched berries from bushes behind the many outbuildings.

Inga often reminisced about the day when a couple of boys had picked flowers for us and my mother had offered them some cookies that Gerta had baked.

I would laugh and remind her, "Those boys weren't interested in us, Inga. They knew how good the cookies were, that's why they brought the flowers."

That was the same summer that my father had become dreadfully ill with typhoid. His fever had run as high as 41 and he was gone for what seemed like months. I never told Mutsch but at the time I was sure Paps was going to die.

It was sometime during 1935 that Inga and I first visited the new Reform temple in Dahlem. It was beautiful inside.

From that day on we pestered our parents to attend services there. I remember the rabbi, a man named Joachim Prinz.[12] His leadership was magnificent. I loved listening to the organ music and the lilting voices of the choir. But most of all I enjoyed staring at the stained glass windows from which shafts of light spread reds, blues, and yellows on the oaken pews. I felt at the time that that had to be the most beautiful temple in all of Germany.

Eventually our parents decided to attend services at the new Reform temple. I suspect their intensified religious interest was a reaction to the spread of Nazi influences.

Despite memories of my warm friendship with Inga and the experiences our families shared that year, this was also the year that my world suddenly fell apart.

When Paps first announced that we would be moving to Japan I pleaded desperately with him. "Why must we go to Japan when Inga and her parents are going to Brazil?"

He told me, "Gerber, the company I work for, has an office in Kobe."

"Why can't the Goldmans go there?" I was sick with the thought of being separated from Inga.

Paps said, "We have to leave our home because of the Nazis. Unfortunately we can't choose where we go. Jules was able to arrange for visas to Brazil for his family so that's where Inga must go. You'll see Inga again someday. I'm sure of it."

It was so difficult saying goodbye to Inga.

---

12 Joachim Prinz served for twelve years as rabbi of the Jewish community in Berlin. After arriving in America in 1937, he would go on to become vice-chairman of the World Jewish Congress, a member of the World Zionist Organization, and a leader in the civil rights march on Washington in 1963 (Fowler, "Joachim Prinz, Leader in Protests For Civil-Rights Causes, Dies at 86").

When we each arrived in our new countries, we wrote letters to one another. She and her family first immigrated to France; then, they fled to South America. Inga told me about Rio and I told her about Kobe. She sent me pictures of herself at the beach, the most beautiful place in the world she said, and photographs of *Pão de Açúcar*, Sugarloaf Mountain. She was learning Portuguese and had already made many friends. "There are so many festivals here," she wrote, "and we dress up in costumes and dance in the streets."

I sent her pictures of our home in Kobe. I told her I had a kitten with a broken tail that is supposed to, the Japanese believe, bring good luck. I didn't tell her kittens' tails are often broken when they're newborns. I wrote instead, "Learning Japanese is difficult for me. As of now I only can read street signs."

The Goldmans visited us in Japan in 1938, without Inga. I was angry with them and with Inga, too. They told me she preferred to stay in Brazil during Carnival. I was heartbroken.

I don't write to Inga anymore. Yet I think of her often. I hope she is happy.

And I'd like to think she still dances in the streets at Carnival time.

Dark Clouds are Everywhere

1932

It was just after our geography lesson ended that I realized darkness had crept into my classroom and was all about us. Fraülein Müller, my teacher, went to the windows and pushed aside the curtains to allow what little light there was into the room. Earlier that morning there were ominous coal-black clouds on the horizon but they seemed so far away. Even though it was only mid-morning it appeared as if dusk had settled over us.

We were told to place our papers aside. We sat motionless, our fingers laced together on the tops of our desks. Fraülein Müller stood erect waiting for our collective and undivided attention. I remember she dressed plainly with blouse collars so stiffly starched they appeared as if they were made of cardboard. Her long straight hair was balled atop her head. She was tall with such big feet!

"Children," she said, "we have visitors today so we'll be going outside into the yard. There you are to form a straight line. When your name is called you'll signal with your arm raised. Then you'll be told either to sit down on the grass or go to a side table where you'll answer whatever questions are asked of you." She clapped her hands three times. "Stand, push in your chairs, follow me. Talking is forbidden."

Once outside she motioned where we were to form our line. We did so quickly.

It seemed like night had fallen. The clouds were dense and dark. A storm was on its way.

All the classes were in the yard, standing in perfectly straight lines. The children were stock-still and mute, our teachers rooted as sentinels nearby. Then our *Schulleiter*, the headmaster, came into the yard accompanied by two men in uniform. I wasn't sure if they were soldiers or police but I guessed they were police.

Immediately I recognized the swastikas on their hats and armbands. One of the men was big and mean-looking, the bill of his cap pulled down to just above his eyes, his face in shadow, his eyes like beacons shining out from within. His lantern jaw was clean-shaven. I knew he was in charge, the leader. As the two of them walked past me I smelled the leather of their boots.[13]

When the soldiers stood at the centre of the yard our headmaster handed a sheaf of papers to the leader and then turned toward the school, leaving us in the yard. The other soldier went to a table situated near a gate that opened to an alleyway. He sat down, opened his briefcase, placed his papers before him, and then readied a pencil.

The bellowing voice of the soldier in the centre of our yard startled me. "I am Lieutenant Colonel Krüger. You will answer to your name as you have been instructed." He gazed about our assemblage making sure everyone was attentive. Then he said, "We begin." There was silence. Then, "Dieter Ackerman."

---

13 The authorities at Ingelore's school that day most likely were an administrative detachment of the SS, the Nazi special police force, later known as the Blackshirts. They were likely registering the Jewish children and teachers on the school's roster. They could also have been doing preparatory work for the coming expansion of the Hitler Youth program that soon would include girls between the ages of ten and fourteen (Mahlendorf, *The Shame of Survival: Working Through a Nazi Childhood*, 91).

The boy timidly raised his arm. The soldier checked the roster and then barked, "*Sich hinsetzen*!" Sit down! Like a vase falling from a shelf, Dieter collapsed on the grass. Another name was called. That child too was told to sit down. Then, another name, and so on.

Fear knotted my stomach. What name will the soldier call me by? Will it be Ingelore Rothschild or Erna Völker? To which name shall I answer? What am I to do?

"Levi Baumstein," the soldier called. This boy was quivering when I saw him slowly raise his arm. Then pointing toward the gate, the officer said, "Proceed to Sergeant Keller." The boy darted to the table as if a rabid dog were chasing him.

More names were called. Some children were told to sit while others were sent to the sergeant. I thought it was a random selection or perhaps a division based on neighbourhoods. As a wave of understanding washed over me my blood ran cold.

The children sent to the table were Jews.

"Adah Metzger." She raised both arms. The colonel's voice barked, "To the sergeant!" She ran to the table sobbing the entire way.

I will never forget those children's names.

I looked at the lines. Most of the students were seated. There were only several boys and girls still standing. I saw conspicuous empty spaces where the Jews had been. The children at the sergeant's table now numbered about twenty.

"Frau Robensohn," the colonel announced. She was the teacher in the classroom across the hall from mine. She stood motionless. Impatiently, the colonel shouted, "Frau Robensohn!" With her arms akimbo she stepped toward the man, then stopped and defiantly remained still. He snapped at her, "You will proceed to the sergeant immediately!" She slowly dropped her arms to her sides, raised her chin, and walked gracefully to the table.

I vividly remember that she never raised her arm.

As more names were called my mind raced. What would I do when he called Rothschild?

Just then the headmaster hastened from the building. "My dear colonel," he was saying as he approached.

"What is this interruption?" the colonel wanted to know.

"There are parents and passersby on the front steps. They see your vehicles in the street and they are wondering if a child is hurt or if there is some calamity with which they can assist."

The colonel looked angry. "And what did you tell them?"

"I told them you were here to conduct a validation of our school's roster. I said it was procedural and customary. They didn't accept my explanation and they're demanding to speak with you."

The colonel pursed his lips. He looked at the sky and then turning to the table he called out, "Sergeant, gather your things." To the headmaster he said, "I see I must handle this annoyance personally. Tell them I will be out shortly. The sergeant will bring that teacher," pointing to Frau Robensohn with an arm as straight as an arrow, "and the children from his table to your office to complete his cataloguing. It will soon rain so be advised I shall return tomorrow to conclude my work here." And with that he marched into the building.

The teachers began yelling, "Everyone inside. To your classrooms!" We dashed inside to escape the first drops of rain beginning to fall. As I ran toward the building I saw Frau Robensohn and the group of Jewish children being ushered to the headmaster's office.

About an hour later the clouds and rain dissipated. In the middle of a reading, noticing how brightly the sun now was shining, Fraülein Müller said, "I see the police took the bad weather with them." I sensed an odious sarcasm in her voice.

At dismissal, my class was taken to the lobby to wait for elders or governesses to record our removal from the property with the school's secretary. Gerta signed the log and we left. On the street she looked at me. "Is everything all right? You look peaked. Is there something wrong?"

"I'm fine, Gerta," I lied, "I'm just tired."

As we walked home in silence I couldn't help wondering what was destined for the Jewish children and for Frau Robensohn.

That night our supper routine began as it always did with Paps talking and Mutsch and I listening. I was tense. I knew the conversation soon would turn to me.

I'd just put some food in my mouth when father asked, "And you, Lorechen, how was your day?"

Everything went dark just as my classroom had earlier that morning. I could smell the leather of the boots. I could see Frau Robensohn and the Jewish children being led into the school building. The entire morning flashed before my eyes.

Reaching for my napkin, I gagged.

Grasping my wrist, Mutsch asked, "What's wrong, Lorechen?"

I retched.

Sensing something was awry, father demanded, "Tell us at once!"

It didn't take long to recount what had transpired at school. I was surprised my parents had so few questions. They understood the implications of that day better than I did.

"And what of Frau Robensohn and the Jewish children?"

I whispered, "I'm not sure."

My parents looked to each other. There were no words between them but there was communication and a clear understanding.

Paps said, "It's the only thing we can do."

My parents decided I would not return to school. It wasn't safe. They said the actions of that day were an affront to Jews, to civility, to education professionals, and to all children and families as well.

"You'll not return to school," father declared.

I protested. "But I enjoy school! Fraülein Müller is a wonderful teacher! I'll miss my friends!"

He said, "No! We'll make arrangements for Gerta to tutor you in the library. Mother will assume some of her domestic duties while she is teaching you."

He stared into my eyes. "You're to remain inside this house when school is in session. We can't have people seeing you on the street, they'll wonder why you're not in school."

"Yes, father," I moaned.

I knew there was no way I could change Paps' mind. Once he reached a decision it was done. Only Mutsch, on the rare occasion, could change his mind.

That night my eerie nightmare returned. This time the deformed demon is wearing the colonel's hat and when I run to my parents' bedroom he's closer to me, just inches away. I awoke more frightened than I have ever been.

The days of attending school were over. I would see a few of my former classmates at synagogue and a handful of others by chance on the street on weekends but I was forbidden to speak with them. I never had the opportunity to explain what happened to me. I never had a chance to say goodbye.

I do not know which is worse: saying goodbye, face-to-face, exchanging a warm embrace, looking forlornly into one another's eyes, the tears about to come; or, the ghostly absence of a conclusion, only a memory of a last encounter, the last hours or days, never knowing it would be the last.

It took just two days for me to realize that Gerta was a strict teacher. She meticulously allocated times for my instruction in science, literature, German language and history, mathematics, European and World history, art, music, and various domestic skills. She scheduled recess periods during which we exercised inside or went for brisk walks several times around the apartment. Although she didn't speak English or French she worked with me when we pored over those language texts, one hour every odd-numbered day for French and one hour every even-numbered day for English.

"Your father will correct your pronunciation," she reminded me.

When we were "at school" she wouldn't tolerate any nonsense. I still laugh when I recall her frantically admonishing Hansi, my canary, for singing too loudly during her tutorials.

"You'll learn your lessons," she said, "and your father will see progress."

After several days Paps, Mutsch, Gerta, and I sat in the library to discuss my comportment. I was relieved to hear Gerta say I was a model student.

"I'm pleased," my father said.

Suddenly there were rapid knocks at our door. We looked to one another. Fear brushed across our faces. Paps rose to attend to the disturbance. He returned and ushered Herr Bayern into the library. The landlord looked tired and wan, his eyes bloodshot. He trembled as he spoke.

"A few days after the attendance sessions were completed the authorities submitted their report. All teachers and students were accounted for save three or four Jewish children, one of them was your daughter. Since there was no report of illness or accident to explain their absences, the colonel demanded addresses. He sent someone from the police station to the Records Hall to examine real estate documentation and confirm the addresses."

"How do you know this?" Mutsch asked.

"I know the man they sent. He's a clerk there. His elderly mother rents from me. Upon his return he verified your address but suggested that they question me first, as landlord, to avoid wasted efforts, rather than come directly here."

"And the result?" Paps asked.

"I told them the Rothschilds no longer live there. They moved to Munich. I showed them the lease. I proposed that the school's roster was in error."

Mutsch was wringing her hands. Gerta and I were speechless.

"And now?" Paps probed.

"The clerk told me if they're unable to locate the girl," he pointed to me, "they'll issue a warrant for *your* arrest. They're on your trail, Herr Rothschild. You must consider what this means not only for you but also for me. They won't stop until they find you. Your wife isn't safe either. No Jewish family is safe. It won't take them long to confirm you're not in Munich. What will you do when they come to your door? What will I do when they demand an explanation for my obvious diversion and the falsified lease?"

Father was calm. It's something in him that I admire to this day. He possesses a quiet courage, he's intelligent, and above all he is fearless.

"I've planned for this, Herr Bayern. We thank you beyond measure for what you've already done for us. I assure you things will work out. No harm will come to you or anyone else."

I had no idea what Paps meant. How could things possibly work out? We had already changed our names. We couldn't change much else.

Conditions Worsen

1933–35

One Sunday, Paps, Mutsch, and I went to the Wannsee for a picnic and a leisurely walk about the shoreline and along the trails that weaved through groupings of flowers and trees. We spent many summer Sundays on that beautiful lake on the outskirts of Berlin.

Paps had a compartment in an outbuilding near one of the docks where we kept our kayak. Handmade of richly veined mahogany, as sleek and as smooth as Mutsch's silk blouses, the boat was perfectly balanced and rode low enough for me to trail my fingers in the water. After each outing we would clean the kayak until we could see our reflection in its sides. It was just the right size for the three of us: Paps in the stern, Mutsch in the middle, and me, a skinny, leggy nine-year-old, neatly wedged into the bow.

Mist was rising off the lake that day as my parents edged our kayak into the water, compelling a mother goose and her goslings to change direction. We watched birds fly through the air and fish nip at insects on the water's surface. In the distance we saw a small beach area. We could barely make out people settling themselves with blankets and chairs.

It was a pleasure to glide through the still water and enjoy the lush scenery and fascinating wildlife. We explored numerous inlets and coves. Then we rowed ashore to land the kayak for an hour or so while we swam in the clear water. We picnicked under the willows growing along the shore.

I said, "It's such a lovely day, please let's stay late!"

My parents smiled. I never wanted those Sundays to end especially since only recently I had learned how to paddle without drenching us.

"All right," they agreed, "we'll stay!"

After lunch Mutsch and I climbed into the kayak. Paps pushed us adrift until he was thigh-high in the shallows. He jumped into the boat causing it to rock from side to side. For a moment we thought we would founder but Paps quickly steadied it as he settled into the stern.

As we were snaking our way about the lake I reclined in the bow facing aft, my legs tucked in at the sides of the boat so as not to press against Mutsch, watching her amidships and my father in the stern. As they rowed, Paps to his left and mother to her right, they swayed like pendulums, their faces crossing back and forth as they switched oars from port to starboard and back again.

Suddenly they stopped rowing, the kayak gliding silently.

"What's wrong?" I asked, seeing the looks of astonishment on their faces.

Paps said to Mutsch, "*Dreh dich um.*" Then he said to me, "Turn around!"

They put their oars in the water on the same side to turn the boat around. Paps saying again, "*Dreh dich um*!" This time there was more urgency in his voice.

"Yes," I said. As the boat continued to swing around I caught a glimpse of something I'd never seen before. We were near the beach area we had seen in the distance earlier that day but we were now much closer. On the shore there were about two dozen men and women. They were naked! Every one of them!

My parents rowed feverishly, the boat racing away from the shore, our backs to the naked people.

"It's time to go," Mutsch said.

The sun was beginning to disappear behind some clouds. Few boats remained on the lake. My parents paddled slowly not wanting to disturb the peace and quiet. Along the shoreline willow branches drooped into the lake. Not even a breeze ruffled their leaves. It was so tranquil, the fish asleep, the fowl off to their nests, the air unmoving, the water like glass.

Suddenly sharp cracking sounds shattered the stillness– ricocheting across the lake scaring the geese into the air.

"What's that?" I screamed.

Paps steadied the boat. He turned this way and that, his ears perked, his eyes searching the shoreline.

"Hush, Lorechen! We're going home!"

While I crouched in the hollow of the bow he and Mutsch paddled furiously toward the shore. They glanced at one another and then at me. When we came ashore Paps moved quickly, pulling the kayak out of the water and returning the boat to the outbuilding without the ritual cleaning.

In the kitchen that evening my parents said hunting was forbidden at the lake so someone must have been shooting unlawfully.

"Will they be punished?" I asked.

"Yes, I'm sure they will be," father said.

He turned to me with a shrug. It was then I noticed that the right side of his face was drooped and his right eye was halfway closed. His head tilted. He was clamping his teeth. He looked away and then went to the library.

"Is he all right?" I asked Mutsch.

"Yes, Lorechen. Another headache is coming on. He'll be fine."

Later, from my bedroom, I overheard snippets of a telephone conversation between Paps and one of his brothers. I sidled out of bed and pressed myself up against my door to listen.

I heard Paps say, "I'm afraid the rampage has started, Alfred. We were on the lake today. Some of the moderates from the Bundestag[14] live near

14 The Bundestag is the lower house of the bicameral German parliament.

there. It was terrifying to hear those rifle shots. I wonder if the Nazis have begun their assassinations."

I wandered into the hallway.

"What do you mean? What are the moderates and who are the assassins?"

Paps was startled by my presence.

Dismissing my concern, he chirped, "Off to bed with you. You've had enough excitement for one day."

He handed the telephone receiver to Mutsch. With a leading hand he escorted me to my room and tucked me into bed.

Over the next few days, conversations between my father and mother stopped abruptly when I came into the room. Something was in the air. I wondered if the assassins from the lake were loose in Wilmersdorf.

About two weeks later I was witness to angry words exchanged among Paps and two of his brothers.

"Go to Holland?" Paps asked in disbelief, the veins in his neck bulging. "It'd be just as dangerous for you to stay here! Do you believe Hitler will respect borders once he carries out his *Lebensraum* policy? No, he'll overtake demarcation lines without conscience!"[15]

My cousin Ullie and her parents lived in Amsterdam.[16] What was so wrong with planning a trip there as Uncle Alfred and Uncle Hans were suggesting, I wondered?

I knew that many of my friends and their families were thinking of leaving Berlin. I thought it was because of what Paps had told me about Europe and America, that things were very bad there too, not just in Germany. When he said there weren't very many jobs what he really meant was that staggering unemployment was the reason for an abysmal lack of opportunities for families to provide for themselves. When he said

---

15 The purpose of *Lebensraum*, a Nazi Party policy, to expand Germany's national and ethnic boundaries in the East was to provide space for the growth of the German population (Bracher, *The German Dictatorship: The Origins, Structure, and Effects of National Socialism*, 47).

16 Ullie's father is Heinburg. Neither "Uncle" Heinburg, nor his wife, "Aunt" Ida, was a blood relative to Ingelore.

that people didn't have much money for food or clothing he meant that the Depression had caused a precipitous fall in the value of all European currencies in tandem with a meteoric increase in the prices of goods and services. When he said there were rising tides of dislike for the Jews he meant that the Nazi-driven cancerous plague of anti-Semitism was rampant in Germany.

Although my father protected me from most of the frightening developments in Germany, in 1933 when Hitler was sworn in as chancellor I can still remember Paps telling me, "An evil man has come to power in Germany. He and the Nazis will destroy all that is decent in this world."

My weekday house detention with Gerta lasted three years. The prevailing climate in Berlin was dismal. I remember many incidents with crystal clarity but others are only vague dream-like recollections.

The last time I had been to school was in May 1932. Gerta had been my teacher ever since, guiding my instruction in various subjects, torturing me with her intense tutorials. Her strictness enabled me to become what my father had hoped I might be one day, "a shining example of a literate, educated, and enlightened young girl." Father was very proud of me, and Gerta, too. Gerta herself remarked, "You're smarter than your counterparts still attending school!" How she knew this I don't know; but, of course, I took her word for it.

Even though the authorities had come looking for me after the incident at the school, Herr Bayern's story about our move to Munich took weeks to investigate. In the meantime, while the hunt for us ensued, father travelled to the Gerber home office in London. There he arranged with a man named Griesbach, one of the owners, to provide documentation not only for him but also for Mutsch and me. The identification papers we acquired all had the surname Völker. Whether Paps was certified as a German national working in England or we as a family were listed as German expatriates travelling to and fro I don't recall. Perhaps they were travel visas. At any rate whatever they were, they were all forgeries. Those papers saved our lives.

One night two policemen and a petrified Herr Bayern came to our home. Paps answered the door. Mutsch and I were in the kitchen. Paps later told us Herr Bayern's face was drained of colour, his eyes steeled with fear, his stubby fingers twitching like the wings of a swarm of locusts.

"Herr Rothschild?" I heard one of the officers demand.

My innards were in knots. I was terrified that I might vomit at any moment.

"No, sir," Paps calmly responded.

There was an avalanche of tension in the air. The policeman then asked, "Who are you and where are your papers?"

Paps presented him with our lease and our identification documents. After careful review the officer apologized for the inconvenience and then apologized to our landlord. After the officers left Herr Bayern remained a moment longer.

"Herr Rothschild," he stammered, "how did you . . ."

"It's fine, Herr Bayern. I acquired the papers in London. They will no longer suspect you and they will have no way of knowing how you helped us. Thank you again for all that you've done. You're safe. We're safe, too. At least for now."

Many things changed soon after, one after the other. In April of that year there were boycotts against Jewish storeowners, the banning of Jews from civil service employment, Jewish judges had to resign, and Jewish professors were let go from universities.

Father said, "I'm afraid during this year the last candle will go out." As it happened he was correct. In August, Paul Von Hindenburg, the president of Germany, died. For my father, this was an especially difficult loss. "It's been virtually hopeless these past few years," Paps lamented, "but with his death there's no hope at all."

Amid the national turmoil our family also experienced unrest. Paps' brothers, Alfred, Hans, and Erich, all were taking flight. Yet, Uncle Sieke adamantly refused to close his factory and leave Germany. His stubbornness caused us great worry. A few years later we learned how his sustained ownership of his factory saved his life. Mutsch and Aunt Jenny were trying to convince Omi and Opa to go somewhere safe as well.

It was a horrific time, the days passed slowly in the expanding fog of fear and dread.

Sometime that fall Gerta and I were in the library finishing our lessons for the day. Gerta sat reading aloud from *Children's and Household Tales*[17] while I lolled on the carpet looking through a book of famous artists' works. I was entranced by the reproductions, Gerta's voice was only a melodic undercurrent in the background.

It was cold that day, the turbulent wind causing leaves to fall at such a rate that we thought the trees, which we could hear scraping against the windows, soon would be bare. The sound of it all was eerily wonderful, the orchestra of autumn trumpeting in full crescendos. Inside it was warm and cozy, my dear Gerta and I sharing a special time together.

Late that afternoon I heard the trap from the mail slot in the front door swing open, then a cascade of letters fall to the floor. Gerta began to rise but I told her I would get the mail.

She said, "All right. Place whatever has come today on the kitchen table."

I closed my book and walked to the door.

There was a large mound of letters haphazardly sprayed about. I scooped them up and sorted them so that each was facing the same way. I neatened the stack and then fluttered it so the right-hand corners whizzed by, the stamps a colourful montage of shapes and sizes. But something I saw took me aback, jogged my memory. More than five years ago Gerta was with me when I first saw the swastika on the poster near my house, how it appeared to move, rather like a wheel rotating slowly. Two of the letters in the stack bore stamps that showed it. One displayed an eagle, its wings outspread, with its talons grasping a disk containing the swastika. The other, a bright red colour, showed an eagle in flight with the swastika as the sun or moon visible from behind the far horizon.

17 A book best known as *Grimm's Fairy Tales.*

A stamp, much like the one described by Ingelore.

Clutching the letters, I ran into the kitchen and threw them on the table. Gerta came quickly.

“What is going on?” she demanded.

I reached into the pile and retrieved one of the letters.

“Do you remember the tree?” I asked her. “The poster when I was little? The broken cross?” I waved the envelope at her.

“Yes, I do,” she said. “But you’ve seen that emblem since then. Why is there such disarray here?

“Don’t you see?” I screamed. “It’s not just in the streets! Now, it’s in our home!”

Nearly a month later, one evening when we sat down for supper my father asked me a peculiar question. Instead of the usual conversation between Paps and Mutsch which I was required to patiently listen to in strict silence and attentiveness. Paps turned to me.

"Tomorrow is going to be a special day," he said. "How would you like to spend a few hours with your Paps, Mutsch, and Gerta? Perhaps looking at wondrous things from wondrous lands?"

I was intrigued. "What do you mean?"

He spoke slowly to pique my curiosity even more. "We could go to a place where there are fascinating creatures, some familiar, some uncommon. I know they would like to see us!"

"The zoo!" I shouted. "Let's go to the zoo!"

The next day the four of us walked along the *Hardenbergstraße*. Paps holding my hand as he and I led, Gerta and Mutsch following close behind. Gerta had a bag filled with tart candies that she nudged into my back continually offering them to me. I reached with regularity. My parents pretended not to see.

The street was alive. People moved about in a rhythm that varied from a slow pace to a scurry. Some had leashed dogs; others carried shopping packages. I saw families with children and clusters of tourists speaking languages foreign to me.

Abruptly Paps stopped. We were in front of a theatre. Pointing to a recess between it and an abutting building he said, "Wait there with Gerta." She and I took the few steps and stood quietly.

From where I stood I could overhear my parents talking: Do we do this now? Is she too young? Will this just be the source of another nightmare? Can't this wait for another time?

I couldn't imagine what was so questionable about visiting the zoo. Then as I looked up I saw an illustration on the brick wall of the theatre. In black letters were the words: *Triumph des Willens*, Triumph of the Will.[18]

---

18 This famous propaganda film directed by Leni Riefenstahl was released on 28 March 1935.

Just then Paps said, "We'll postpone our visit to the zoo. Instead we're going in to see this movie. It may be disturbing. If it bothers you, then tell me and we'll leave."

He arranged for our entry. The darkness was tangible. We found two seats in one row with two directly behind. Gerta and I sat in front of Paps and Mutsch. In a few moments the screen started to come alive. Paps leaned over to say in my ear. "Tell me when you want to leave."

The screen filled with a multitude of clouds, then an aerial view of a large city emerged. I asked Gerta if it was Berlin and if we might be able to see our house.

"No," she whispered, "it's Nürnberg."

There were parades with throngs of people lining the avenues. Then I saw swastikas on banners and flags, on buildings, on the armbands, badges, and medals on every soldier's crisp uniform, on buntings attached to the windows of homes, many of them strikingly similar to ours and in large disks held in the grasps of foreboding iron eagles. They were everywhere. Then a plane landed from the heavens. Hitler appeared.

Father leaned over again, "Shall we leave?"

"No," I said.

There was a large crowd gathered and a man—I believe it was Rudolph Hess—at the podium. After he finished his address several men, one after the other, made speeches.

One line in particular is etched in my mind and still echoes in my ears: "*Eine Nation, die nicht zu halten ist seine Reinheit der Rasse sicherlich untergehen*." A nation that does not maintain its racial purity surely will perish.

Then I heard Paps say to Mutsch, "The die is cast."

He rose, taking Mutsch by the arm. "We're leaving immediately."

And so we did.

Sand Falls Through the Hourglass

1935–36

During the mid-1930s waves of Jews crashed against German borders in an attempt to escape the growing web of Nazism, anti-Semitism, and oppression. Many of my relatives and friends were among them. They scattered across the frontiers to Eastern Europe, North and South America, Australia, Africa, and the Orient.

In many cases comfortable lives, beautiful homes, successful careers, and loved ones were left behind. Many of those fleeing were met by the frustration of language barriers, loneliness, and in some cases abject poverty. All were terrified by the hunt.

I know of this first-hand. My friend Ullie and her parents fled Berlin to settle in Amsterdam for a time before moving on. They disappeared into the night to avoid detection. From somewhere in the south of France, Ullie sent a photograph of herself sitting on top of a split-rail fence, her long slim legs dangling. She and her parents were staying in a sleepy little town nestled among large expanses of vineyards and horse farms. They'd been wealthy in Germany but I didn't know if they'd been able to take their money with them.

In Berlin, Ullie's mother and Mutsch often took us to a museum or a park and, for a special treat, to a bakery on the magnificent *Kurfürstendamm*, a boulevard lined with shops, restaurants, and hotels. Ullie and I had so much trouble choosing among all the luscious pastries!

Those days of innocence—how our lives have changed.

My parents knew it was imperative that we leave Germany to escape the coming wolf pack. The predatory fascists and anti-Semitics, both ferocious and savage armies, had already begun to run riot in Germany. Paps told me that he had been planning our departure for over a year. I remember the dining room table littered with documents and maps, hundreds of Deutschmarks, train and ship schedules, newspaper clippings, and addresses of family and friends. But all the evidence of his plans was swept aside whenever I came near. For months heated discussions took place only while I was asleep. My parents wanted to spare me, believing there was no profit in alarming me more than was absolutely necessary.

The whole family was making plans. I remember Uncle Hans saying, "We don't have to worry. Conditions won't become too intolerable for us here. If they do then we can go to Holland."

My father took issue. "No, brother. We already discussed this. It won't be safe anywhere in Europe."

"I agree with Kurt," Uncle Alfred remarked. "Those in Austria and Czechoslovakia are as fearful as we are. It's said that Hungary, Poland, Belgium, and Holland will not withstand the advancing Nazi juggernaut. Will France and England fall as well? You may wish to stop in Holland, but it's paramount you continue on. I'm going to Australia."

Omi and Opa were reluctant, avoiding discussions about what to do or where to go. Mutsch believed it was their resolute faith in the goodness of people and their optimistic view of the German citizenry who they believed wouldn't stand much longer for the vise of fascism clamping down on the freedoms and dreams of the proud and decent German people. Believing that the Nazi tide would subside they were content to remain where they were.

Uncle Sieke stayed in Berlin. He had no family of his own. His life was his factory so he remained behind.

As Uncle Hans continued mulling over his choices my father tried to convince him to relocate to Africa. Hans' work with the Gerber Company already had afforded him the opportunity to do business in Cape Town and he had made the trip from South Africa to Germany and back again many times.

I don't recall Uncle Erich or Aunt Jenny ever being present at these discussions. Perhaps they already had left Germany.

Just after the New Year in 1936 my parents clarified the procedures and strategies necessary to prepare and then to execute their plans for departure. They thought of things I didn't imagine. Some were so basic while others so astute. The first questions they answered were: Where will we go? When will we leave? But the one I felt was the hardest of all to answer was, what will I take with me?

Mutsch and I were in the library one afternoon. She was knitting a scarf for Paps. I was lying on the rug finishing lessons Gerta insisted I complete.

"Lorechen" she whispered, "come sit with me."

I went to her, nestling close.

"We must talk now of our upcoming trip. Your father and I have done much planning. You need to start your planning, too. You'll make a list of the items you'll bring. Then think about arranging an area in your bedroom where you'll keep those things of greatest importance and necessity. Paps and I will evaluate what you've chosen and then we'll pack whatever you've selected. You understand we've no room for non-essentials."

"I understand. I'll choose my clothing, books, toys, the mementos from my shelves, Hansi and his cage, my easel and colouring pencils, paper, my dolls and marionettes, things like that."

I was oblivious to what was coming.

With tragic frustration in her voice, she said, "We'll see, Lorechen."

The next day I was reminded again to make my list of things I would bring. I prepared an area two metres square in the corner of my bedroom.

Rather than writing everything down, I assembled my possessions and placed them in the designated corner. The heaviest things, I decided, should be at the bottom so I began with books. After a few hours my teetering pile was taller than me and it did not include Hansi in his cage. For the most part I felt it was a good beginning. I ran to summon Mutsch to see my handiwork.

"Mutsch!" I said, running into the kitchen. "Come see the work I've done!"

She followed me into my bedroom. When she saw the patchwork tower of my belongings, she gasped, covered her face in her hands, began sobbing uncontrollably and then hastened from my room.

"Mother!" I called after her. "What's wrong?"

Her bedroom door slammed shut. I heard muffled sounds. She was crying into her pillows. It didn't take long for me to realize how childish I was being–I was deluding myself. Our voyage was not like moving to a new home. Of course not. We were to run for our lives.

As I grew up, I gradually understood what my parents knew to be true: belongings are only material things, what matters most is family and friends. Leaving our possessions behind was nothing compared to the other losses we faced.

In those early weeks of 1936 we finalized the preparations for our departure. Paps and Mutsch worked tirelessly to make sure that when it came time to leave Berlin we would be swift and safe. My father later revealed to me many of the agonizing struggles he and Mutsch had endured during those countless days of preparation: moments of haste and dispatch, trying to tie together loose ends that arose at every turn. But, he admitted, the most difficult campaign for them was to prepare me.

I have always felt my father to be a man of determined action, not only one who is quick to respond to matters at hand but also one who would always spare Mutsch and me as much anxiety and worry as he could.

"I remember one night," he mused years later, "when we had to decide what to do with our possessions. It seemed only proper to be charitable with them since we couldn't possibly bring them with us. Your mother and I decided we'd offer our things to relatives and friends who planned on staying in Berlin: to Gerta and her family and to Herr Bayern."

"Gerta was heartbroken when we first informed her of our plans to leave," Paps recalled. "She couldn't stop crying. Mutsch embraced her and thanked her for all she'd done for us, from those first few days after you were born through all the good times and of course, through the horrible tribulations forced upon us during the recent years."

Mutsch offered Gerta most of her wardrobe including the furs, silks, and linens along with many of her shoes, scarves, blouses, and trousers. My mother gave her a gold necklace threaded through three red gemstones. "The garnets represent our hearts," mother said to her. "Think of us every time you wear it."

All the larger pieces of jewellery, save Mutsch's gorgeous diamond wedding ring, Paps sold—money would be a necessity for what lay ahead. Before mentioning it to me, my parents offered my toys to Gerta to give to her brothers. When I learned of this I was so angry, inconsolable. But my father reasoned with me and I learned what it is to be generous, altruistic, and benevolent.

"We wanted to leave everything undisturbed until our return," Paps said, "We thought our stay in Japan would be short. We imagined coming back to Berlin, to family and friends, to Gerta, and prospering as we had in the old days. I was insufferably naïve then, Lorechen. We all were."

A few days later Paps and Mutsch left the house to meet Herr Bayern at a café. I'm told their meeting was mostly one of silence, the words unspoken but the feelings and understanding explicitly clear.

At their parting, Herr Bayern, with tears in his eyes said, "My wish, Herr Rothschild, is that you'll return to Berlin safe and sound. Of course I'll accept the items you've pledged to my family. But in the meantime, while you're gone, I'll lease your home as it is with all that remains there with the expectation that these egregious abuses of decent German people, Christians and Jews alike, will pass. Upon your return you will find everything as you left it."

My parents and I would see Herr Bayern one more time before we left Germany.

Everything Worries Me

February 1936

Mutsch hurried me along as we exited the grocery store onto the frozen sidewalk. The sleet was like needles falling from a thousand pine trees, the slush gathering at our feet as we trudged along. The oddest thing was the thunder. Roars of it barrelled across the black sky. But with our scarves, boots, and woolen gloves we weren't too uncomfortable as we went home.

Just as we were approaching a butcher shop Mutsch pulled me toward an alcove covered by an awning. She was shivering.

"Mutsch," I asked, "shall we go inside? Look at the steam on the window glass!"

"No, Lorechen," she said, her teeth chattering, "just hold my hand and let me rest."

People plodded by, heads bent, their bodies leaning into the wind. Just then a man sidled by us, opened the door, and eased his way inside. I felt Mutsch flinch. She released my hand and hastened toward the street. I heard her cough and then she vomited into the gutter. She had her arms wrapped around her midsection. I ran to her.

"Mutsch, are you all right?" I screamed.

She composed herself, wiping her lips and chin with a tissue from her pocket. "Yes, I'm fine. It was the smell of the meat when that man opened the door. The odour overwhelmed me. I'm fine now. Let's go."

We changed out of our damp clothes as soon as we arrived home. Gerta was preparing the next day's lessons but when she realized Mutsch and I possessed a chill she went to the kitchen to prepare hot cocoa.

While she was at the stove I snuck up behind her. She stood erect, her posture always beyond criticism. I was flushed with the thought that soon I would have to say goodbye to her. She turned to me, smiled, and then said softly, "Come to me."

We took the cocoa to the table. Gerta pushed aside the papers that were spread about. Evidently Paps and Mutsch had been reviewing them the previous night and uncharacteristically had left them there. Mutsch, Gerta, and I sat down. The warm cocoa was frothy with a rich aftertaste of bitter chocolate.

As I sipped, one of the papers protruding from under some others caught my eye. It was written in Italian. Even though my French and English studies had been going well, I didn't speak or read Italian. But I did recognize the word *ospedale*, which was similar enough to the English word *hospital* and the French word *l'hôpital*. The German word *Krankenhaus* is so very different.

A wave of fear rolled over me.

"Is Paps ill?" I demanded, pointing to the exposed page. "That's information for a hospital. Are his headaches more serious?" Mutsch looked at me and then Gerta. "Tell me, is father ill?"

I was terrified by the thought of my father suffering any more than he had already. He often described his headaches as blinding. He would direct me to close the shades so no sunlight would aggravate him. Frequently I had to be very quiet and if I needed to speak I was to do so in a whisper.

Mutsch reached for my hand.

"It's not for your father, Lorechen," she stammered, "it's for me."

I jumped to my feet and screamed as loudly as I ever have. The vision of my mother vomiting in the street passed before my eyes as did images of my father during his many headache attacks. Then came a flash of the ogre from my nightmares, about to clutch me at my throat, laughing, knowing my parents had vanished.

I bolted from the kitchen. Suddenly I crashed into what felt like a tree trunk. I was stunned. Then Paps took me in his strong arms and lifted me up. I was kicking frantically, shaking my head from side to side as forcefully as a piston in an engine. My father tightened his embrace.

"Lorechen," he gasped, "what's wrong?"

Mutsch and Gerta hurried from the kitchen. Mutsch was holding the brochure from the Italian hospital waving it in the air. Paps saw it.

"I see," he whispered, "now you're aware."

He carried me into my room. The commotion had set Hansi to screeching. Gerta snatched a pillowcase and placed it over his cage. Hansi fell silent.

I must have fainted because the next thing I knew I was sitting on my bed. I looked at my father, his eyes were warm and tender with concern. Gerta sat beside me, her arms around me. Mutsch knelt at the foot of my bed nervously wringing her hands.

I grilled Paps about Mutsch and the hospital spluttering questions between sobs and shallow breaths. He knew I was afraid and thinking the worst. He tried to calm me as best he could.

"Lorechen, I'm fine. Mutsch will be fine as well. For the past few weeks she's complained of stomach problems. She'll need a minor operation to correct what's bothering her. It's nothing major. We've chosen a hospital in Italy because there the doctors specialize in abdominal . . ." he stopped for a moment, ". . . curiosities for which they are renowned in their ability to remedy. No other facility we know of, none in Berlin certainly, has such a reputation."

"What's wrong, mother?"

"You know, with age come some challenges."

"But you're young," I protested.

"Thank you, Lorechen, but at times I don't feel as I know I should. This operation will make me even better prepared to take care of you and your wonderful father."

"So," I reasoned, "Paps will go with you to Italy and Gerta and I will remain here?"

They looked at each other.

Paps said, "No, Lorechen. Mother will go by herself. This is only a minor procedure. She couldn't go alone if it was anything major. She'll have the operation and convalesce there for a few days."

I retorted, "Oh, I understand. Mutsch will be in Italy while Gerta, you, and I will carry on as usual."

Paps replied, his voice now sharper and higher-pitched, frustration causing him to speak faster.

"You will listen carefully. Mother is to go to Italy. She'll remain there until she recovers. I need to go to London to wrap up my business affairs before our departure. Have you forgotten what lies ahead for us? We need to leave Berlin. We will be hunted down if we don't."

"But what of me?" I was stricken with terror. "Am I to be alone?"

"You'll go to Amsterdam. You'll wait there for us."

"But—"

"You'll wait with Uncle Heinburg, his wife, and Ullie. You will—"

"But, I—"

"Silence!" he shouted. "Don't you understand? I'd be with your mother if I could. I must go to London. You're going to Amsterdam. It is done."

He stormed out of the room.

Mutsch sat down on the bed beside me.

"Will we be apart for long?" I asked.

"We'll be separated for a time that's all. Each of us will be on our own but only for a little while. We'll meet in Italy and then begin our voyage to Japan."

My mind raced to offer alternatives so I could be with either Mutsch or Paps.

"I know what you're thinking," Mutsch said, "but you can't come with me. I'll need complete rest to be strong enough for the next part of our adventure and your presence would be . . ." she was searching for the right word, ". . . counterproductive. The long trip, especially the part of it across Siberia, would be too strenuous for me if I have not regained my strength. You'll do as we say. You'll go to Amsterdam."

"Why can't I go with Paps to London?" I persisted.

"You can't. His business there demands his presence not yours."

"Then I'll stay with Gerta at her house!"

Now she was panting with rage. "Have you forgotten? The Nazis are still looking for your father and they continue to look for you. They know he's not in Munich. It's only a matter of time before they retrace their steps to look for him here in Berlin. You may not stay at Gerta's house. She's already done so much for us. If you're there it will put her in danger. We'll not ask her to harbour a fugitive! You must leave Germany!"

"But—"

"Ingelore!" Mutsch shouted. "Enough!" She hurriedly left the room.

Gerta got up, kissed my forehead, and said, "I'm sorry, but it is decided."

What at first appeared to be a family trip filled with exciting adventures now played out as three separate and distinct journeys each fraught with menacing risk, danger, and the possibility of being left behind. Would we ever be together again? I didn't understand. Why should I go to Amsterdam, Mutsch to Italy, and Paps to London? Why couldn't the three of us go together to each place?

With overwhelming regret and hideous embarrassment I write of those next few days. Because I suffered from ignorance and selfish immaturity I was uncontrollably incensed. I was being obtuse. As it often the case when one encounters unimaginable tragedy, I could not believe that the fate of others could also be my own.

I pouted for days. My parents absorbed as much of my petulance as they could. They made dozens of attempts to further explain the necessity of our plans. They tried everything: reason, analogy, threats, guilt, fear, and as a last resort, bribery. Finally, it was Gerta who made me appreciate what they were trying to do for me.

"Your parents are doing the right thing," she said. "Look at what's happened over the past few years and especially over the past two months. The Nazis not only have transformed our country but they've also crept into Berlin and into our daily lives. They've altered the ways we can choose to live."

"But you're a Christian. You're not affected," I countered.

"Everyone is affected, Ingelore. I'm very much affected."

I knew she was at her most serious because she had called me by my given name no more than five times in all the years we had been together. Although I have had other friends, no one has ever been as close to my heart as Gerta. She *is* my heart.

"We just want to be left alone!" I said.

She thought for a moment. "Do you see how our world is changing? No longer can a Jew marry a German. No longer can I be your housekeeper. No longer can–"

"–Why not?" I interrupted.

"There are laws. Right now your father and I are breaking the law. A German woman cannot be a housekeeper for Jews anymore. And the marriage ban between a Jew and a German, the Nazis say it's because of the sanctity of Aryan blood. Another law says your parents can no longer vote in elections. And if your father were, say, mayor of Berlin, he'd need to step down. Another law concerns our national symbols. I'm afraid this is only the beginning."[19]

"So, when I'm older I can't marry a German who's not a Jew?" I asked.

"No, you cannot."

"When I'm an adult, I can't vote?"

"No," she said.

"Once I finish my university I won't be able to work for the government?"

"No, you will not."

---

19 The overview Gerta presents here is of the *Nürnberger Gesetze* (the Nuremberg Laws) that were passed on 15 September 1935 and made effective the following day. The section relating to domestic workers, however, was not binding until 1 January 1936 (Shirer, *The Rise and Fall of the Third Reich*, 233).

Then I asked, "What do you mean when you say there are rules about national symbols?"

Gerta looked exhausted. "Because you're a Jew you cannot display the German flag or the German national colours. But," she added disdainfully, "you can display the Jewish colours in, around, and outside your home."

"See," I said, "Jews do have some rights!"

She became angry. "Don't you understand? The Nazis *want* the Jews to display their colours. It'll make it easier for them to find you! They won't be your colours. They'll be a target."

"But—"

"No! You must understand! They are wolves. They will not stop hunting!"

She cupped my chin in her palm. "The worst thing is that they are telling you who you can love. Think, my angel. When the time comes and you fall in love with a German boy, or a Christian, and you are swept away with feelings of happiness, the law will tell you that you may not couple—" She stopped abruptly.

I was curious. "Couple? What do you mean?"

"You know what I mean," she said. "You want to be in love, you want to kiss, and then you want to . . ." She stopped again. ". . . and then you want to couple."

"That's not such a bad thing, Gerta."

"But it's against the law! If you're caught, both you and your German boy will be imprisoned and made to do hard labour in a work camp somewhere. Do you see now? The Nazis have altered the way you may choose to live!"

My time of revelation had come. It was swiftly followed by my time of remorse. I felt terrible about the way I'd acted with my parents. I understood now how grave the situation was for Jews and how necessary it was for us to leave Germany. What my parents had decided I must do was for my safety and well-being. I should have been more cooperative and not so insufferably contrary. I needed to apologize to them immediately.

That evening as soon as we sat down for supper Paps recited his usual blessing, offering thanks for the bounty before us and so on. I was stunned when he added, "We're also thankful for our progeny, our only child, who matters most to us."

I burst out crying.

"Paps, Mutsch," I wailed, "I'm sorry. I've been a dreadful daughter these past few days. I'm so sorry."

Mutsch reached for my hand as father came to kneel down beside me.

"We love you, Lorechen," he said. "There's nothing more important to us than you. We've done what we feel is best for you. You need to be strong now. We all do."

I wept uncontrollably, "I've been a disgrace to you both."

"Hush," father said. "You are no such thing. We love you and we are proud of you. Look at what we have been through already. Are we weaker as a family? No, we are stronger."

"I was so worried about your headaches all the time and then you said you were going to London." I looked at Mutsch. "I am so scared thinking that you have to go alone to the Italian hospital. I'm tired of the shadows all about us, everywhere we look and everywhere we go. I don't want to be away from you."

"We understand," Mutsch said. "It's been very demanding and burdensome for you. But as your father says, we must carry on."

"I've never been apart from you. I'm afraid of being on my own even if it's only for a few days. What if we are separated? I worry that we might never reunite."

All of a sudden another wave of grief engulfed me.

"And what of Gerta?" I bawled. "What will become of her?"

We Say Goodbye

April 1936

Our final weeks in Berlin were full of a litany of heartbreaking farewells. I cannot count the number of times I have said goodbye. I lament them all.

The last days in Wilmersdorf flew by. My parents attended to tasks written on lists, crossing them off as they went. Our house was busy, Paps scurrying here, Mutsch toiling there, oftentimes bumping into each other while arranging trunks and boxes destined for family and friends.

Gerta was coming and going running errands. She returned from one mission with the rail tickets we would need: one ticket to Paris for Paps and then another to Calais where he would board a ship to London; transit for Mutsch to Switzerland where she would transfer to Merano, Italy; and, one for me to Amsterdam.

I stayed busy cleaning up everywhere. I remember folding most of my father's formal wear and dress garments with care so as not to wrinkle them. Herr Bayern would come by soon to pick them up.

I packed a rucksack that was to be my only luggage for the trip. I received it from Gerta. It had been her father's, left behind after a furlough he had enjoyed at home during the last weeks of the Great War. Shortly after his return to combat he was killed.

"Carry this and know I'm with you every step of the way," she said with tears in her eyes. "Perhaps I will visit someday."

Several of my friends already had emigrated with their families. I didn't know where they had gone until after my arrival in Japan. Their leaving had broken my heart. Spread across the globe, they were quite literally worlds away. Most of Paps' and Mutsch's friends, too, were planning their escape. For some, their departures didn't come quickly enough.

And so my father was to leave for the London office of his company at the same time. Mutsch would go to the hospital in Merano and I would be off to Amsterdam.

Paps explained that he needed to move his assets out of Germany. Dozens of pieces of jewellery, candelabra, silver tea sets and cutlery, religious items, Meissen porcelains, crystal vases, diamond rings, broaches, earrings, and pins were shipped to the London office of the J. Gerber Company. They would be inventoried then sold, converted into British pounds. Some of the money would be used to buy life insurance policies for him and Mutsch, some would be kept for travelling and most would be transferred to the Kobe office so it would be there waiting for us. Paps needed to be present to oversee this meticulous work.

Omi and Opa decided to remain in Berlin. In her youth, Omi had fled from the pogroms in Russia. When I begged them to come with us Omi said they were too old and too frail this time to start anew.

Paps' oldest sibling, Aunt Jenny, had married a Christian. He was the president of the Hamburg Import and Export Bank. When confronted by the Nazis he was given the choice of losing his position or his wife so he went underground with her. First hidden by French and Belgian partisans they would be on the run for many years, afraid for their lives.

Uncle Hans and his wife Lotte escaped to Argentina, lived there for six years and then returned to Berlin. Lotte was born a Christian and converted to Judaism when she and Hans married. Some of Lotte's family survived the relentless Allied bombing of Berlin and were still living there.

We would see Uncle Sieke in Warsaw in a few weeks at a last family reunion with Mutsch's sister and her family. Then we would continue across Poland, our final destination as far away as we dared imagine.

Even though we cried our wishes for speedy and safe travels and sobbed the belief we'd meet again, tacitly we knew there was little hope of either happening.

And the worst of the parting was yet to come.

Literally and figuratively, we drew the curtains on Friday, the seventeenth day of April, 1936.

I awoke that morning to a commotion. I jumped out of bed for the second time, the first being several hours before when my nightmare had awoken me again. This time I rose out of curiosity and not out of paralyzing horror. I dressed and found Herr Bayern and two men in our home. They were in the last stages of taking trunks and boxes outside and loading them onto a wagon.

"Well," he said, "there she is! It's been a long time, Fraülein Rothschild. Or is it Fraülein Völker?" He laughed, extending his hand. I didn't take it, deciding instead to hug him about his midsection. He patted my head.

Father said, "Herr Bayern will take some of our things and keep them safe. His friend," he pointed to one of the other men, "is Herr Ackerman. You remember his son Dieter from school." Of course I remembered Dieter.

Now acknowledging Herr Ackerman, Paps said, "He also has helped us. When we had the trouble with the police it was Herr Ackerman, the clerk at the station, who alerted Herr Bayern of the investigation. If it wasn't for him then we'd have . . ." He did not finish his thought but I knew what he was going to say.

Is it more sorrowful to leave without words than to do so with them? Mutsch and Paps embraced Herr Bayern, each of them kissing his cheeks. "Your home will be here, Herr Rothschild, waiting for your return," he said. Then he, Herr Ackerman, and the other man left. As I looked at Mutsch and Paps I saw a weighty silence between them.

When Gerta came by we went to my room to evaluate what I'd packed in the rucksack. "Mutsch told me to include underclothes," I said as I dumped the rucksack's contents onto my bed, "socks, blouses, and as many trousers and sweaters as I could fit. There's room only for one dress. I'll wear my sturdiest shoes."

"And the pencils, the writing paper, and the envelopes?" she wondered.

"I'll write to you, my family, and friends."

Gerta sorted through the items. "And what's this?" she asked, holding up a pouch Mutsch had made. It had a lanyard attached to it so I could wear it around my neck.

"Look inside," I said.

Gerta opened the pull strings and took out my identification document. "It makes me sad that you again must deny your name. But you'll need to be Erna Völker at least until you leave Germany. Good, your rail ticket is here, too."

After sifting through the garments one more time Gerta said, "Well done." Her eyes were puffy. "We must refold everything neatly now."

As we repacked the rucksack she said, "I want to thank you again for the clothing you won't be taking with you. Your mother has been so kind in that regard too. I've been lucky enough to find another family to work for as a housekeeper. It's a German family of means with three daughters, the oldest not quite ten, so if any of your things don't fit them now they soon will. They will delight in them."

"Is the man of the house kind?" I asked.

"Yes," Gerta said. "But of course he's not as nice as your father. Nor is their family as pleasant as yours. There'll never be a family for me such as yours." We hugged each other. "And thank you again for all your wonderful toys," she said. "I gave most to my brothers and some to the girls I care for now. I constantly badger them to stop their playing and attend to their chores." She laughed.

Just then Hansi let out a barrage of chirps. "Oh my," I said, tears welling up, "what'll become of you?"

"I'll take him home, if you'll allow it," Gerta said. "That way, when he sings, I'll think of you."

Finally, Paps, Mutsch, and I were at the door as Gerta came from my room carrying a book and Hansi in his cage. We all were overcome.

"Your father didn't allow you to bring the hundreds of volumes from the library," Gerta said, her humour easing the dread of what we knew was coming. "But, he'll allow you to bring this one. Take it and whenever you read from it remember the many times I've read it to you." It was our old frayed copy of *Children's and Household Tales*. I can still hear her now, reading aloud in the snug recesses of our library all those years ago.

Our last embrace came on the front steps where Paps and Mutsch had placed their suitcases. I had my rucksack on my back. Paps closed our door, locked it, and handed the key to Gerta. She said, "I'll see to it that Herr Bayern receives this later this afternoon."

The four of us linked arms, swaying back and forth. We poured out words of love, appreciation, and gratitude—dozens of memories were whispered through our tears.

Gerta gathered herself. "I pray to St. Boniface your voyage will be safe. I pray you'll return soon. I'll pray for each of you every day of my life."

Gerta kissed my forehead, picked up Hansi's cage, and walked away. We stood there watching her get smaller while her shadow grew longer. Just as she turned the corner, she raised a hand to us without looking back, then disappeared from view.

The trolley ride to the train station was short. Our car was almost at capacity. Many passengers were carrying packages, suitcases, and bundles and I suspected those people, too, were on their way out of Germany. I heard Paps say to Mutsch, "Isn't this ironic? This trolley is taking us away from our home and from one another, but it was also a trolley that first brought you to us, Lorechen." Mutsch placed her hand on Paps' wrist. "Yes, darling, it is indeed an irony." To this day that moment saddens me beyond words.

When we arrived at the rail station it was overrun with families lugging whatever belongings they could carry while pushing and dragging what they could not. Parents pulled their children along as if they were stubborn horses resisting their reins. The movement of the crowd swept elderly couples along.

We approached the platform for the train to Amsterdam. I could see that most seats were taken. Then a piercing whistle blew. A conductor, shouting to be heard over the clamour, alerted everyone to the train's imminent departure.

Paps hugged me. "It's time, Lorechen." He kissed the crown of my head a dozen times. "You be careful. When you arrive in Amsterdam Uncle Heinburg will greet you at the station. He'll care for you until I come from London. We—"

Mutsch interrupted, "And then both of you will come for me." She kissed my cheek.

I stepped back to look at them. "I'm frightened I'll never see you again," my throat closing.

I turned away, gingerly stepped from the platform into the rail car, and then sat in the first empty seat I found. I looked out the window. Paps and Mutsch were crying. As the train began to creep ahead my mother blew me a kiss. I waved to her.

In a moment they were gone, and I was on my own.

PART TWO

On My Own

Holland 1936

The man seated next to me was snoring. He was a well-dressed man about Paps' age. Earlier when I boarded the train and stumbled over him to sit at the window, he said, "You're travelling alone. I'll watch for you."

The train was knifing its way westward, the sun softly setting in the distance.

There were no empty seats. The car was littered with travel bags, cartons wrapped in newspaper, and assorted other luggage. Could these people all be tortured innocents on their way out of Germany?

I felt safe with the snoring man next to me so I crouched down in my seat and began to doze, the motion of the train lulling me to sleep. I'm not sure how long it was before I felt a jerking movement. My eyes popped open.

"This is just a stop," the man said. "After a few minutes, we'll be on our way." Then he asked, "What's your destination?"

"Amsterdam. I'm going to my uncle's home," I said.

"Good," he smiled, "that city is my destination as well. I have business there."

The train crept along and then resumed cruising speed. I fell back asleep.

The next thing I remember is waking to the sounds of a harried commotion. Several people were craning their necks to see down the aisle. I began to stand but the man next to me put his hand on my knee. "Don't get up. Remain seated."

Then a sudden horror presented itself. Three soldiers entered by the doorway at the front of the rail car. They wore the swastika, just as the police from the schoolyard had years ago. The heels of their boots thumped as they made their way to the first row of seats.

"Show us your papers!" they barked in German.

Everyone fell silent. It was as if time stopped. Then the commotion resumed as everyone readied to present their documents. I reached into my shirt pulling on the lanyard of my pouch to retrieve it. I opened the drawstrings and pulled out my paper and my ticket, holding it in my trembling hand. I repeated the words "I'm Erna Völker, Erna Völker," in my head.

The man next to me said, "We're at the border." Pointing to the soldiers he whispered, "They'll decide who will pass into Holland."

Two of the soldiers began examining the passengers' documents while the third remained at the front door. At first I hadn't noticed but there was a fourth soldier at the rear door. The man next to me followed my gaze.

"That's so no one exits into the next car," he said.

As the soldier checked the people in the row ahead of us, the man leaned over and whispered in my ear, "I'm your grandfather, Karl Langer. We're going to see our family in Amsterdam. Do you understand?"

Now that the soldier was upon us I could smell the leather of his boots. Herr Langer nonchalantly handed his papers for review. The soldier returned them and then took mine from my quivering hand.

"Are you related?" the soldier asked.

"For your information," Herr Langer said with a staunch tone of authority, "this is my granddaughter. We're going to visit our family in Amsterdam."

I was holding my breath. Father had told me to expect this kind of confrontation.

The soldier returned my document to me. "Very well, Herr Langer. You and your granddaughter are permitted to continue on."

Just then the soldier a few rows ahead called out. "This family is to be questioned." A young couple with two children was hurried to the front of the car whereupon they were told to get off the train. "And this one," he said as he forcibly pulled a man from his seat, "is to be detained indefinitely."

The soldiers finished their examinations and then proceeded to the next car.

Herr Langer exhaled, "That was unfortunate." I wasn't sure if he was referring to the people who had been escorted off the train or to the indignity to which we had all been subjected.

When the train pressed on I was heartbroken to see a dozen people, some of them children, gathered in a knot of fear, the German soldiers leading them into the station house.

"It's done," Herr Langer said. "Try to relax now. Soon, we'll be in Amsterdam."

The train ride passed quickly. I regret that I didn't see more of the countryside but the darkness was thick. All I could make out were a few polders protected by massive dunes and dikes.

Before long the train began to decelerate.

"Prepare your things," Herr Langer said. "We'll be at the station momentarily."

I checked my pouch, tightened its drawstrings, adjusted the straps of my rucksack, and then sat quietly. As the train crawled into the station I saw dozens of people, some standing and some sitting on benches, all huddled with their belongings, ready to board. Others were waiting for loved ones. As the sea of faces passed I searched each one, looking for Uncle Heinburg.

The train stopped. Everyone rose at once, rushing to gather belongings. Some passengers were rude, pushing and shoving, handling their luggage without regard, hitting each other in the knee or leg. I heard many obscenities as they exited the car.

"Are you ready now?" Herr Langer wanted to know.

"Yes, I'm ready."

We left the car. As we made our way along the platform, I stopped after just a few steps. Herr Langer, who I now realized was a great deal taller than I'd thought he was, towered over me.

"Thank you," I said.

"You're welcome. I'll stay until you find your uncle."

I began to feel a fire of nervousness. The crowd on the platform had thinned. My uncle was nowhere to be found. I felt dizzy and nauseous. What will I do if Uncle Heinburg does not come for me? Where will I go? What will become of me?

"You're alarmed," Herr Langer said. "Don't worry. I'm sure your uncle will be here shortly." He reached into his vest and took out his pocket watch. "See? The train was nearly twenty minutes early."

As we walked into the station house I saw Uncle Heinburg running toward us.

"Forgive me," he shouted, "I didn't know the train would be early! You must be so upset! But now I'm here!"

He hugged me. "You look wonderful. So big now! How long has it been since we . . ." He stopped when he saw the tall man standing next to me.

"Good sir, you'll kindly step away from my niece," he barked.

"No, uncle," I pleaded. "This is Herr Langer. We travelled together all the way from Berlin. He's been so kind–a wonderful travel companion."

"I see," Heinburg said. "I apologize, Herr Langer. Thank you for all you've done for my loved one."

Herr Langer reached down and gently lifted my chin, tilting my head up. "It's been my pleasure, Fraülein. I'm sure you're safe now so I'll say goodbye."

We exchanged a short embrace. Then, Herr Langer left.

"I'm glad you're here," Uncle Heinburg said. "Let's go now. Ida and Ullie are waiting for you at the house. They're so excited!"

It was late when we arrived at Uncle Heinburg's home. Aunt Ida and Ullie already were asleep. I was ushered to a small room off the kitchen that served as a storage area. Canned goods and other household items were in boxes off to one side to make room for a cot. Uncle Heinburg kissed me goodnight and then retired. I placed my rucksack under the cot, pulled down the linens, took off my shoes, and collapsed on the mattress. I was exhausted.

The next morning after a wonderful reunion with Aunt Ida and my cousin Ullie, we sat down for breakfast, gabbing the entire time, my curiosity about them only slightly overtaking their curiosity about Paps, Mutsch, the rest of our relatives, and me. We talked for hours, each of us contributing news and memories.

Outside the city was alive with colour. It was tulip time in Amsterdam. The flowers' petals and sepals glowed like stained glass all along the avenues.

On my third day in Amsterdam I went for a walk on my own. I returned with a bouquet of tulips a gardener in a park had given me. "Everyone's so nice here," I said to my aunt, "and nobody's called me a dirty Jew."

Ida was horrified. "Why would they call you such a name and what makes you say such a thing?"

"That's what some children in Berlin called me, even those I played with for years. Paps says it's one of the reasons we left Berlin. But I guess things are different here."

"Yes," she assured me, "of course they are."

Aunt Ida had no idea what was on its way. None of us did. Four years later, when my parents and I were in Japan, news reached us that Dutch Jews were running for their lives from the Nazi advance. It took only a few days for the country to fall. Uncle Heinburg wrote that thousands of Jews were arrested, some sent to concentration camps, and others were forced into slave labour. Many were shot dead where they were standing.

Looking back I still can't come to terms with the striking contrast between the delicate tulips of Amsterdam and the iron waves of tanks—the relentless legions of soldiers crushing that beautiful country underfoot, destroying its warm and friendly people.

Ten long days had passed since I'd left my parents weeping on the platform of the station as my train pulled away. I didn't know if Paps had made it to London without incident and if Mutsch had arrived safely in Italy. Was her operation successful? Had she found relief from her discomfort?

I tried to remain positive. I chose to believe my parents would persevere because they'd always been good people—virtuous and kind. During prayer times at the synagogue in Dahlem, I kept telling myself only the wicked are punished.

Ullie and I were outside, skipping along one of the canals, when I saw Paps.

I raced to him and leaped into his outstretched arms. He was smiling, his eyes filled with tears. We embraced for what seemed like hours.

At the supper table that night Uncle Heinburg recited words of thankfulness to which he added a benediction for Mutsch's safety and speedy recovery.

Paps and I readied for the journey to Italy. My uncle, my aunt, and Ullie wished us well asking us to remember them to our relatives. They came to see us off at the rail station with tears of joy and sadness.

I lament all the times I've had to say goodbye.

Together Again

April 1936

When Paps and I left Amsterdam bound for Brussels I wondered why we couldn't take a more direct route through Germany to Italy. After all, our forged papers had worked and neither of us had aroused suspicion. When I questioned Paps about this he was reluctant to explain not wanting to worry me.

As our train hurtled across the countryside he finally told me, "It's necessary to avoid crossing into Germany. No Jew is safe there."

"But we travel as the Völker family," I said, "and when I was questioned at the border on the way to Amsterdam there were no problems. Everything was in order."

He looked at me. "I've kept it from you until now but there's been another arrest warrant issued for me. The Nazis set upon my company offices in Berlin and examined its records regarding employees and their whereabouts. They learned that I'd forwarded all my financial business to London. They surmised that I was planning an escape. By cross-referencing the records from the roster at your former school it was easy for them to positively identify me and my relationship to you.

They know who I am. They know who you are. We must continue to travel without re-entry into Germany."

It was difficult for me to imagine my father as a fugitive. His alleged offenses could only be a tragic misunderstanding. His heritage and his faith were his undoing. It was a pathetic injustice that the root cause of the prejudices against him was something over which he had no control.

We arrived in Brussels. The first leg of our journey was complete. At the station Paps verified the particulars of our upcoming travels. "We must remain alert because if we miss our connections there may be complications." Next, we went to Luxembourg. From there to Strasbourg, in eastern France.

On the train, I wrote to Gerta. It had only been eleven days since I left her but already I missed her terribly. I would write to Omi and Opa, too. I hoped they were safe. Paps told me he was grateful I was thinking of his parents. I would also write to Uncle Sieke.

At the station in Luxembourg we had time to stretch our legs and walk about. The large crowds carrying luggage mesmerized us. I wondered if they were running from something too. We made our next connection with no trouble.

In France, we were safe. As we were leaving the Strasbourg station I got to show off in front of Paps when I had a conversation in French with a teenaged girl seated in front of us.

I must have fallen asleep because the next thing I remember is our train approaching the station in Basel. Again, Paps and I checked our tickets and schedules for the next connection. When the train stopped we made our way to the designated platform. The train to Merano would be leaving momentarily.

"We've travelled approximately eight hundred kilometres," Paps said. "We've maybe three hundred more. In a few hours we'll reunite with Mutsch and our family will be together again."

The train chugged along straining to climb the steep inclines of the mountainous terrain of Switzerland. There was snow everywhere at the higher elevations.

I decided to read from the book Gerta had given me. The story was *Rotkäppchen*. Paps said, "It's a favourite of mine, too, Lorechen, the little girl in her red clothing on her way to her grandmother with a basket of food. It's such an endearing tale."

I read silently and then closed my eyes imagining Gerta's voice reciting the words, remembering our sessions in the library. I swooned with delight at the memory of the sweet intonations of her voice.

And then my ogre appeared, dressed in a black fur overcoat, chasing me through the rail cars. He limped after me just a few steps behind. I ran past startled passengers, far enough ahead of him to crank open the doorway, step precariously onto the wavering iron platforms between the cars, and then slam the door behind me. I ran through several cars and then I entered one where I found Paps. I screamed as I hurried toward him, "Father! Save me!" He had his head down, reading from a newspaper. He didn't look up. Overwrought with terror, I tried desperately to open the next door. Would the monster catch me? Would I fall between the cars? Would I die at his hands?

"Lorechen," I heard my father say as he tried to shake me awake. "You were screaming in your sleep. You're safe. You're here on the train with me." I composed myself. Paps embraced me assuring me all was well. "Soon we'll be with your mother."

And so it was. In less than an hour we found ourselves in Merano, Italy. We walked the short distance from the station to the hotel where Mutsch was staying. Dusk prevailed as we made our way, the early evening air crisp and clear.

The hotel was surrounded by a semicircular area of lawns with fountains and flowerbeds leading up a slight slope upon which the hotel sat twenty metres away. We walked up the pathway, both of us bubbling with excitement. And there near a stand of trees was Mutsch looking off into the distance. She was munching on grapes completely oblivious to our approach.

I ran to her. At the sound of my footsteps, Mutsch turned, the grapes dropped from her hand, and she immediately extended her arms calling out, "Lorechen! Lorechen!" We embraced. I buried my face in her dress.

She smelled fresh and clean. Seconds later father came and encircled Mutsch and me in his strong arms. We were together again, the three of us, swaying in a caress as our tears came with Paps kissing Mutsch, all the while my parents squeezing me nearly to death.

"You look so well," Paps said, "so healthy and so tan!"

Mutsch said, "I'm well, my darlings. Everything's fine. A day or two after my arrival I was up and about. The doctor said I had fared exceptionally well. Now I'm as good as new!"

"I missed you so much," I said. "I was scared we never would be together again."

"Yes, of course, and I've missed you as well. So much so." Her eyes were tearing up again. "But now, let's go inside. There's someone I'd like you both to meet."

We walked into the building. As we came to the front desk Mutsch said in Italian, "This is my family, Anna." The woman, about Mutsch's height but much heavier, looked up. "Very nice," the woman said. Then after we exchanged greetings she said, "Now it's time to eat!"

Anna ushered us into the dining room. Candles glowed everywhere. The aromas of sharp cheeses, pungent garlic, and sweet sauces filled the air as she led us to a table.

We sat, arranged our napkins, and then sipped water from stemmed goblets. "And so," Paps said to Mutsch, "you look so . . ." He stumbled to find the right word, ". . . so, so . . ."

Mutsch laughed. "Yes, I've gained some weight. Anna insists I eat my spaghetti and bread at every meal, even breakfast!"

It was wonderful to be together again each of us safe and well. We chatted without stopping, Paps detailing his trip from Berlin to London and then onto Amsterdam, and my telling Mutsch of my voyage from Berlin to Amsterdam—the incident at the German border made her gasp. She wanted to know about Uncle Heinburg, Aunt Ida, and Ullie and I told her how they took very good care of me and how I enjoyed the tulips. Then Paps and I took turns recounting our exploits from Amsterdam to Italy.

Our reunion in Merano lasted three days. The weather was perfect, warm and sunny with a slight breeze and at night the air was dry and refreshing. We talked about our family and our dearest friends whom we'd left behind. No word had come yet from Gerta, Omi and Opa, or Uncle Sieke, although my letters to them surely must have been delivered by then. I'd written my return address as Mutsch's hotel since Paps said there'd be no other chance to receive mail until we arrived in Japan. Mother hadn't heard from anyone.

On one occasion I overheard Paps and Mutsch talking about his brothers, Hans, Alfred, and Erich, and his sister, Jenny. My parents didn't know of their whereabouts and they were extremely worried.

I remember Paps asking Mutsch whether she felt strong enough to carry on.

"You're prepared to travel?" he asked.

"Yes," she said, "though the doctor wants to see me on Friday for a final examination. That's six days from now! I know we can't wait that long. We must proceed. I'm fine. I've notified his office and cancelled my appointment."

"You're sure then?"

She smiled at him, clasping her hand about his wrist. "Yes, darling. I'm fine, I'm sure. I'm ready."

At our evening meal Paps reminded us of what the next part of our journey would entail. "From here we will go to Vienna. We may be interrupted at the Austrian border. The Nazi influence in that country is great, Lorechen, so you'll need to make sure your pouch is secure. Then we'll enter Czechoslovakia and make our way to Prague. We don't know what the political situation is there. Once we leave that country we'll be in Poland. I hope it will only be matter of days before we see Mutsch's sister in Warsaw. Our journey is far from over and there may be many . . ." he looked pensively at Mutsch, ". . . many situations that will test our resourcefulness and resolve."

I knew I wouldn't rest well on that last night in Italy.

"Lorechen," my father was yelling, "it's time to get up! You've slept enough, young lady!"

I sat up, groggy with sleep.

"Paps, Mutsch," I whispered, remembering what day it was. "It's time to leave already?"

"Yes," Mutsch said, "we must pack our things and be on our way."

That morning, at breakfast in the hotel's dining room, we reviewed our tasks and plans for the day. Our schedule included arriving at the train station, purchasing our tickets, and boarding the next train to Vienna.

"*Si mangia il maccheroni di questa mattina*?" I heard behind me. I turned to see Anna, her apron splashed with sauce. She was bright-eyed, smiling. Mutsch translated, "She wants to know if I will eat the macaroni this morning."

"*No, grazie,* Anna," mother said. "We're leaving today. *Grazie di tutto.*"

Anna opened her arms to Mutsch. They embraced. With tears in her eyes, Anna said, "*Dio sia con voi e la vostra famiglia.*"

"I'll miss Anna," mother said as we left the hotel, "she's been very kind to me. She's looked after me every day. When we hugged her last words to us were, 'God be with you and your family.'"

At the station Mutsch and I waited for Paps to purchase tickets.

Returning, he said, "The train will leave in twenty minutes. Let's go to the track now."

Paps insisted I have a window seat. "Remember to take in the landscapes and topography, Lorechen. Already you have passed through six countries. Someday you may choose to write about your travels!"

The landscape of northern Italy is nearly beyond words. I relished the expansive, craggy mountains, the verdant fields, the netted lemon orchards, pockets of small villages glistening in the late morning sunlight, august churches perched on hills, and sleepy dirt roads meandering through meadows and grasslands. The scenery of that trip to Vienna hypnotized me. At the time I considered Italy to be the most wondrous of lands.

Seven Hundred Kilometres, More Goodbyes

May 1936

Paps and Mutsch had been holding hands for a long time. They decided to stretch their legs. "We'll walk along the aisle, Lorechen," Paps said. "We won't leave the car." They traversed the length of it several times continuing to hold hands.

Not more than a minute after they sat down the train reduced its speed. Father looked tense, "We're near the Austrian border."

The door of the car opened. Two uniformed men entered. One was fair, of average height. The other was swarthy and heavy around the midsection. Their uniforms were similar but not identical. Each had an official-looking emblem sewn onto the sleeve. Father noticed. "They're police," he whispered. "See the colours of the badges? One is with the Italian authorities, the other is Austrian."

The taller man, the Austrian, addressed the passengers in German. "You will have your tickets available for review." The other officer repeated the instructions in Italian.

"Lorechen," Paps said, "get your document ready. If you're approached don't speak unless I indicate that you may." Paps held our train tickets. It was not long before the Austrian came to us.

The man's facial features were pronounced. "Your tickets, please," he said. He took a moment to review them. "Very well. We will cross the border soon. We apologize for the inconvenience."

Paps exhaled in relief.

"Why does the train slow down to verify tickets?" Mutsch suddenly asked. This made Paps and I snap our heads in her direction.

"Excuse my beloved, sir," Paps said haltingly, "but she's inquisitive, more so than is necessary."

The policeman stared at Mutsch. My hands shook in my lap.

"What's your name again?" he asked.

Mother swallowed hard. "Ernestine Völker."

"It's routine, Frau Völker," the officer said, "if we need to remove undesirables who are trying to enter Austria we can stop the train quickly and escort them off at the border." He studied her for a few more seconds. I could hear my heart pounding in my chest. Then he continued on his way.

Paps stroked his forehead with his thumb and forefinger. Then he said, "In the future, my dear, in a similar situation you won't speak unless I indicate that you may."

Well that was a first, Paps admonishing Mutsch and me with the same words!

I must have been asleep when we crossed the Italian border into Austria. We disembarked in Vienna and then walked to the main section of the station. We stopped at a bistro for something to drink. Paps ordered tea for himself and coffee for Mutsch. All I wanted was cold water. After studying the train schedule posted on the wall, he said, "I'll go to the ticket booth now. You will both stay here. Don't leave one another's sight. Be alert, watch our baggage."

The lobby was busy. I tried to guess who was late and who was early. I silently wished them a pleasant welcome on their return home rather than for safe travel away from it.

Father returned hastily. "There's a slight problem."

"What is it?" Mutsch asked almost losing her breath.

"The agent informed me that all persons desiring tickets must be present at the time of purchase. We must go to the booth together. We'll need to show our papers to the agent."

"Will there be trouble?" Mutsch asked.

"I don't think so," Paps said. "Just follow my lead and try to relax."

As I looked into father's eyes I knew he was suffering from one of his headaches. I saw lines of stress in the skin at his temple. His right eye was beginning to tear, blinking more rapidly than his left. He sensed my concern. "I'm fine, Lorechen, just a slight headache. Gather your rucksack. Let's go."

At the booth my father requested three tickets to Prague.

"Your papers?" the agent asked.

I took mine from my pouch and gave them to Paps. He reached into his jacket and found his and Mutsch's. He handed them to the agent who studied them for a few moments, looking at each of us as he perused them. Then he slid the papers back to Paps.

"What's your destination?"

"We request passage to Prague."

After Paps paid the fares the agent produced three tickets. "Proceed to track four and ready your papers and tickets for boarding."

I looked to Mutsch. She seemed poised to inquire again about procedure but her look suddenly changed to one of resignation. I'm sure she heard Paps' admonishment in her head.

As we turned away the agent asked, "Your purpose in Prague?"

Again I heard my heartbeats. Paps appeared dumbstruck.

"Sir?" father asked in disbelief.

"Your purpose in Prague, Herr Völker?" the agent persisted.

Mutsch approached the booth. "We're going to a specialist. My husband suffers from severe acute headaches and will undergo a day or two of tests. Don't you see his discomfort?" She edged Paps closer to the agent's window, pointing her shaking finger at Paps' face.

The agent saw the manifestations of pain on Paps' brow and eye.

"Very well. Proceed to track four."

We withdrew from the booth and made off through the crowds.

Paps said, "Thank you, my darling. Your quick thinking was—"

She interrupted him. "You're welcome. I needed to protect my husband."

When the train arrived we stepped back to allow passengers to exit. As the last few disembarked a soldier appeared at the doorway. He looked menacing, another man with pungent leather boots and the frightening swastika on his sleeve, another reminder that we were being watched, shadowed, our every move regarded with suspicion.

The soldier demanded our tickets and papers. He studied them all the while looking at Mutsch. Father was getting impatient.

"Is there a problem?" Paps demanded.

"We verify everyone's identity," the soldier said matter-of-factly, "so no one leaves our country who should not."

Paps reiterated what Mutsch had told the ticket agent. "Shall I not proceed to Prague to try to find relief from what afflicts me?" I thought Paps was being too brazen. I was nervous. "I suffer," he added.

The soldier tensed. "We scrutinize everyone leaving our country," he said. "You are German, you understand, don't you?"

"Yes, of course," Paps said, "I apologize for being meddlesome."

With that we inched passed the soldier, entered the railcar, and found seats. The exchange had been exhausting and we exhaled with overdue relief.

We continued our odyssey, the monotony of travel taking hold of me. It was now early evening. The train pressed on to Prague. The panorama flitting by was that of thick darkness interspersed with needles of light from villages and outposts. Black clouds hid the stars.

I asked Paps if he too felt the tedium of our travel.

"Yes, Lorechen, I do," he said, holding my hand. "But it's necessary. We must remain positive and dedicated. It'd be perilous to be in Germany now. The Nazis are looking for both of us. They're making life miserable for Jews. There's persecution everywhere. Our trip to Japan will be long but when we arrive I'll be able to resume my work and provide for you and Mutsch, and we will live in relative comfort, free from oppression."

"I'm starving," Mutsch interjected.

"Yes," Paps said, "let's go to the dining car. I have our tickets handy. We'll need to take our belongings."

When we came to the dining car several groups of people were seated. Our presence didn't interrupt the diners. The aromas in the car were pleasant. I recognized sauerbraten, the billowing smoke of cigars. We found an unoccupied table and sat down.

We decided on simple but filling meals. I didn't know how hungry I was until I began eating. Our schedule had only allowed for breakfast and supper, we had to forgo a midday meal because of haste and expense. Paps told us we would need to monitor our expenditures and use restraint so that the money he possessed would see us all the way to Japan.

During our meal Paps said, "We'll have travelled approximately seven hundred kilometres from Merano to Prague."

"It has already been a long journey," Mutsch said, "travelling across Europe. Now together, we continue on."

After supper we returned to our railcar. I tried to read my book but soon dozed off. A few hours later, Paps woke me. "We're here, Lorechen, in Prague."

We encountered no resistance or inconvenience in Prague. We bought tickets to Warsaw and then proceeded to the platform.

The architecture of the station was remarkable. Its cavernous lobby had a lofty dome, sculpted busts and statuary, and magnificent stained glass windows.

There were no police, no Nazis, and no questions about who we were or where we were going. There were no blatant or probing stares. In fact, it was as if we were invisible. The only request casually made of us was, "May we see your tickets?"

We were now on our way to Warsaw to see family and rest for a while before our pilgrimage would take us out of Europe and into Asia where we would begin our trek across Russia to the Orient.

Sleep came easily to me once we left Prague. When I awoke I saw slivers of light on the horizon. Paps was asleep, Mutsch leaning against him. They were holding hands.

The passengers near the front of the railcar began to stir. We must be close, I thought.

The train coughed, waking Paps and Mutsch.

Even before the train came to a stop I saw Aunt Irma wandering along the platform's edge looking into every window as the cars went by. I could hear her high-pitched voice yelling for her sister, "Doris! Doris!" It was so amusing, Aunt Irma lost in a sea of people, everyone else knowing exactly where they were going. When we got off the train she ran toward us. She was just as I had remembered her, a fat little lady with big brown eyes and a warm engaging smile.

"How are you my dears?" she said embracing Paps. "And how are you, my sick little sister!" She hugged Mutsch and then kissed her cheeks. Without waiting for an answer she chirped, "You look so well! Merano has done wonders for you!"

She then turned her attention to me. "Here's my favourite niece!" she said, bending slightly to crush me in an excited embrace. After kissing me, she stepped back to look at us, and her eyes clouded. I knew she was happy to see us yet she looked so sad.

Aunt Irma came to Berlin only a few times a year so I didn't know her well, but I felt her warmth and sincere concern for us.

At a dinner in Berlin a few years earlier, I had learned that before I was born Irma had married a Pole and then moved from Berlin to Warsaw. He died shortly thereafter so I never knew him. She remained in Warsaw in the home that he had built. Whenever she came to visit she would bring chocolate tarts filled with fruit. They were delicious. I had always liked my Aunt. She was jolly and cuddly.

I noticed a girl standing behind her. My parents embraced her. "This is Stella," Irma said to me, "you two have never met." She was Irma's daughter, older than me, just as plump as my aunt and as shy as her mother was gregarious.

Stella said hello, we smiled at each other, and then the five us went to the waiting room. "We have two hours before our departure," Paps said.

As we were making our way Stella asked, "Are you excited about going to Japan?" She spoke perfect German even though Polish was her native language. "It's so far away," she mused.

"Yes," I said, "I'm very excited. Wouldn't it be fun if you and Aunt Irma came to visit after I learn Japanese? Then I could teach you both!"

Stella said, "Yes, I'd love that!" Paps, Mutsch, and Aunt Irma, like most parents, preferred not to make decisions without careful thought, and they told us we'd have to wait and see.

All of a sudden I saw Uncle Sieke! I jumped into his arms and hugged him with all my might. Paps said to me, "I'm sorry we didn't tell you sooner, Lorechen. We knew of his plan to come here but we didn't say anything for fear of disappointment. At the last minute the German government granted him permission to come to Warsaw, but only for two days."

I was so excited to see my Uncle Sieke. I adored him. I have fond memories of Uncle Sieke taking me for rides around Berlin in his big, black shiny car. He was the first person in our family to own an automobile. I thought he was the most handsome man I had ever met, after Paps, of course.

"Please, come with us to Japan!" I begged.

He laughed. "Maybe soon. Then we'll have a big reunion!"

Fate was not that kind.

Several years later we learned that when Uncle Sieke returned to Berlin from Warsaw he was arrested and sent to a concentration camp. As it turned out his wealth made him one of the fortunate Jews. The Nazis wanted his factory. By that time Uncle Sieke's factory had diversified to include the production of miner's helmets, lights, and other equipment used by workers in the extraction of iron ore and other minerals necessary for the manufacture of steel and armaments. They offered to release him on condition he leave Germany after selling his factory to them for ten Deutschmarks! It was worth ten thousand times more! Further, he could obtain an entrance visa to any country that would have him. The

Nazis acquired his enormous factory, his life's work, for almost nothing. He obtained a visa to Australia and left Germany several weeks after his release from the camp, penniless but free. I remember seeing a picture of him in Australia, a haunting photograph of him sitting on a park bench dressed in linen trousers and a short-sleeved shirt. On the inner part of his lower left arm a striking, dark blue six-digit tattoo is visible. We were relieved to hear that Uncle Sieke eventually became an Australian citizen. Although he started with nothing he established a career and an affluent business. He lived there until his death many years later.

Aunt Irma died in the Warsaw Ghetto Uprising of 1943. Stella survived, but her husband perished during an air raid. Months later, having begun her pregnancy a matter of weeks before her husband's death, Stella gave birth to a son. When the little boy was three he died after stepping on a land mine buried beneath the road near their house.

But that day at the Warsaw station we didn't know any of this. Amid tears and promises to meet again soon, we said our goodbyes to Aunt Irma, Stella, and Uncle Sieke, and we unenthusiastically boarded our train to continue the long journey to Japan.

A Major Catastrophe

May 1936

We travelled uneventfully across the Polish border into Russia. Villages flanked by military installations of some sort and huts with guards armed with rifles peppered the way. When we arrived at the station in Minsk we had time for a quick rest and a light meal.

We approached the next train that would take us to Moscow with amazement. Its enormous locomotive was resting at the platform, breathing a steady tempo, expelling bursts of steam from its sides and iron chimney. Paps noted, "There are many more cars, Lorechen," he said pointing to the locomotive, "so the power needed to pull them is much greater."

We made our way along the train looking for the railcar assigned to us on our tickets. Railway personnel were assisting passengers looking for their appropriate boarding locations. On his own, Paps discovered ours. We found seats at the front of the car. No sooner had we put our baggage down than two Russian soldiers entered through the doorway. They stopped in front of us. Both were dressed impeccably in tailored uniforms but I cannot recall if they were carrying weapons. Just then one of the soldiers said something to Paps.

Father was bewildered. Of course! None of us spoke Russian!

Paps asked him in German if he spoke German. The man replied, "*Nyet*," which we obviously gathered to be the Russian word for *no*. Then Paps asked both of them in French if either spoke French. "Nyet." Paps made one last effort, this time in English. Both responded, "Nyet." I felt my insides cramping. I was petrified that we would be escorted off the train, orphaned in the middle of a wilderness, wrestling with the prospect of having to retrace our steps while the train departed without us.

Mutsch stepped toward them. She used two fingers to draw a small square in midair. Then she placed her palms together, then opened them slowly as if they were covers of a book. The soldier's eyes opened wide. "Dah!"

"They need to see our documents," she said.

The soldiers checked our papers. Within a few minutes they left us to proceed along the aisle. The three of us watched as they reviewed the papers of a middle-aged couple in the seats next to ours. They'd seen what had transpired with us so they knew to present their documents. The soldiers finished with them, continued down the aisle, and then exited into the next car. We never saw those two soldiers again, not once during our trip between Minsk and Moscow. We never saw them get off the train at any of the stops. We never knew where they stayed while on the train, if they were on it at all. It was a mystery to us.

I was worried that our inability to understand and speak Russian would pose problems along our nine thousand kilometre journey from Moscow to the eastern terminus. The train would make dozens of stops along the way with those soldiers, or others, checking everyone's papers frequently. "There'll be interaction with the police. I'm sure of it," Paps commented.

There was a slight jolt when the locomotive came alive. It slowly started to churn its wheels, strenuously pulling at a snail's pace until the train reached a leisurely speed, the engine and its long line of railcars clearing the station. We were on our way.

Paps stood up. "I'm going to walk along the aisle. I won't be gone long," he said.

Mutsch closed her eyes. I was not sleepy so I opened my rucksack to retrieve my book. I was flipping through it just as father came back. Mutsch opened her eyes. Both of us noticed that Paps had a peculiar look on his face.

"What's the matter, dear?" Mutsch asked.

He sat down and said in a low tone, "You won't believe it but of the people with whom I've chatted . . . it's incredible . . . they all speak German!"

Immediately Mutsch and I perked our ears as if we were hunting dogs. Up until that point the bellowing locomotive had rendered all conversations into unintelligible rumblings and undertones that we assumed were spoken in Russian. With the police expected to patrol the train frequently we thought everyone was whispering so they would not draw attention to themselves. Now with careful scrutiny we heard the distinctive sounds of our native tongue! What a fortuitous circumstance!

I asked Paps, "Do you know if any of them speak Russian?"

"No, I don't, Lorechen," he said. "A man told me there'll be a meeting in the club car for passengers occupying the first three railcars within the hour."

Anxious still, I asked, "Will this make it easier for us to get by without understanding Russian?"

"Let's not worry, Lorechen. Not everyone on this train speaks German and certainly not everyone speaks Russian. Perhaps we'll be fortunate enough to meet people who speak both languages."

When we entered the club car an hour later there were people all about. I heard music in the air! Everyone was speaking German! It was extraordinary! As we walked down the aisle father conversed with many of the passengers—it was as if he knew everyone but of course he did not. I'm sure all of the travellers were relieved to be able to understand one another.

We learned that some passengers were running from the Nazis just as we were. But I also recall two couples seated together, dressed in magnificent clothing, wearing what surely was couture. They could have been German aristocracy. As we passed by, they bragged in stilted authoritarian tones that they were on their way to the Orient to vacation for a few months. Others were not as favoured. There were some who were obviously tired and beleaguered, most likely from prolonged travel. Those with temporary visas hoped to reach their destination before their expiration condemned them to alien status.

A thin woman in her late twenties entered the car. Quietude descended upon everyone. She was wearing a police uniform. Her brown hair was straight as nails, her shoulders perfectly level, unmistakably perpendicular to her tall linear frame. She was very attractive.

"Good afternoon. My name is Katya. Is there anyone who does not understand me?" she asked in less-than-perfect German. "Raise your hand." No one did. She continued. "Very good. I'm your tour guide and travel companion.[20] Feel free to consult with me when you need information or if you have problems or concerns. Now I need to remind you of procedures." Her voice suddenly changed from warm and compassionate to frigid indifference. "You may not leave this train without me nor wander off by yourselves at the stops we will make. Carry your travel documents and identification papers on your person at all times. Never let your valuables out of your sight." Then she smiled. "We'll become friends. When we arrive in Moscow you will detrain. Those continuing on will find assistance locating connections. Passengers ticketed for the Trans-Siberian Railway have an approximate ten-hour wait until

---

20 The Intourist employees were the regular police and border guards of the People's Commissariat of Internal Affairs, more commonly known as NKVD. The Cheka (Extraordinary Commission), a Russian State security agency established and organized by Stalin in 1917 to combat counter-revolution and sabotage, was succeeded by the State Political Administration (GPU) in 1922, which in turn was reorganized in 1934 as the NKVD. In 1946, the NKVD and the NKGB (a separate unit of the NKVD) were renamed the Ministry of Internal Affairs and the Ministry of State Security, respectively. In 1954, they were combined into the present-day KGB (or the Committee of State Security), a group that was finally dissolved in 1991 (Medvedev, *Let History Judge: The Origins and Consequences of Stalin*, 652, 657–58, and 878).

its departure. For those passengers, during that time I'll provide you occasions to become familiar with the train and your compartment, give you an opportunity to freshen up and escort you to supper. After your meal, you will retire for the evening. Tomorrow, I'll take you on a sightseeing tour lasting perhaps an hour or two. I'm here to make your time with us as pleasant and comfortable as possible. I'm available at all times to answer questions and help in any way. Consider me not as an official but as your companion. I promise to do my best to continue to speak German though I'm sure I will need your help with vocabulary and pronunciation."

I whispered to Mutsch, "Doesn't she look like Gerta?"

She didn't answer me.

Katya then said, "You're free now to return to your railcar or," raising her arm and pointing to the windows, "remain here to view the scenery. Avail me any time. Thank you for your attention." She left the car.

For the next few minutes no one said anything. Then everyone seemed to rise at once to leave. Paps turned to Mutsch. "Something's not right here," he said with concern in his voice. "We must figure out what it is."

I had many questions for Katya. What were those buildings with armed soldiers as sentries I saw dotting the countryside? When will we get to Moscow? Is that going to be the only stop where we'll be able to leave the station and venture out?

Mutsch knew what I was thinking. "You'll wait for an appropriate time to pose your questions to Katya and only when one of us is with you. Do you understand?"

"Yes, mother."

We made our way back to our coach. As the train rumbled on I day-dreamed about our arrival in Moscow and Katya's promise of sightseeing in the fresh air. I was anticipating the variation in our routine that had been rather monotonous up until this point.

For a while we read, played word games, and watched the scenery as it flashed by. We passed more villages and military installations. We saw lush farmland worked mostly by women wearing babushkas and long skirts, their sad-looking donkeys milling about nearby. At crossings, people waved to us. What were they thinking? Did they wish they could join us?

By now Paps had established acquaintances with several of the passengers. His charismatic personality and outgoing manner made it easy for him to strike up conversations with strangers.

I closed my eyes for a moment and the next thing I knew Mutsch was waking me up.

"We're in Moscow, Lorechen. Get your things ready."

When the train stopped everyone scurried to gather their baggage. We were the last people off. On the platform we saw Katya waving her arm. Thirty passengers huddled around her. Railway personnel escorted us to her.

She spoke loudly, her voice carrying above the din of the station, "The Trans-Siberian connection is on track three. I'll take you there right away. Before we board, you will ready your documents and tickets. They will be reviewed. We allow you one hour to enter your compartment, stow your things, and freshen up. Then we'll proceed to the dining car. After supper you will return to your compartments and retire for the evening. At eight o'clock tomorrow morning we'll meet on the platform for our sightseeing tour. When we return there'll be a short wait. Then the train will continue on through the city of Moscow, making several stops before arriving at its final station in the city's environs. It will depart from there for all points east." She surveyed the group waiting to see if anyone had any questions. "Very well then. We proceed to the train."

The Russian police evaluated our documents then we entered our compartment. The coach was brand new, the interior luxurious. In the main room, there were royal blue upholstered daybeds and mahogany panelled walls. Everything was polished and spotlessly clean. Our quarters even had a separate room for my parents and a smaller room for me with a lavatory in between. Indeed, the accommodations were deluxe! Mutsch and I put away what little clothing we had in a beautiful credenza below the window in the main room of our compartment.

Paps looked at his watch. "It's time. We should go to supper."

In the dining car, waiters in tuxedos stood ready to serve us. We introduced ourselves to the other passengers as we walked by their tables. I noticed that the conversational music made by the other passengers was different this time. Not only did I hear German but also French and English. I recognized Italian and then guessed that the lilting guttural utterances emanating from one table was Czech. What we gathered from the bits and pieces of conversations we heard was that many of the passengers were refugees, as we were, bands of harried transients distancing themselves from the spread of the Nazi web in Europe.

After we sat down I said, "I'm disappointed there are no other children my age. I can't be the only child on this train."

Paps said, "Don't worry, Lorechen, there'll be so many interesting sights! You won't be bored. Just wait until we get to Lake Baikal!" I wanted to know about it right away but Paps had only heard about it so I would have to wait.

We ate a delicious meal. They served enormous portions. Mutsch, who had gained some weight during her convalescence, had a difficult time making healthy choices from the train's menu. Since leaving Italy she'd been trying to monitor closely what she ate. She found what she thought would be a good diet choice: caviar! She would eat her way across Russia and Siberia on that comestible alone! Within a day or two the waiters remembered her fondness for it and, no matter what Paps and I ordered, a large bowl of the pickled sturgeon eggs would be placed at her setting.

During our meals, Paps would often eavesdrop on conversations at nearby tables. Mutsch and I would be gabbing and he would appear to be listening but his eyes would shift from left to right and up and down as if exercising them that way would make it easier for him to hear.

At dinner the next evening, Paps leaned toward us. "I understand there are increased tensions between Hitler and Stalin," he said softly. "Matters of ideology, a likely point of conflict between the two men, will surely lead to a serious and prolonged confrontation.[21] It sounds as if Spain will be the next battlefield of wills. Can war in Europe be far behind?"[22]

Mutsch spooned a dollop of caviar onto a cracker. "I'm sure of it, too," she said. "No wonder everyone in the club car spoke German."

"What do you mean?" I blurted out.

"Lower your voice, Lorechen," she said. "Don't you see? We Germans are being watched."

"Because we're Jews?" I wondered aloud.

Paps snapped at me. "Don't dare say that for all to hear!" he whispered harshly. "We're travelling as Germans on this train not as Jews! This is a first-class passage. It's assumed that we are business people, intellectuals, or perhaps doctors or lawyers."

"Remember those two couples in the club car on the previous train?" Mutsch asked. "Their elegant clothing? Their sparkling jewellery? They are well-to-do, very important people. They're being watched. We all are. Every German on this train is being watched because we're seen as

---

21 Traditional anti-Semitism, honed by Stalin over many years, was seen by his successors as a fundamental element of the Russian psyche (Shlapentokh, "Putin's Jewish Anomaly Comes as a Surprise"). During Stalin's reign, anti-Semitism was introduced as official Soviet state ideology. However in the late 1930s, during Stalin's Great Purge—that saw the execution of more than half a million Soviet citizens, including almost all of the Bolsheviks who played an important role in the Russian Revolution—neither ethnic nor religious Jews were targeted. But in 1939, after Germany and Russia signed the friendship pact, Stalin handed over a large group of German antifascists and Jews who had fled the Gestapo to the Soviet Union (Lewis, "Why Russian Jews Are Not Russian"; Medvedev, *Let History Judge*, 435).

22 The Spanish Civil War (1936–39) was indeed a battlefield for clashing ideologies, in effect a dress rehearsal for World War II. Spain's Republican Coalition, which had come to power 1931, was under attack from both communists and fascists and in the general election of February 1936, the communist-influenced Popular Front, an electoral coalition, swept into power. Both Hitler and Mussolini backed Franco, the leader of the party, while Stalin supported the Republic, saying, "The liberation of Spain from the oppression of fascist reactionaries is not the private affair of the Spaniards but the common cause of all advanced and progressive mankind" (quoted in Crozier, *The Rise and Fall of the Soviet Empire*, 53–58).

capitalists, as potential threats to the Russian proletariat. We're being kept together."

"You're right," Paps nodded. "Now," he said to me, "finish your dessert because we'll return to our compartment and then your mother and I need to discuss our strategy for whatever confrontations may be in store."

On the way back to our rooms I made a silent vow that in the future I would think before speaking. I was terrified that I might be the cause of some trouble that would endanger my parents and me.

When we returned to our railcar a porter was leaving our compartment, holding our towels from the lavatory. He spoke to Paps in French. "Sir, for the entirety of your trip the windows will be washed at every stop. At night, the tables will be tucked away and your bedclothes turned down. Linens and," he directed our attention to the towels draped over his arm, "lavatory cloths will be exchanged daily as well."

Paps thanked him. Then the porter moved on to the next compartment. Mutsch and I went inside while Paps stepped onto the platform to enjoy a cigar. I asked Mutsch, "Won't this be a wonderful trip, mother?"

"Yes, dear," she said, "it'll be fascinating to see Moscow in the morning. I'm sure we'll have a splendid time. Now it's off to bed, we have to be up early. Sleep well, darling."

I kissed her twice, saying, "One is for you, the other is for Paps when he returns."

In the lavatory I washed my face and hands. I thought about how much fun we'd have the following day. While drying my face, I stared into the mirror. I looked drawn and tired. "Well," I whispered to myself, "everyone in Russia has been so nice. I only wish Gerta and some of my family and friends were here to share this with me."

Once in my room, I settled into bed–it was so comfortable! I began thinking about Katya showing us Moscow tomorrow, seeing things I'd only read about in books. I closed my eyes and entered into a blissful slumber.

A jarring motion stirred me from my sleep and I got out of bed to see if my parents were awake. Paps was finishing dressing. "Good morning,

Lorechen. Did you sleep well? Mother is in the lavatory and will be ready shortly. You should get ready. We'll go for breakfast and then meet Katya for our tour."

I felt another jolt and then a slight movement of the railcar. "What is that?" I asked.

Paps said, "The train is being shunted from its place here to a better position for fuelling and the loading of supplies for the long journey."

When we entered the dining car it was nearly empty. Paps said, "It looks like many of the passengers prefer to sleep than to sightsee. Maybe with a smaller group Katya will be able to show us more things."

For breakfast we were served crusty black bread, thick raspberry jam, eggs, a bowl of caviar for Mutsch, fresh fruit, and steaming tea served in a richly decorated silver samovar.

Suddenly, father stood up. "I need to return to our compartment. Finish your meals. I'll be back in a moment."

I looked at Mutsch. "Is something wrong?"

"No, dear," she said, helping herself to another cracker and lathering it with caviar. "Perhaps he prefers, you know, to use our own lavatory."

We finished eating and then waited for what seemed like an eternity for Paps to return.

"Why is Paps taking so long?" I complained.

A fog of worry settled in the air. Mutsch stared down the aisle in the direction father had left. She glanced at me, then returned her gaze to the aisle. Just then Paps appeared in the doorway, his face frozen with fear. "What's wrong?" Mutsch asked, wringing her hands.

He threw up his arms and yelped, "I can't find my wallet! We have no money, no papers, no documents!"

This was a crushing blow. Paps and Mutsch were now among those passengers who were worried about their temporary visas expiring but in our case we had no documents at all. Suddenly we were foreigners in the most frightful sense, literally lost inside Russia.

"It must be in your jacket," Mutsch sputtered. "Lorechen, where's your pouch?"

I felt my neck. No lanyard. "It's in my room, Mutsch."

Paps patted his pockets, then rifled through them. "We must ask for help," he said. Then he called out, "Waiter! Waiter!"

The maître d' came to our table.

"May I be of assistance?" the elderly man asked in German.

Father explained the nature of our distress. At once, the man summoned three other staff members. The four of them began scouring the dining car, scanning the aisle, looking under tables and chairs, fluffing tablecloths, checking in plant pots, and pulling away curtains to examine windowsills. Paps and Mutsch rummaged the area surrounding our table and would do so a dozen times over the next five minutes. I stood paralyzed. I knew we couldn't travel without documents. Not knowing what to do, I took three slices of bread from the serving tray, crammed two of them into my pocket and then began nervously eating the other.

Suddenly Paps and Mutsch interrupted their foraging. They were staring at me in disbelief. "Lorechen!" my father yelled, "What on earth are you doing? Don't stand there and eat! Help us find my wallet!"

I stuffed another piece of bread in my mouth and dropped to my knees, crawling about underneath the tables in search of Paps' wallet.

After about twenty minutes the maître d' returned. "I'm sorry, Sir, there's been no wallet found. Be assured my staff and I will continue to look for it."

We rushed back to our compartment. Paps said, "Lorechen, you search the lavatory from top to bottom. Mutsch will look for your pouch in your room and I'll begin here," he said pointing to their room. After a few minutes of searching I saw Paps looking through his pockets again and I heard Mutsch raking drawers.

As I was turning the lavatory upside down I heard a knock at our door. Father opened it. It was Katya and three railway personnel. Evidently the news of Paps' missing wallet had spread.

She pushed passed Paps into our compartment. "We're here to help," she said. Then, turning to the railway personnel, she barked orders in Russian. Immediately they began stripping the beds, turning over the cushions, looking in every corner, under the tables and bed frames, even lifting the mattresses. They checked the windowsills and behind the curtains. Mutsch was scouring through our valises and my rucksack.

It was obvious. Paps' wallet and my pouch had vanished. And with them our identification documents, tickets, Japanese visas, and money.

After about an hour, Katya addressed the railway personnel. She must have told them to stop because they bustled to the door and left.

Mutsch panicked. I started to cry when I saw the fear on her face. She began to sob uncontrollably. "What'll happen to us without identification and without money? What will we do?"

Katya was quick to comfort us. "We've done what we can for now. We'll continue with our original plans. We'll go on our sightseeing tour. I'll take full responsibility for you. While we are on our tour all available staff members will persist in searching for your missing items. When we return, if they haven't been found, I'll make arrangements to replace your documents and tickets. I'm sorry to say I'm not sure what I can do regarding the replacement of your money."

Even though we didn't find the wallet or my pouch I thought things would be all right since Katya had promised to help. I was still looking forward to seeing Moscow but I could tell my parents were in no mood to go sightseeing.

Katya sensed that we needed some time as a family. "I see you need to discuss your preferences. I'll wait outside on the platform. When you have decided what it is you would like to do then come out and let me know." She closed the door behind her.

Paps said, "I'm doubtful that Katya will be able to help much more than she already has." Then he lowered his voice to just above a whisper. "We won't be able get new passports from the German embassy since we're not who we say we are. We're trapped. We can't travel through Russia without papers and it is unlikely Katya can vouch for us the entire way. But worst of all, we've lost the visas that Herr Griesbach procured for us through the Japanese embassy in London." My father shook his head. "Because of carelessness, our situation is beyond remedy."

A Bad Situation Becomes Worse

May 1936

My parents needed to discuss our next step. I knew I wouldn't have a say and so I wandered into my room. From my window I saw Katya standing among some other passengers gathering for the sightseeing tour. I was wretched at the thought of missing the excursion. Shrugging my shoulders, I dug into my pocket to find another piece of bread. At least I wouldn't be hungry for a while.

I could hear my parents talking in their room. I assumed that a long discussion meant that they already had decided to forgo the sightseeing tour and were now preparing their rebuttal remarks to my expected complaining. I was resigned to the fact that I would miss my chance to see a magnificent city, the grand Moscow, its treasures once so close but now so far away.

The next time I looked out Katya and the group had moved further along the platform. In the distance I could see a water fountain that previously had been blocked from my view. My throat was dry and my stomach bloated from the bread.

"May I get some water?" I asked Paps, pointing to the window of their room from which Paps could now see the fountain.

He stopped talking. "Yes, but I'll come with you. I don't want you out there by yourself."

We walked to the fountain. By this time Katya and the others were nowhere to be seen. She must've assumed we wouldn't be joining her.

"I'll hold the spigot," Paps said. "Take a drink but don't touch the nozzle with your lips."

Leaning over I had the strangest sensation. I wasn't dizzy but I thought the platform was moving. Out of the corner of my eye I could see the train, which looked stationary. And yet I still felt as if I were moving.

And then it occurred to me.

"Father!" I shouted, "The train is leaving!"

His head whipped around so forcefully to look that I thought he had broken his neck.

"Quickly," he yelled dragging me by my arm, "we must get back on the train!"

We ran toward the train but by then it was propelling itself along the platform's edge. The locomotive and the next few coaches, one of them ours, already had gone by. The train was rapidly gathering speed. We were screaming and waving at the passing cars, none of which, incredibly, had their windows open. Then we saw the dining car go by and then more coaches. With a final torrent of dust the last car passed. We saw the tail end of our train disappear in the distance around a curve. It was gone.

I broke down, tears streaming down my face like rain.

"There's no time for crying," Paps said, "we must think."

"Paps," I sobbed, "should we wait here by ourselves? How will we catch the train? What'll happen to Mutsch? She's all alone?"

Everything was tragically clear. Paps and I spoke no Russian. We had no papers and no money. Katya had already gone. Mutsch, alone on the train, had no papers and no money.

For the second time in a matter of hours we were lost inside Russia.

We stood motionless on the deserted concrete platform for what seemed like an eternity. I looked to Paps expecting that by now he had come up with a plan. Instead I saw the marks of pain on his face, his right eye nearly closed, the furrows of his brow pronounced, his eyelid fluttering like a leaf.

"Are you all right?" I asked.

"No, Lorechen, I'm not," he replied, massaging his temples with his ring finger and thumb. He pulled me toward the station's entry doors. "Perhaps someone in here will be able to help," he said.

The station was quiet. Only a few people wandered about. Four men were seated at a table, their chessboards between them, their eyes riveted on the pieces. One of them rose and began walking toward us. He was older than Paps, not as tall, and as wide as two of Paps put together. His gait was uneven, leaning to the right every time he lifted his left leg. He had a greasy complexion and a greasy smile. I didn't like the looks of him. When he approached us Paps tried to communicate in three different languages but the man understood none of them. He looked at his watch and then motioned for us to follow him.

My father hesitated. "Supposing the train backtracks?" His mind raced with the different options. Should we stay here? Should we go with this man? Should we search the station for police? Should we wait for Katya to return?

Finally, Paps said, "We can't wait here. Our train's left and I suppose there must be another station in Moscow. Perhaps that's where Mutsch is. Let's follow this man and hope he'll understand the nature of our distress. Maybe he'll know what to do."

The man led us out of the station onto a busy street to a bus stop. He tried hard to communicate with gestures. I didn't understand him at all but Paps must have caught some meaning because just as a rickety old bus pulled up Paps said, "We'll board this bus now, Lorechen."

Looking forlornly at the man, my father pulled out his empty pockets and held them while shaking his head from side to side. The bus came to rest in front of us. Our mysterious benefactor stepped onto the bus, reached into his own pocket, and paid not only his fare but ours as well. As Paps and I boarded, the man spoke with the driver who kept looking over his shoulder at us.

We made our way down the aisle. A thin, kind-looking woman smiled at me as I passed by. I was still so upset that I just looked away. The bus jerked forward. The man joined us at the rear of the bus. I noticed several workmen, their front teeth sparkling with gold fillings, pointing at us and talking rapidly. I saw a little girl, seated on her mother's lap cradling a ragdoll, staring open-mouthed at me.

After a short while the man touched my arm and then pointed out the window. The bus slowed as it came upon a square similar to the piazzas we had seen in Merano but this one was incredibly vast, breathtaking in scope, and wondrous in its seemingly endless panorama. I marvelled at the massive buildings and the majestic onion-shaped domes, some gilded others decorated with stone carvings. I saw a magnificent church and what I thought to be a stately museum. Hundreds of people were bustling by.

Paps said, "This is Red Square, dear, you've seen pictures of it."

We exited the bus. Children gaped at us while their mothers, dressed in drab and shabby clothes, tried to hurry their charges along. I saw stern soldiers standing at attention, guarding the entrances to government and municipal buildings. The man with us stopped, letting us look around for a few moments then he gently urged us to follow him. He led us through several side streets where I saw beggars and skinny, scantily clad women huddled in doorways.

As we walked, Paps said, "Let's keep pace, Lorechen, our friend here is moving faster now. We can't afford to lose him." It was surprising, the old man was moving quickly, limping and leaning, swinging like the pendulum of a clock.

We came to another square, a much smaller one, and stopped in front of a flight of stairs that disappeared into the ground. Our benefactor turned to face us, smiled and said, "Yes!"

Father was astonished. "You speak English?"

The man shook his head and said, "No."

Apparently that was the extent of his foreign language capabilities.

My nerves were brittle. "Paps, I'm worried about Mutsch. Where is she? When will we see her? What are we doing here? Where are we going?"

I could see my father was also worried. "We must stay with this man. I have a feeling he knows what he's doing. In an hour, if we're not reunited, then we'll go back to Red Square to find the British or American Embassy."

The man gently pushed us in the direction of the stairs. When he descended Paps and I looked at each other before following him into the bowels of the earth.

By this time I had reconsidered my initial impression of the man who was no doubt our benefactor, patron, and guide.

At the bottom of the white stone stairs was the Metro platform. I'd never been in an underground railway station before. I wasn't sure what to expect. But then I remembered the descriptions I had read of the Moscow subway system. The few pictures I'd seen of it were breathtaking.

I was awestruck as we emerged from the stairwell. Fine oil paintings of Russian folk in native costumes, powerful land and seascapes, still lifes, and beautiful children's scenes were displayed along the white stucco walls of the platform, each of them illuminated by glowing chandeliers suspended from the cavernous ceilings.

"I see you're quite enchanted," Paps said, "so take a good look because I doubt we'll see another subway station like this anywhere in the world."

I stood open-mouthed, craning my neck up and down from left to right, oblivious to the passersby. I was trying my best to absorb the wondrous art and amazing architecture of the station.

Suddenly, our benefactor pulled us along. At the ticket booth he paid for our fares again and then urged us to the edge of the platform. Within minutes a train charged into the station and came to an almost silent halt. The doors opened, we boarded, and the doors slinked closed behind us.

The train left the station and entered a tunnel. At each subsequent station we waited to see what our patron would do because we didn't know how long we'd be on this train. Three or four stops later our angel of an associate yanked his head as if to say the next one would be ours. Sure enough, when the train pulled into the station he quickly disembarked taking care to look over his shoulder to confirm that we were following him. He burrowed his way through the crowded platform with Paps and me trailing behind in his wake.

We came to a flight of stairs. When we reached the top we were in another station above ground. The man motioned toward a bench. Paps and I sat down. For a short time, our guide took a few steps away and as the people passed by he was out of our line of vision. I panicked at the thought of him disappearing into the crowds.

When he came back Paps pointed to a clock on the wall, looked at the man to engage him, and then made train-like puffing noises. "Soon?" he asked.

The man smiled and shook his head no.

"I wonder if that means he didn't understand me. Or maybe the train Mutsch is on won't arrive at this station," Paps sadly mused.

When I saw the worry on my father's face, his brow still creased, his right eye nearly shut, I couldn't help myself. I started to cry.

"Don't cry, Lorechen," he said, "this station looks like a major terminal. I suspect our train will arrive momentarily."

I didn't believe him and I wasn't convinced that Paps believed himself. He sounded more cheerful than he looked. But I was grateful that he was attempting to calm my fears.

Father tried again, waving his hands, making all kinds of shapes, trying desperately to communicate. Will the train come into this station?

The man replied, "No."

Then a train pulled in. "Ours?" Paps asked. The man said, "Yes." But it wasn't. Another, and then a third and a fourth arrived. Each time the man nodded in the affirmative but not one of the trains was ours.

By then we had been at the station for almost three hours. I was thinking at any moment Paps would grab my hand and we would return to Red Square so that we might find a friendly embassy.

More trains arrived. Paps and I sat as disconsolate and despondent as either of us has ever been. Then another train came puffing into the station, this one much larger than the others. We looked at the man—his face was without expression.

We stared into the passing windows of the slowing train. It came to a screeching halt.

"There's Mutsch!" I shrieked.

Standing at the doorway of the railcar, Mutsch was frantically looking about the station. Then she saw us. She nearly fell down the steps in her haste to rush to us. We ran to her and then hugged and kissed. It was another blessed reunion.

For the moment, all our worries were forgotten because our family was together once again.

Our guide, the man whom I originally thought to be an errant dullard and totally unaware of both our dilemma and danger, was the one who had taken us from utter desperation to the sweetest reunion of all. He watched us embrace from a few feet away, a look of satisfaction on his face. Without hesitating, Paps motioned for him to join us while he rattled on to Mutsch about our benefactor, giving a brief summary of our travels in our quest to find her. After hearing how he had helped, Mutsch hugged him. He blushed the colour of crimson.

Amid the commotion and din of passing travellers, baggage being dragged along, and crying children, we heard someone yell, "There they are!" Katya and her sightseers were coming our way. Everyone was smiling and some even applauded. It was a heartening spectacle.

Paps again recounted what had happened and then asked Katya to convey our deepest appreciation to our guide for his assistance and generous kindness.

"And now," Paps said to the group, "may I ask someone to help me reimburse and reward this man for all his trouble. As you know, I've lost my wallet and I'm without papers and money but I don't want to let this opportunity for reward slip by." Promptly, everyone reached into pockets, opened handbags, and took out wallets.

While Paps was talking to the group, Katya had been speaking to the man. Hearing the last few words of what Paps said, she held up her hand to signal for attention. Then she placed her arm around the man's shoulder. "Everyone, that is not necessary. This is Zurinoff. I've known him for a long time. He's a former railway employee, retired these past three years, and he's pleased to have been of help. Our laws require all present and former government representatives to aid and assist foreigners especially when they are in distress. It's our way, the Russian way. He would be punished severely should he accept any kind of payment for what we all understand to be the call of duty. Look at him," she said turning toward him, "and you'll see how happy he is to have ended the separation of the Völker family. This proves again how much pride *Gospodin*," she stopped, realizing she had momentarily switched languages, "rather, I should say *Herr* Zurinoff, and all of us employed by the railway service take in our duties and obligations to tourists in our beloved country."

"Well," Paps said, "it's too bad he can't be rewarded for his civic and patriotic pride! Please, thank him most sincerely and tell him that as far as my daughter and I are concerned, he is our saviour." For the next few minutes, Zurinoff spoke rapidly to Katya, gesturing for emphasis. He had a look of embarrassment about him and then one of marked contrition. It seemed as if he was apologizing for something. When he finished, Katya replied to him, her voice stern, as if she was reprimanding him. For the life of me I couldn't fathom why.

"Herr Zurinoff wishes to apologize to the Völker family for his ignorance."

"Ignorance?" Paps asked. "What ignorance? It's because of him that my daughter is reunited with her mother and me with my wife!"

Katya pointed her finger at Zurinoff. "As I mentioned before, he's been retired for a few years. He and his fellow retirees come by the station a few days a week to maintain their friendships. However, he failed to note that several weeks ago the master schedules for the incoming and outgoing trains have been changed. It's no wonder he escorted you from there to the bus, then to the subway, and finally, to here. When he saw the Express moving out of the station he wrongly assumed it was beginning its last passage through the remaining Moscow stations before departing for the Orient. He was unaware that the train merely was being moved into the rail yard onto a different set of tracks."

"Nonetheless," father piped up, "if it wasn't for his efforts, my daughter and I would've had no idea of what to do or where to go to rendezvous with Mutsch."

"Yes, of course," Katya said, "and that's why no disciplinary action will be taken against him. In fact, it's fortunate he knew to escort you to this last city station to meet the Express. If he had chosen any of the ones in between I'm quite sure you would have been late at every one."

"In any case," Mutsch said extending her hand to Zurinoff, "it's because of this man that I'm with my family now." Katya then said something to Zurinoff. He smiled in his awkward way, bowed before us, waved his hand, and then disappeared into the crowds.

Katya said, "You'll want to talk for a few moments. I'll return to the train. We leave in thirty-five minutes from now. I'll watch you from the railcar. We needn't be separated again, yes?" We all laughed!

It's the strangest thing. When terror or fright is relieved humour manages to take over so quickly.

Several people from the sightseeing group stayed back, eager to hear of our adventures.

Paps asked Mutsch, "What happened while we were separated?"

We returned to the bench. The group huddled around. As if on cue, we all turned to make sure Katya would still be able to see us. I saw her watching from the railcar, waved my hand to her, and she acknowledged by waving back and smiling brightly. Everyone else waved back as well.

Mutsch told us, "When the train began moving I ran from our compartment into the corridor and toward the exit door but by then it had been closed. I screamed! Then I ran through the adjoining cars looking for someone who could help me. There was no one! When I reached the dining car I saw a waiter and the sous-chef leaving the kitchen. I cried out to them."

"Didn't you see the maître'd'? He understands German."

"No, Lorechen. And then the train seemed to stumble on its tracks jerking to a halt. I thought it had crashed into something. Then it started to creep backward, then forward, then backward again and with another jolt it picked up speed. Within a few minutes I was back at the station only this time on the opposite side of the platform."

Paps was staring at her. "But how's that possible?"

Mutsch flapped her hand. "The train was being pushed and pulled into the rail yard. It was switching to another track and then reversing into the station!"

"So it was gone only for a short time!" Paps said in wonderment.

"Anyway," she continued, "you can imagine my terror when I realized you and Lorechen weren't on the platform. I was distraught. So I remained by the exit door of our railcar the entire time. Hours went by and then I saw Katya returning with the sightseeing group. As soon as she boarded I ran to her to tell her of our misfortune. She calmed me down and told me you and Lorechen would be found and that I wasn't to worry."

Paps reasoned, "So when we saw the train pulling away it would have been only a little while until it came back on the other side of the platform?"

"Yes," Mutsch said, "and when Katya and I realized that you both had left the station she said it was likely that one of the railway personnel had come to your assistance. She told me all the employees know the timetables and where the trains go. Even though Herr Zurinoff didn't know of the revised schedules he correctly anticipated with time to spare how long it would take to catch this train based on the old schedule and obviously he managed to coordinate its arrival here with your arrival as well before it would leave Moscow for good." Mother was breathing quite rapidly now.

"All right," Paps said reaching to clasp our hands, "the ordeal is over. Come, hug me now so you will be calm for me."

We overheard a few of the people from the group talking. Some were saying that compared to the tale of our exploits their sightseeing excursion had been dull!

A loud whistle shot through the station. Everyone froze. We turned as one to look at the railcar. We saw Katya waving her arms, beckoning us to return to the train. We ran to her.

As the door of our railcar closed behind us, Paps, Mutsch, and I stood still, then embraced each other, a cluster of happiness and gratitude.

The train gathered speed as it made its way out of the station away from the city of Moscow beginning the long trip across the vast Russian landscape to the Far East.

The Truth is Revealed

May 1936

I sat by the window in my room thinking about Gerta, my relatives, and friends I had left behind in Berlin. It was time to write letters again to remind them of me, to tell them how much I have been thinking of them and how much I miss them.

The view of the Russian countryside was bleak. After leaving Moscow proper, the terrain gradually became untamed and undeveloped. I saw small huts, muddy farmlands unattended with bony and gaunt cows and goats lolling in the pastures, and makeshift pens filled with scraggly chickens. What roads there were, were unpaved, furrowed from the wagon wheels that scarred them during hard rains. This country looked as if it had slept for decades while Moscow had been wide-awake with progress.

I thought about my parents, knowing they still were worried about our missing papers and money. At this point we had no need for them. Nevertheless I was more than curious to learn what had happened to my pouch and Paps' wallet.

The first stop of consequence was a city that seemed to be cut in half by a river. In the distance, mountains riveted the countryside. I can't remember the name of the city but I still have pictures of it in my mind. There was bustle on the roads and sidewalks.[23] I wished I could have walked around but I knew I couldn't.

We settled into a routine which included going to the dining car at meal times to chat with other German passengers. I heard my parents discuss politics with them, including what everyone presumed would be the forthcoming clash between Hitler and Stalin. But they also talked about future plans with families and friends and never-ending worries about relatives who had remained in Germany.

I believe a day or two passed, the only relief from the monotony were the stations along the route. Even though many passengers would step off to walk about the stations, Paps, Mutsch and I never left the train. When word was passed along to inform us of delays, we remained snug in our compartment. We wouldn't venture even to the dining car when the train was at rest.

The next day there was a knock at our door. Mutsch answered and invited Katya to come in.

"Hello. Are you well?" she asked.

"Yes, we are," Mutsch replied. "Is there any news of our possessions?"

"No, not as yet. We are continuing our investigation. Try not to worry. My staff and I will resolve the situation I'm sure of it." Then pointing to me she asked, "May I borrow the little one for a short while?"

Paps inquired, "For what purpose, Katya?"

Katya extended her hands. I grasped them in mine. "I'd like to escort Fraülein Völker to the club car. We have some fine scenery in this part of my country and some notable points of interest coming up. It will be a good geography and history lesson for her."

Paps said, "Yes, that's fine. How long you will be?"

"No more than twenty minutes," Katya said reassuringly.

She and I left the compartment and briskly walked to the club car. We sat down.

---

23 The city must have been Novgorod, which is situated at the convergence of the Volga and Oka Rivers. At this point along the Trans-Siberian Railway route, Ingelore and her parents had travelled approximately 300 kilometres from Moscow.

"In a few minutes we'll pass a demarcation point," she said. "You'll see no particular distinction when we do but I must tell you of its significance."

My first guess was the equator but then I realized that was silly. We were nowhere near it. Perhaps it would be a medieval fortress or a natural wonder.

"Look in that direction and soon you'll see," she said pointing.

All I could see was an endless sprawl of land, the mountains in the distance seeming to erupt from the horizon. There were no buildings, no animals, nothing, just a vast stretch of uninhabited land.

"I don't understand," I said.

"Yes, I know," she said. And then with particular emphasis she screeched, "There!"

Still nothing.

"We've just crossed from Europe into Asia," she informed me. "We're not far from a wonderful city, Katherineburg, our first stop in Asia." I didn't see anything out of the ordinary but I understood the implication. The country of Russia is so incredibly vast that even though we were inside its borders we were entering another part of the world.

"There are unique and provocative stories about that city," she said moving closer to me.

"I'd love to hear," I said.

Katya closed her eyes to gather her thoughts. "You're familiar with myths?" she asked.

"Yes. I've read many Greek myths. I'm fond of several of them."

"Well," she said, "there were mammoths—enormous creatures now extinct—that roamed about this very area thousands of years ago." I nodded my head. She continued. "Because there was no end to the discoveries of their bones, tusks, and teeth, many believed that they still lived underground. They believed the movements of the mammoths caused the earth to tremble and open up. Today we know that what they were describing was an earthquake. The native peoples thought that the mammoths were responsible for the upheaval of massive boulders that would appear on the landscape, ripped from the earth, thrown onto the surface into prominence. Some reasoned that the erratic courses of the rivers were due to the waters wishing to avoid the mammoths burrowing below."

"Fascinating," I said. "I have heard of other stories that helped to explain things which at the time had no other explanation."

"Yes. You're a very intelligent young girl." Then Katya stood up. "But we must return you now to your parents or they will worry."

She escorted me back to my compartment where she cordially thanked me and bade my parents goodbye. Paps and Mutsch wanted to know everything about my interaction with Katya. I told them about the mammoths.

They were as spellbound as I had been.

The next morning I woke up and looked out my window. It was incredible how the landscape had changed. Expecting the same dreary scene that had followed us from Moscow, I was delighted to find colour and vibrancy as far as I could see. I was captivated. Suddenly I heard Katya's voice in my parents' room. I went to see what was going on.

"Good morning," Katya sang to me. "Are you well?"

"Yes, thank you. Have our things been found?"

"No." Katya said, "But you may be pleased to know that overnight we entered into the western reaches of Siberia."

"It's beautiful!" I said.

"Did you see the flowers?" she asked.

"Yes, I did. I saw pink, white, and purple wildflowers spread about like an endless carpet."

"And?" She was testing me.

"And low-growing bushes with yellow blossoms close to the tracks. They swayed in the wind. But it's strange, I didn't see any birds."

She placed her hand on my shoulder. "You're very observant, little one. Oh, they're there, almost everywhere. The speed of the train might have frightened them away."

"I understand," I said. "I wonder how different this place looks in the winter covered with snow!"

The four of us shivered at the very thought of the cold.

At lunch one afternoon I looked out to find drab buildings and dense groups of concrete structures on the outskirts of the city we were approaching. Here was another Russian town cleft by two rivers—one much wider than the other. As the train crawled into the station I looked to Paps and Mutsch. Knowing our routine I said, "Should we go back to our compartment?"

With my question still hanging in the air, Katya entered the dining car and stood at attention just inside the door. She looked around at the diners. I saw a waiter jump to, hastily bringing her a glass of something. I assumed it was vodka, but who knows. As she continued to scan the car it appeared that she was looking for someone. With a cold stare she surveyed the tables several times. Paps waved to her when her line of sight crossed his but she didn't respond.

The train stopped. When I looked out the window I noticed a placard with a white background and four black letters, O, M, C, and K. I was overcome with fright. Scores of police officers were pacing about. Most carried pistols and many had rifles.

Paps and Mutsch saw them. They were as fearful as I was.

"What do we do now?" Mutsch asked Paps.

"If we hasten to our compartment that only will arouse suspicion. We'll stay at our table."

We saw Katya making her way toward us.

Paps whispered, "Lorechen, you will eat your meat and bread. Mutsch, you will continue to enjoy your caviar."

Katya stopped at our table. We exchanged stilted and forced pleasantries. Paps suggested that she join us for lunch.

"No, thank you, Herr Völker, not this time," she said rather coldly.

There was a commotion at the front end of the railcar. At the doorway two Russian police officers appeared carrying carbines.[24] We froze in our seats.

---

24 Special NKVD police units were organized not only in every large oblast but also in nearly every city. Almost all gathering places, including railroad stations and trains, educational institutions, parks, theatres, and even libraries were under constant surveillance by NKVD operatives (Medvedev, *Let History Judge*, 657).

Katya snapped her fingers. "Please, everyone, don't be frightened. These officers will be with us for a while. Our request is that you go about your routines."

The armed personnel walked the length of the aisle and then entered the next car.

"What's that all about?" father wondered.

Again, Katya addressed the group. "The officers will be with us until certain situations have been resolved. There's no cause for alarm. Return to your food and to your conversations!"

Katya then turned to us. "I see that you are concerned. Don't worry. The officers are on maneuvers. They'll disembark within the next day or so." She then looked down at the large bowl at Mutsch's setting. "I'll leave you now to your caviar, Frau Völker." She left.

I didn't like the way the police had strutted about, their long rifles strapped across their shoulders like suspenders, their expressionless faces. I wondered, did they board because of our missing papers? Were they monitoring our every activity? If so, then why wasn't Katya concerned?

I did not sleep well that night and I am quite sure neither did my parents. When we awoke the next morning we quickly dressed and made our way to the dining car. We seated ourselves, ordered, and then waited in silence. I saw Paps' eyes moving from left to right and up and down. He was listening in on a conversation at the next table. As usual Gregori, the waiter who knew Mutsch's culinary predilection, brought a large bowl of caviar and placed it at her setting. He lingered next to her, pausing from his duties, I imagined, to receive an acknowledgement from her.

Just then Paps leaned to the adjacent table and said to the couple seated there, "Yes, we were as well. But I did learn from the railway personnel that the police officers we saw are with the NKVD and they're searching the train for persons possessing passports stolen from tourists at our last stop. It's best to keep your eyes and ears open."

Gregori left our table hurriedly without waiting for a response from Mutsch.

Ten minutes later another waiter brought food for Paps and me. After our plates were presented Mutsch whispered, "By the way, darling, I didn't hear anything about stolen passports. Are you sure you are well-informed?"

"Not now, Dottie."

That was the first time in several weeks I'd heard Paps refer to Mutsch as Dottie. In the past, whenever he would use her nickname it meant for her to be quiet, not to ask questions, and to go about her business as usual. "Yes, darling," she said to him.

We felt the train slowing down. The man at the table next to us told Paps a stop was not scheduled at this time so we guessed there was a sharp turn ahead. The train's motion decreased rapidly. Within a minute it stopped. I looked out. We were in the middle of a vast expanse, no station or village anywhere to be seen.

Paps craned his neck to see along the side of the train. "There are several police vehicles just beyond the tracks," he said.

Moments later police officers entered the dining car causing everyone to flinch. Mutsch reached for my arm. They marched toward us. My stomach lurched. Please, I thought, I do not want to vomit now. I was terrified they would demand our papers and when we could not produce them they would arrest us, take us off the train, and throw us in prison. Mutsch appeared as if she would faint. The policemen gathered at our table. One of them motioned for the other diners to leave. They did so quickly. This is the end, I thought, Paps, Mutsch, and I were at the mercy of the Russian police.

Katya entered the car. I didn't know if that meant we were saved or if we were condemned. She was carrying a small burlap bag. There was something in it. I closed my eyes and began to pray it wasn't a pistol. She stood before us, her expression blank yet foreboding.

"Herr Völker," she said in a low monotone.

"Yes, Katya?" father asked.

"I'll now inform you of a discovery we've made."

The colour drained from Paps' face. Mutsch was shaking. I imagined what Katya was about to say. I felt I would lose consciousness.

You are not *Völker*! You are *Jews*!

She slid her hand into the bag and presented Paps' wallet!

"I'm sorry for every inconvenience you and your family have suffered because of blatant dishonesty. And here, little one, is your pouch."

"Thank you," I said weakly.

"We've apprehended the porter who was assigned to your compartment and one of the waiters, Gregori, his accomplice. They are the thieves." Paps, Mutsch, and I exhaled as one. I felt the knot in my stomach ease and gradually unravel. My thumping heart slowed. Mutsch let go of my arm, leaving fingernail impressions.

"Thank you, Katya," Paps said. "We're so grateful."

With trembling hands Paps opened his wallet and my pouch, dumping the contents onto the table. Everything was there. He flipped through our tickets, travel documents, Japanese visas, and our money. Nothing was missing!

"Let me order you food and drink," Paps said, "and for your officers as well." He opened his wallet and withdrew some bills. "Please let me reimburse you for your time and effort."

Katya barked at the policemen. They left the dining car. "That's not necessary," she said. She patted my head and then followed the officers out. "Look there," Mutsch said as she peered out the window. The porter who had serviced our compartment and Gregori, the waiter, were now in fetters and were being escorted to the police vehicles. In a matter of moments the doors slammed shut and they were driven away.

We heard a loud whistle and the train lurched forward, gathering the momentum necessary to carry us onward.

We slept well that night.

We regained our countenance and our composure the next morning although we still had fresh memories of the frightful confrontation with the policemen. We were less worried and we felt more relaxed. Paps reminded us not to let our guard down. If the Russians discovered us we would be considered the worst kind of impostors: German Jews masquerading as German Christians.

When we asked Paps to explain how he knew of the NKVD and its search for passengers in possession of stolen passports he wouldn't answer us directly, he shrugged his shoulders or said news travels fast in the confines of a train especially when it has to do with law enforcement activities.

Paps' cavalier replies didn't sit well with Mutsch.

We were halfway through our breakfast meal when Katya entered the dining car. I waved excitedly to her and she smiled back as she walked toward us. When she arrived at our table Paps jumped up, shook her hand, and said, "Good morning, Katya. Please join us."

Standing behind me she grasped my shoulders. I really wanted to learn more about her and find out how such an attractive woman ended up bossing policemen around. I was sure she wouldn't sit with us but perhaps she would remain long enough for me to pose at least one question.

"I'd be delighted," she said.

I was so surprised! Paps brought a chair over from an adjoining table. A waiter arrived to take Katya's order before she had finished adjusting her napkin. "Eggs, fruit, and vodka," she said.

Paps told her again how indebted and grateful we were to her for her assistance in recovering our things. She smiled. "It's the Russian way."

When the waiter returned with Katya's order, she didn't waste any time before addressing Paps. "I'm curious how you knew of the NKVD and its hunt for the thieves with stolen passports."

This was what Mutsch was waiting for. "Yes, dear," she commented dryly, "do tell us."

He stammered. "Katya, I'm reluctant to say anything that . . ."

"I know," Katya said, "but you must confide in me. I didn't know that the NKVD were on the train."

Paps' face drained of colour. He was nervous.

"Well, if I must," he said.

"Please do," Mutsch and Katya implored simultaneously.

We broke into laughter at their curious duet! Paps realized that he would have to explain sometime so he told his story.

"A few days ago when the porter was leaving our compartment I remembered my first impression of him. I didn't like the way his cold eyes looked into mine. I thought it odd that he spoke in French since all the other porters in the first few railcars spoke German. Anyway, when I realized my wallet was missing, I immediately suspected him. Then, one night while I was in the club car by myself, Gregori, Mutsch's favourite waiter . . ."

He stopped to smile at Mutsch, who blushed.

He continued, ". . . passed through the car on his way to the front of the train. That was unsettling to me. One of the other passengers had mentioned that the kitchen staff had accommodations near the back of the train, practically the last car. There'd be no reason for any waiter to be this far forward. Also, I did notice that every time we were in the dining car Gregori made it his business to come to our table with Mutsch's caviar, even when another waiter already had begun to serve us."

Katya asked, "Then why didn't you bring this to my attention?" She had not touched her eggs or fruit but I did see her swirl a mouthful of vodka then swallow hard.

Paps was contrite. "It was only a suspicion, at that time baseless. But, then I thought sometimes a rumour has more power than we imagine it will."

"And that's when you made the comment about the NKVD to the man at the next table," Katya concluded. "You were hoping Gregori would overhear and then do something rash that would give away his guilt?"

"Yes," Paps said, "I didn't want to make unfounded accusations."

Katya waved her empty glass as a waiter passed by. "It's extraordinary that you would conceive of such a ruse."

The waiter returned, placing another glass in front of Katya. She flicked her hand at the eggs and fruit. The waiter removed her plates.

"You may be surprised to know, Herr Völker, that I was conducting my own investigation and also presumed that your porter was responsible. Passports are worth, how does the proverbial saying go, their absolute weight in gold?" She drank from her glass. "We were monitoring the interaction between the porter and Gregori. When Gregori left the dining car in search of the porter we knew for certain. We already had the porter in custody by the time Gregori arrived, and well, you can imagine his look of shock and surprise. In my country stealing is a capital offence. They will be dealt with accordingly."

Katya stood up, apologized again for our inconvenience, and then patted the top of my head. "You know I'm in charge of all the enforcement officials on this train. We would never request the help of the NKVD. There's no need to."

She winked at Paps, quickly trying to conceal the smile that crept across her face. "In the future, though, please leave this kind of thing to me, yes?"

She handed money to the waiter and then left the dining car.

Mutsch turned to Paps. "You never cease to amaze me, my darling," is all she could think to say.

Our Secret is Safe

May 1936

Boredom overtook me. There's only so much to do on a train. A fog of repetition and a cloud of monotony were passengers, too, always with me. I read my book several times, played word games with Paps and Mutsch, dallied in the club car as the train hurtled through the Russian landscape, danced in the corridors on my way to and from the dining car, fell into naps during the day, and wrote letters to Gerta, Omi and Opa, and my other relatives and friends. I'd run out of paper but Katya graciously had given me handfuls of flyers, pamphlets, and information booklets, most printed on one side, their other side blank. "Direct your reader's attention to the opposite face of the paper so they'll see where you are," she urged, "a souvenir of sorts, yes?"

We came upon a river over which a bridge was built. As the bridge came into view I was doubtful it would be strong enough to bear the weight of the train. For several increasingly fearful moments I imagined that when we were halfway across its span the bridge would collapse, throwing the entire train and all its passengers into a watery grave.

As we crossed I felt the bridge swaying from left to right in cadence with the train's forward motion. The massive supports beneath squealed in an effort to bear the load of the train. This is where our voyage ends, I remember thinking. But the train cleared the bridge. It proceeded slowly, a distance of perhaps several hundred metres, before it stopped at an enormous station. I saw a placard with letters of which I only can recall the first: H.[25]

I placed my nose against the window. There were hundreds of people coming and going on the platform. The station was cavernous, much larger than any I'd seen since we left Moscow.

Paps entered the compartment from the corridor. "We'll be here for a few hours while the train is restocked with food and supplies, Lorechen," he said.

Just then Mutsch came from the lavatory. "Can we walk about for a while?"

Paps frowned. "I know it's been tiresome to be pent up all these days but Katya told us we're never to leave the train without her. Let me see if she might escort us and some other passengers on a brief stroll about the station."

Mutsch and I looked out at the platform, as forlorn as young children peering into a candy store.

"I'm sorry," Paps said as he reentered the cabin. "Katya said there are no plans to detrain. Apparently, there would be too much commotion with other trains boarding and workers bringing supplies aboard and it would be too difficult to monitor everyone."

Mutsch and I were disappointed. "There mustn't be enough police to do so," Mutsch reasoned.

We had imagined parading around the station, if only for a short while. Perhaps we could sneak off the train and stand on the platform near the doorway to our car. The fresh air would be a welcomed treat. We haven't been on solid ground for quite some time.

---

25 The station Ingelore is describing is in Novosibirsk on the Ob River.

Mutsch looked at me. “I know what you’re thinking but it’s best that we stay where we are rather than risk any sort of incident that would draw attention to us.”

And so, Paps and Mutsch retired to their room. I nestled down on my bed, peering out my window with envy, longing to be among the people moving about.

For hours workmen and police swarmed the train, hustling on and off like bees at a hive, buzzing from task to task.

When the train eventually left the station it rolled out of the city and its environs and began to barrel through a dense and endless forest. I recognized evergreens of all sorts, including firs, spruce, and cedar. The view was so monotonous I fell asleep. For the first time in a rather long time the rhythm of the train was soothing.

Hours later I woke up. The scenery had not changed. The forest was as green and as dense as it was hundreds of kilometres before. Had we not made any progress?

Another day passed. On our way to the dining car that afternoon, a German passenger told Paps our next stop would be Krasnoyarsk. All across Russia I had a terrible time with most place names but this one has stayed with me.

We were well into our meal when Katya and four policemen entered the car. She smiled, waving at us. I saw her point to a vacant table. The men rushed to ready a place for her. One pulled a chair back. Katya sat and then the other policemen did as well.

“It’s impolite to stare, Lorechen,” Mutsch said.

“I know but it’s so interesting how she commands such respect from the men,” I said.

“Perhaps it’s respect tempered with a hearty dose of fear,” Paps said with a slight chuckle.

“Yes,” I said, “I’m sure it is.”

We were about to leave our table when I saw Katya animatedly talking to the policemen, her hands gesturing a point of clarification or one of insistence as they scribbled in their notebooks.

“Lorechen,” Mutsch said, “you’re staring again.”

I turned away. "Sorry," I said.

Leaving, we smiled at Katya. She returned a radiantly happy face to us.

I looked back one last time, and I know I was staring again. This time I noticed Katya's policemen did not appear cheerful at all.

With my temple pressed against the window in my room I saw the perfectly parallel tracks burrowing through the thick forest. We were on our way again, the train barreling through the countless legions of trees. The next stop was not for several hours and I was determined to make the most of the time. I would read from my book and enjoy once again the fairyland magic that had captivated me from the first readings in the library of our home in Wilmersdorf with Paps and Gerta.

I must have fallen asleep because I was startled awake. I hit my head on the window when the train slowed down. Then it came to a screeching stop. We were not at a station but in the middle of nowhere, the trees flanking the long line of railcars, sentries at their posts.

As Paps came into our compartment I heard him say to Mutsch, "There are mechanical problems with the locomotive. We'll have to wait here until maintenance personnel and parts can come from the next town."

"How long will it take?" I asked.

"I don't know, Lorechen, so we'll have to be patient."

For once, I was frustrated not to feel the motion of the train. I was annoyed and disappointed to be stuck in the forest, hundreds of kilometres from our next stop. Paps and Mutsch also were discontented.

The sun was beginning to set. Paps suggested we freshen up and then go to the dining car for an early supper. "It's Friday so let's say a prayer before we go."

We joined hands and bowed our heads. In Hebrew, Paps said, "We lift up our hands and our hearts to the Lord. We are grateful for our safety and beg for the safety of our family and friends wherever they may be. Bless Omi and Opa, bless my brothers and my sister, bless the siblings and family of my beloved Doris, and bless all our friends who we hold close to our hearts. We lift up our hands and our hearts to the Lord." We stood motionless for a time and then Paps and Mutsch recited another prayer. "Blessed art thou, O Lord our God, King of the universe, who hath such as these in His world."

"Mutsch," I whispered, "I don't recall that prayer. What is it?"

She cupped my chin in her hands. "On seeing beautiful trees, Lorechen, there's a prayer for that. And we've seen so many!"

Katya was seated in the dining car when we arrived. I waved to her and she waved back. Paps said, "Why don't you ask Katya if she'll join us for supper, Lorechen." Paps and Mutsch went to find a table and I skipped over to Katya.

"Hello, little one," she said with a warm smile.

I was so excited to see her that I blurted out, "My father asks that you please join us for supper."

"No, thank you," she said. Her eyes darted toward Paps and Mutsch, eyeing them coldly. Then she looked at me but said nothing. Her gaze was searching, almost annoyingly probing. Finally she said, "Tell your father I need to speak with him in private after you finish your meal."

"Yes, Katya," I said.

At our table I told Paps what Katya had said. Mutsch was concerned. "Do you have any idea what this is about?" she asked Paps.

"No, I don't." Then he asked me, "How did Katya seem when she said that? Was she angry? Upset? What was the tone of her voice?"

"I believe she is bothered by something," I said.

Katya stayed at her table the entire time we were having supper. She did not have any food brought to her, just a small glass that was filled several times. I thought, it must be vodka.

Paps stopped at Katya's table on our way out while Mutsch and I waited by the door. After a few minutes Paps joined us and we left. Along the corridor I kept turning back to see the expression on Paps' face. He looked as cold as a stone in winter, his expression blank.

Inside our compartment he sat hunched over on his bed with his head cradled in his hands.

"What's wrong?" Mutsch asked as she sat down beside him.

"It's Katya," he said in a whisper. "On her way through the corridor to the dining car she overheard us talking in our room. She wants to discuss it with me first thing tomorrow morning."

"That's all right," I said. "We were just praying. I'm sure Russians pray, too."

Mutsch was horrified. "Did she hear us speaking in Hebrew?"

"I don't know."

Mutsch was gasping now. "What'll we do if she accuses us of being Jews?"

Paps and Mutsch stood up holding hands. "I don't know," he said.

"Katya is our friend," I said.

"Yes, Lorechen, she is, but it may be her duty to report the presence of Jews. If she does ask, I'll deny it," he said. "She's seen our papers. We have come this far with our charade and we will not give up now. If she accuses me, I'll say I was speaking in a German dialect."

Mutsch let go of Paps and began feverishly wringing her hands. "No!" she cried out, "No! It is enough! We are who we are! I will no longer hide our faith! You'll tell her the truth!"

I was terrified. What would happen to us? Here we were in the middle of the forest, the police on our train. Would we be taken away like Gregori and the porter? Would we suffer the same fate?

The next morning Mutsch stirred me from my sleep. "Right now, Lorechen, up and dressed," she said. I rose quickly. I didn't feel any motion, the train must still be stagnant in the forest. Quickly, I changed from my nightclothes and met Paps and Mutsch in their room.

Paps looked weathered. His right eyelid was flittering. For the first time in my life, I saw the impact that worry and age were having on him.

He took a deep breath. "I'll go meet with Katya."

As soon as Paps left, Mutsch blanched before my eyes. "I'm so worried," she said, "that after all this, after all we've done, we will have failed to keep you safe." She was crying.

"Mother," I said, "you and father have never failed me."

We embraced for a moment. "Thank you, Lorechen." She was still crying. She sat on the bed. I sat beside her, held her hands, and rested my head on her shoulder. "Please don't cry. I love you and Paps more than anything. I'm so blessed to have you as parents."

"You're my angel," she said. "But right now you need to take a walk for a bit, maybe to the dining car for some breakfast. You can even have a cookie."

"Yes, mother."

"But don't leave the train," she said. "We're stuck here and there's no telling when we'll be moving on. We don't know what will transpire between your father and Katya so when they have finished speaking and he returns we must be near one another in case . . . so quickly go . . . quickly."

She got up, kissed my cheek, and then went into the lavatory. From inside she reminded me, "Do not leave the train. Come right back."

While strolling through the corridors I passed several passengers who regarded me with greetings. I felt the warmth from outside as I crossed from one car to the next. When I got to the club car I saw the two couples from several days earlier, the ones with the jewellery, again impeccably dressed, their clothes of shining rich fabrics neatly pressed, the women's coiffures flawlessly arranged, the men's perfectly knotted neckties. I sat down in the first seat, as far from them as possible. But within a few minutes they left the club car to walk along the gravel edging of the tracks. It was then that I saw scores of people milling about outside. I was the only one still in the rail car.

The windows to the car were open, allowing cool breezes to enter as I stared out at the wall of trees. I was snapped out of my daydream when I saw a massive flock of birds flying in formation, winging their way from north to south. Although they were far away, they looked to be swans or geese. Moments later I saw a large elk and its calf peeking out from in between two large trees. They stood still, staring at the sleeping iron monster in front of them. They were ready to cross the tracks but couldn't because the train was in their way and there were people all about. They disappeared back into the dark forest.

Just then I heard footsteps in the gravel below. I looked down and saw the top of someone's head, the hair on it as straight as nails. I knew it was Katya. Right behind her was Paps. They walked a few more steps and stopped. I heard Katya say that she required an explanation.

"For what?" Paps asked.

Katya held Paps' arm. "I'm concerned about what I heard last night as I passed by your compartment."

"I don't know what you mean," Paps protested. "Perhaps my wife and I were talking too loudly. I'm sorry if we disturbed you."

She let go of Paps' arm. "That's not what I'm talking about," she said curtly.

Paps insisted again. "I don't know what you mean."

They walked a few more steps. I tiptoed to the next seat. I worried that I might be discovered but I couldn't help myself.

"Do you consider me a fool?" Katya asked.

"No," Paps said right away, "of course not."

"Then I'll say what needs to be said. When I overheard you I realized what you were doing. You were praying. I recognized the language you were speaking–it was Hebrew."

Paps stammered, "Please, Katya . . ."

"That will do," she snapped. "I tell you now that I know you are Jews. Your documents and visas must be forgeries. Perhaps you are fugitives. Is that what it is? What crimes you have been accused of I can only surmise."

My blood turned to ice.

"Please, Katya," Paps tried again.

"Silence!" she huffed. Then, in a calmer and friendlier tone, "I'm charged with monitoring the movements of those who are a threat to my country, my government, and my people. There are subversives and dissidents everywhere."

"But you know we are no such things. We mean no harm to anyone."

"Yes, I know," she said. "You are nothing other than transients. You, your wife, and your adorable little one are on your way to Japan. You're in search of a better life, especially for your daughter. I'll do my best to help you accomplish your goal."

"Then I owe you an explanation," Paps began. "We are–"

Katya interrupted him. "I see it in your eyes now, you needn't clarify anything. You've assumed many risks and have managed to overcome them so far. It's remarkable. However, there are risks for me, too. If other authorities meet this train then there may be trouble. Especially if my superiors demand a closer accounting of who is on this train. If they're not satisfied with the information I provide them . . . well I may be in an awkward position. If it comes to that your safety may be compromised, but I'll do what I can."

Paps offered his hands. "I'm indebted to you and your staff for everything you have helped us with. I can't ask nor can I expect any more than what you already have done. Please accept my heartfelt appreciation and my boundless admiration."

"It's odd," she said, reaching for Paps' hands, "how there's such disdain in your country for people like you, as if you're the cause of everything that ails your Führer. This can't be." She turned, releasing his hands. "After all, we are the same underneath, you know, as people, aren't we?"

I saw them smile at one another. Then they walked back along the side of the train. I jumped out of my seat and ran the entire way back to our compartment.

I told Mutsch everything I had overheard. As I rattled on she glowed with relief and joy. She couldn't have looked happier.

Shortly after Paps burst into the room, his face lit up with excitement.

Mutsch thrust herself at him. "I know, darling, I know!"

Paps stopped abruptly, his feet suddenly welded to the floor. He was astonished. "How do you know? What do you know?"

"Our angel here," Mutsch said pointing to me, "overheard from the club car. It seems we have a little spy in our midst." She playfully tugged on my tresses. "By chance she was privy to your conversation with Katya, what with the open windows, and she told me everything. I'm so relieved!"

Paps smiled. "Amazing," he said. To this day I remember that smile. I took it to mean that he believed my eavesdropping was purposeful, in some way helping us with a problem affecting our family. I now know it was sheer luck to be in the proper place at the proper time.

I'm sure my parents were thinking about the same things I was, that we were now shielded from suspicion and danger, that we were so very fortunate Katya was the supervising police officer on our train, and that we were indebted to her beyond measure because she pledged to carry our pretense so our safety would be assured.

"It's all well and good," Paps said, "for Katya to be our guardian and keep our secret secure, however the lesson is that we can't be careless." He spoke slowly, with the tone of his voice cautionary. "Imagine what might have happened if an officer had passed by and heard us praying or perhaps a passenger with no decency toward Jews? We must be more careful. Do you understand?"

Afraid to speak, both Mutsch and I nodded our heads.

Paps said, "The next time we'll whisper our prayers to the Lord. He'll hear us, I'm sure of it."

Just then three deafening blasts of the train whistle pierced the stillness of the forest and the quiet of our compartment. At once we could hear voices yelling, "Quickly! Now! It's time! All aboard!"

And then we heard the continuous crunch of gravel as the people outside scrambled toward the train.

A commotion developed in the corridor with an avalanche of footsteps, the people on their hurried way to their compartments. Again, the whistle blared three times and then there was that sudden jerking motion. We were on our way!

An hour later Paps ushered Katya into our compartment. I heard her say we would be at our next stop soon. Then she gasped, "Oh my, where is the little one?"

I exited from the lavatory and with abandon I rushed to Katya, hugging her with all my might.

"There, there," she said, rubbing my back. "For a moment I thought we left you in the forest!"

I stood on tiptoe and kissed her cheek. She blushed. "Anyway," she said, stepping back, "I want to inform you that at Krasnoyarsk we're scheduled for only a fifteen minute stop. I don't recommend leaving your compartment."

"Of course," Paps said. "We'll tidy up our cabin and ready ourselves for lunch after the train leaves the station."

"Very good," Katya said. "Then it'll be on to another station and then . . ." she placed her arms around my shoulders, ". . . it'll be time to see a wondrous spectacle."

"What is it?" I asked.

"In about ten hours we'll come to Lake Baikal. It's so incredibly vast that we'll be travelling along its shoreline for days."

"I'm excited to see it, Katya," I said.

"And I'm excited to show it to you!" she said, touching my nose with her fingertip.

We were at the station no more than twenty minutes before we heard the screeching whistle and felt the slow movement of the train. I watched as we passed the limits of the city and then clanked along an iron bridge over a large river before we were on our way again.

Later, reclined on my bed munching on cookies I took from our dining table that day, the light went out.

Although it was mid-afternoon it was as dark as night. Rain fell on the roof with such force it sounded like rivets were being hammered into it. Nature's orchestra was in full force with all its staccato and vibrato, the clash of the elements in a magnificently discordant song. The storm was churning in the same direction as our train, chasing us for several kilometres before overtaking us, its intensity so great the train slowed considerably to safely navigate the bends and turns through the forest. At this rate it was going to take us a lot longer to reach our next stop so I decided I would make myself snug and take a short nap.

The train whistle woke me. I perked up, looked out my window and saw that we had reached another station. It was still very dark but it had stopped raining. I could see puddles on the platform.

Mutsch came into my room.

"I see you're awake now, Lorechen. How was your nap?"

"It was fine, mother," I said. "Where are we? When did the storm pass?"

"A few hours ago. I'm not sure what the name of this city is but I imagine we'll depart shortly. Those whistle blasts are hard to ignore!"

Then she said, "It's past seven o'clock. Your father and I are hungry. Will you come with us for supper?"

"No," I said, "I'm not hungry." The cookies were still heavy in my stomach. "I'll stay here. I promise I won't leave our compartment."

"All right. Your father and I will return shortly."

As soon as they left I went to freshen up. Then I cleaned up the evidence left behind on my bed from my snack.

A knock at the door startled me. With fear creeping up my back and neck I went to the door. My nightmare sizzled in my mind.

"Yes?" I said, "Who is it?"

"Little one, it's Katya."

I immediately opened the door. She greeted me with her wonderful smile. I was so happy to see her! "Aren't you feeling well?" she asked. "I met your parents in the dining car and they said you chose to remain in your compartment."

"Oh," I said, "I'm fine. I guess I had too many cookies at lunch."

"Well then, I wanted to check on you and tell you that by tomorrow morning you'll be able to see Lake Baikal on the horizon. Look at the colour of the water and carefully scan the shorelines. You might be able to see the seals."

"That would be wonderful!" I said. "Will we have a chance to . . ."

"Go swimming?" she asked. I nodded. She laughed. "No. But at the next station we'll have a long stop for supplies so we'll be able to leave the train for a few hours. However, this time I'll escort you so we don't have a similar situation as the one where, well, you know!" We both giggled. "Anyway," she concluded, "you'll watch the horizon tomorrow, yes?"

"I will, Katya." She leaned toward me, looked into my eyes, and kissed my forehead. "You're special," she said. Then she left.

When Paps and Mutsch returned I told them about what Katya had said about leaving the train at our upcoming stop and escorting us to sightsee.

Paps was laughing. "As long as we don't wander off to a fountain for a drink!"

Parting is Such Sweet Sorrow

June 1936

At the age of eleven, almost twelve, on the cusp of adulthood, it was difficult for me to comprehend fully the forces that were at play during that stage of my life. But I now understand that at that time I was a fragile and skittish fox, fearful of the hounds at my heels, a willowy impressionable young girl who tensed at every shadow and a dutiful daughter who worried about her parents. Yes, our voyage was necessary. It was paramount to escape the Nazi oppression in Germany that certainly would have dissolved our way of life in Berlin. I deeply regret that I wasn't able to do more to help my relatives and friends flee as well.

By early June of 1936 I had been on a train nearly every day for three weeks. But our trek across Eastern Europe into Asia wasn't over and Japan was still far away, farther than the distant horizon. For some reason I thought of Hansi, my canary, in his cage, unable to fly. It occurred to me that I was in a similar situation. The confines of my compartment, the corridors, the club car, and the dining car were not the brass spokes of Hansi's birdcage but part of an iron sheath that enfolded me along my way. Hansi and I were experiencing the same fate, trapped in a world that seemed never to change.

The next morning I saw pieces of azure horizontal stripes peeking through the tops of the trees, bold splashes of colour abutting the soft blue sky. The lake was not far off, just as Katya had said. That meant an extended stop, a respite, and a chance to get off the train, to walk in the fresh air, and see some interesting things as well.

As I was putting on my trousers Mutsch came into my room. She was wearing the only dress she had with her.

"Mother," I said, "you look beautiful!"

"Thank you, dear," she glowed, "and for you, please wear your dress as well. We want to look our best today. Don't you agree?"

"Yes, of course." I took off what I was wearing and searched for the one dress I had brought along.

As the train pulled into the station I was overcome with relief. Another leg of our journey was realized and we were safe. Then eagerness surged through me like a tide. I couldn't wait to disembark.

There were hundreds of people on the platform, most with more luggage than they could carry, children prancing along, couples, the elderly, the alone, all in a frenzy to get where they needed to go. Police were standing at the doors to the station and near the doorways to the railcars. Because we were stopping for a few hours they needed to monitor who was getting off the train and make sure that no one else attempted to board.

We were ready! We fled down the corridor and onto the platform. Katya was already there. She was with a policeman a dozen or so metres from the car behind ours, waving one hand while holding a whistle to her lips with the other, tooting short blasts to gain everyone's attention. We hurried to her. There were eleven people in our group, all of us eager to get going. The two fashionable couples from a few days ago were among us, their clothing superb, the women's hair in appealing order, and, of course, their jewellery shining in the light slicing through the station's windows.

"Does everyone have their papers and tickets?"

Mutsch leaned over to Paps. "Are we prepared?"

"Yes, darling," he said patting the lapel of his jacket, "I have everything we need."

When our group was quiet and attentive Katya laid out our plan. "We'll be taking a bus into the city. The bus will take that bridge across the Angara River. We will get off the bus at its first stop and then proceed to some points of interest including shops, cafés, museums, churches, and other places. But please," she implored, looking at me, "let's stay close together as we go." Like ducklings waddling behind their mother we ambled with Katya, catching glimpses of our surroundings while feverishly peering ahead to make sure she was in front of us.

Our group left the station. Within a few metres we came upon an unadorned cubicle that served as a bus stop. As we gathered ranks, Katya told us that the governing body of the Russian railway system had set aside bus tickets for passengers to take sightseeing trips at extended stops under her supervision. Our wallets would not be necessary. She reminded us to stay close together and then, to reassure the two couples with the jewellery, she said the police officer standing beside her would be accompanying us, as was customary.

The bus approached and then stopped. Katya grabbed my wrist and ushered me to the first row where we sat down. Paps and Mutsch were behind us. The two couples with the jewellery found benches farther back and the other sightseers plopped down wherever there was room. The policeman stood at the front of the bus.

As we crossed the bridge Katya said, "I have a special treat for you, little one."

"What is it?" I wondered.

"There's a quaint café where this bus will stop. Our group will assemble there. Then one part of our group will go one way to some . . ." she scrunched up her nose as if she had smelled a skunk, ". . . really featureless and humdrum tourist places. But the rest—which will be you, your mother, and your father—you'll go to see some special houses, a magnificent church, and other fascinating places."

"Yes, Katya," I said, "that sounds much better."

We got off the bus and followed Katya and the policeman to the café. We huddled at its doorway.

"This is where we will meet later this afternoon. We have exactly two hours. We'll reconvene then."

Then Katya addressed the group. "Fräulein Völker and her parents will pursue a sightseeing course to my left while the rest of our group will head off to my right."

The woman with the wrist full of gold bracelets asked her gentleman companion, "Why are *they* being singled out and separated from our group?" she asked disquietly.

"It's all right," I whispered to her. "Katya wants me to see some really interesting things —something special, but more suited to a child."

"I see," the woman said condescendingly.

The larger part of our group walked away. I was puzzled because Katya went with them. The policeman came over to Paps. "I'm here to accompany you as Katya has directed."

"Wait!" I screeched. "I thought Katya would be guiding us."

"No. I'm your guide. My name is Alexi. Follow me."

He started on his way. Paps and Mutsch didn't seem overly concerned. "Let's go with him," Paps said. I was heartbroken that Katya wouldn't be with us. I didn't understand why she chose the other group.

The policeman was very cordial. He took us to see several houses decorated with intricate trim. "These," Alexi told us, "many years ago, were the homes of the families of exiles, those writers and thinkers sent here as punishment for their participation in a revolt against our Czar."[26] Then a short while later, "This is the Kazan Church. Note the incredibly intricate architecture." Alexi didn't say much, but when he did speak I found myself eager to listen.

---

26 Czar Nicholas I came to the Russian throne in the midst of the Decembrist Uprising of 1825, an anti-Czarist rebellion. Loyal troops suppressed the revolt and six months later, leaders of the conspiracy were executed while officers were sentenced to penal servitude in Siberia (Feinstein, *Pushkin: A Biography*, 138–39).

He led us through some foreboding side streets to several streets with enormous brick buildings. There was a great variety in this city, variety everywhere.

Two hours later, as instructed, we arrived back at the café. As we approached, I saw the other sightseeing group had already arrived. Through the window I could see that everyone was seated, conversing, laughing, and gesturing among themselves, the steam from their hot beverages wafting in the air.

But I didn't see Katya.

Alexi opened the door. Mutsch entered, then Paps and I stepped in. Everyone stopped talking at once. I saw only blank expressions on their faces. The air was thick with silence. Time seemed to stop. I was horrified. Had I done something wrong? The seconds seemed like hours.

Then, from the rear of the café I heard a familiar voice. "Who are we here for today?"

There was no reaction from anyone.

Mutsch turned to me. "Lorechen, close your eyes."

"Yes, mother," I said squeezing my eyes shut. A knot of guilt was tightening in my stomach. There was a commotion, first of chairs being pushed back, then people standing, then handbags, napkins, and cutlery being moved and then that familiar voice singing out, "*Herzlichen Glückwunsch zum Geburtstag*!"

I opened my eyes. Everyone smiled as brightly as I had ever seen. And there was Katya, holding a cake, one lit candle at its centre.

"To our guest of honour!" Katya bellowed. Everyone applauded. Room was made for us at a centre table where Katya placed the cake. It looked delicious, a square concoction of layers topped with flowery swirls of icing and nuts sprinkled on top. Voices chirped all those nice things said at birthdays. I staggered with surprise.

"Mother," I asked in between shallow breaths, "what's this? It can't be my . . ."

"Yes, Lorechen," she said, "it is your birthday. Well actually not until tomorrow. Your father and I and Katya and our friends from the train wanted to do something for you. Happy Birthday, darling." She kissed my cheeks.

"But . . ." I stammered.

"But nothing," Katya boomed. "Here's your cake and here . . ." Katya reached out to one of the women with the jewellery who rushed to hand her two packages enclosed in what looked like butcher's paper. Katya gave them to me. "I'm sorry for the wrapping but in Siberia we must do with what we have!" Everyone laughed.

"I don't know what to say," I whispered.

Mutsch urged me to open the packages. The first was a diary, covered in the softest leather, its pages lined.

"That's from your father and me. We love you very much. With it you may wish to record your experiences, for future reference and enjoyment."

It was difficult for me to speak. "Thank you, mother," I said.

"And this," Katya beamed, handing me the other package, "is from me. Use it often and as a remembrance of me."

I opened it. Inside was a drawing pad and two dozen coloured pencils. I looked up at her. "I'm so . . ."

"Draw your recollections of our beautiful country and our majestic cities, won't you?"

"Yes, of course I will." She kissed my forehead.

Someone suddenly shouted, "*Mangeons du gâteau*!"

"Yes!" I said. I blew out the candle and then cut the cake.

"Your manners, Lorechen?" Mutsch asked.

At once I stood up. "Thank you all for this wonderful surprise party. I'm so grateful." I looked to Katya. "Thank you for everything." Then I looked to Mutsch and Paps. "Thank you for today and for everything that you have . . ."

Just then I felt dizzy. A memory flashed before me. I smelled sauerbraten and *Bienenstock* cake. I saw Omi and Opa with Gerta portioning plates just as the waiter was doing here. I saw numerals on a calendar, the twenty-fifth of May.

I realized it had passed by, forgotten and neglected.

I had failed to remember Paps' birthday.

"I know what you're thinking," Paps said pulling me to his side. "It's nothing. Just to have you safe is what matters most. You're here with us, we're with friends, and at this moment we have the opportunity to celebrate with you, albeit a day early!"

"I'm so sorry," I said.

He kissed my cheeks. "Everyone," he boomed, "may I now tell you of the day our Lorechen came to us? Let me see, at dawn there was a slight mist of rain . . ."

I knew what was coming. I stood up, walked over to Katya and asked her if we could step outside for a few moments. "Of course," she said.

On the sidewalk, she explained the planning for that day. "Your parents asked the German passengers if they wanted to participate in a celebration for you. I'm surprised those two couples, you know who I mean . . ."

"The ones with the jewellery?" I asked.

"Yes. I was surprised they were interested. One of the women, the skinny one with the black hair and the fancy hat, she was the first to voice interest! So, with her help this sightseeing trip was arranged. But we needed time to get ready so we sent you and your parents off by yourselves so the rest of us could prepare."

"Paps and Mutsch knew?" I asked.

"Of course! It was your father's idea. After you left with Alexi, and before I left with my group, I asked the baker to fashion a cake by the time we returned. We came back twenty minutes before you arrived. Your father had given me money to purchase the diary. Your parents wanted to do something special for their dearest one."

"I feel terrible. I forgot Paps' birthday!"

"As your father said, it's nothing. He's grateful that both you and your mother are safe and that the three of you are together. For him that's gift enough."

"And the pad and pencils?"

She smiled. "It's something I wanted to do for you. I'd like you to remember your voyage in my country and I hope you'll remember me. You will draw pictures, yes?"

"I shall do some later this evening," I said.

We were about to go back inside when Katya placed her hands on my shoulders and leaned over to me, "You've much to remember. And I know in my heart that I'll always remember you, little one."

We returned to the train just in time to scramble to the dining car for an early supper. We were hungry from the day's adventure and Mutsch could not wait for her bowl of caviar. The pieces of cake at my party were delicious but very small!

Later that evening I took out the pad and coloured pencils and tried to draw a portrait of Katya in her uniform. Unfortunately, I realized what I knew from my days in Wilmersdorf when Gerta would read and I would draw on poster board: I was better with inanimate things. I didn't yet fully understand proportion and scale when it came to the human body and face.

After a few tries I looked out my window. The horizontal stripe of Lake Baikal, much wider now, stretched from one end of the horizon to the other. We were rapidly approaching it. Even in the fading light I saw that it was as clear as crystal. I didn't know how far we were from it but it was enormous, dividing the sky from the terrain as far as I could see. It was as vast as an ocean, utterly breathtaking. I remembered Katya telling me that there were towns and villages along its edge and sure enough, as our train sped into the dusk, lights became visible in the distance.

I alternated between drawing on my pad and reading my book and then I dozed off. I was startled awake by the train rattling to a stop. There was a hint of dawn. Wherever we were, we stayed only long enough for some passengers to detrain and others to board.

Mutsch and Paps greeted me with a celebratory cascade of good wishes, hugs and kisses, and repeated declarations of love and thankfulness on this, the precise date of my birth.

"Please," I said, "don't fuss. I'm so happy and so grateful for the wonderful surprise yesterday. I love you both."

"You are our joy," Mutsch said.

When the train arrived at a station that afternoon I saw a placard with four Russian letters of which only the last two looked familiar to me. At lunch, Katya told us we'd linger at this stop for a while because many passengers intending to board were Chinese on their way to Manchuria. This would necessitate an examination of travel papers. Even though many of the railway employees in the station spoke Chinese only one of Katya's subordinates did.

We didn't leave our compartment.

I saw dozens of people inching their way toward the loading doors as Katya's police thoroughly checked papers. It then occurred to me that this was the first time I had seen so many people of a different race. I was fascinated by what I observed. I wished I could talk with them, learn about them, know something of their lives. And then, of course, I could share my story too.

After an hour we left the station, travelling east, always looking behind us, to see if our shadows would be overtaken, distancing ourselves from what we cared for most, our beloved Berlin, our dear family and friends, and our former way of life.

Much later, after spending time in the club car sketching scenes of the countryside, I entered our compartment to find my parents' valises on their bed, their folded clothing piled beside, both of them arranging their belongings for packing.

"What's going on?" I wondered.

They stopped what they were doing. With sadness in his eyes Paps said, "Lorechen, there's something we need to tell you."

Mutsch took my hand. My nerves awoke.

"What is it, mother?" I asked.

Paps stood near me. "Well, Lorechen," she said, "in less than an hour we'll arrive at a town where it'll be necessary—"

"—We can't be at our destination," I said.

". . . no, but it'll be necessary for us to switch trains."

I was bewildered. Why? I thought this train would take us to the end of Russia and then we would sail to Japan. Did something happen? Please, I thought, not another detour to a hospital. Is Mutsch all right? Is father suffering again from his headaches?

"Lorechen," my mother scolded, "are you daydreaming? You must listen."

Paps didn't wait for a response. "We're to change trains. You'll pack your belongings. When we arrive at the station we'll exit to find the train that goes to the border. We will cross into China."

"Yes, father, I understand," I said. "So everyone will change trains? I'm so glad we'll all be travelling the same route."

I stood up, eager to go to my room to begin packing but Mutsch braced me with her arm.

"Lorechen, it'll just be us and a few German passengers."

I stopped breathing. Where will Katya be? Why must we leave her? Will we be without police protection? Will we be safe? For so many days this compartment had been home. I didn't want to leave it.

I heard my father's voice. "This train will continue on through Russia to Vladivostok. We're to go a different way. Our next train will travel through Manchuria and China and then to Korea. It's the safest and quickest route to Japan."

There was no breath inside me for words of protest. This would be another sacrifice. More lost friends, another moment of sorrow and sadness when we would leave our friends behind in order to maintain our distance from our relentless oppressors. But I knew that we must continue our flight to freedom. I was resolved.

"I understand, father."

Mutsch embraced me. "I'm sorry, Lorechen, but we must persevere."

After packing my things I sat by my window for my last look at the Russian landscape. There were rolling uplands that swelled into mountains. I was so despondent I nearly became ill.

Paps called to me. "A policeman has come to tell you Katya is in the dining car and that she'd like to speak with you."

I ran to meet her.

She was seated alone in the dining car, a glass of vodka in her hands. She looked up, smiled at me, then waved with enthusiasm for me to come to her.

"Sit," she said pulling out a chair for me. "Can I order you something? Tea? Perhaps some cookies?"

"No, thank you, Katya," I said, sitting.

She sipped from her glass. "Well, by now you know what will occur shortly. I'm disheartened that our paths will separate. I won't have the delight of seeing you every day. I know where you and your parents are going but of course I can't go with you."

"I'll miss you so much," I said with tears beginning to well.

"Now, now," she said trying to comfort me, "there can be no tears when friends reflect on shared memories, only joy. You understand I'm a better person for having to come to know you, little one."

I repeated myself. "I'll miss you so much."

"What is the well-known phrase? Parting is such sweet sorrow, yes?"

Abschied ist so süß Leid.

I never will forget those words.

Abschied ist so süß Leid.

She stood up extending her arms to me. I rose and clasped her hands in mine. We stood there for a few seconds smiling at each other. Then she let go of my hands and wrapped her arms around me. She hugged me for a long time.

"I'll miss you so much," I said again, embracing her with all my might.

"Yes, yes," she said. "Care for yourself and for your parents. Always be safe."

As we released each other, Katya kissed the top of my head, touched my nose with her forefinger, and said, "Farewell, little one."

A Token of Friendship

June 1936

When our train came to a stop at the next station Paps and Mutsch looked at each other sorrowfully. We said nothing as we exited the railcar to begin the search for our next train. I was saddened by my goodbye with Katya and I couldn't stop thinking of her. The arrow in my heart from our farewell that day is still with me.

There were people everywhere. Paps directed us to a train bound for the Russian border city, our last stop before we crossed into Manchuria. There were no police, so we entered the train swiftly. We were about to board when I noticed the two couples with the jewellery approaching us.

"We meet again," one of the women said.

"Good day to all of you," Paps offered politely.

The taller of the two men directed three railway employees to bring their cartfuls of luggage to the train. There must have been two-dozen pieces in all. As the employees struggled with the valises and packages fumbling their way onto the train, the tall man looked at me. "We had quite an enjoyable time at your party," he said, "right about now I would enjoy another piece of your cake."

"Thank you again for attending," I said.

He was sleek in his appearance with his dark gray topcoat and his coal-coloured trousers. His derby was tilted on his head. He had smoky blue eyes. Although he was handsome, his countenance was one of disdain, persisting even when he smiled. For who or for what does he hold such contempt, I wondered.

"Let us be formal for now. Herr Schrader, at your service," he said to my father, touching his index finger to the brim of his hat.

Paps said, "Our pleasure, Herr Schrader." Then, turning to Mutsch and me, "My wife, Frau Völker and our daughter, Fraülein Erna."

"I present my wife, Frau Schrader," he said. As she extended her hand I heard the clatter of her bracelets and saw the sparkle of gemstones on her lapel. Her beauty was rather unremarkable other than her tight-knit curls that burst from beneath the brim of her cloche hat.

Just then the whistle sounded. Without formally meeting the other couple, the seven of us hastened to board through the rear doorway of the car. A railway employee signalled for Herr Schrader and the couple travelling with him. Their compartment was at the front of the car while ours was aft.

"Please join us for supper," Herr Schrader said as he and his companions passed us.

"Yes, of course," Paps said.

No sooner had we opened the door to our compartment than the train lurched out of the station. We were on our way. Although we were looking forward to completing another leg of our journey we were also somewhat dispirited. With every departure came more goodbyes.

The accommodations were very nice. The compartment was tidy, not as large as the last one but with enough room for a bed for Paps and Mutsch, a cot for me, a chest of drawers too large for our meagre belongings, and a bench seat beneath its only window. The lavatory was much smaller.

We went for dinner. Many of the diners looked like business people, perhaps traders or shopkeepers, neatly dressed but with a style of clothing that seemed not European but Asian. Several of the waiters were

Russian. Some were Chinese; their distinct facial features a constant fascination to me.

We sat down. A Chinese waiter handed us menus. Mutsch whispered to Paps, "Our first challenge will be to inquire if there's caviar." Mutsch said the word in German, French, and then in English. The waiter responded in broken French. "*Oui, madame, je vais mettre un peu du caviar.*" Then he hustled toward the kitchen to fetch some.

Herr Schrader, his wife, and their travelling companions entered. Paps waved to them then slid an adjoining table toward ours to make room for everyone.

It is shameful of me but I did envy them—their expensive clothes, their shining jewels.

When everyone was seated Paps said to Herr Schrader, "Please be so kind as to introduce your friends."

"Of course," he said. "May I present Herr and Frau Beck?" Then he said to them, "The Völker family." Our waiter returned with caviar for Mutsch. Then in a rather authoritarian tone Herr Schrader said, "I'll order cocktails for us. Your daughter will have mineral water." He ordered in French, the waiter nodded and left.

"Your destination, Herr Völker?"

As the women fidgeted with their napkins, their gold and silver bracelets sounded like delicate pieces of glass shattering.

Paps answered. "We're bound for Kobe, Japan. The company I work for has opened an office there and my services are required. And you, Herr Schrader?"

I could tell this was going to be a tedious conversation so instead of listening I scrutinized our newly introduced supper guests, the Becks, doing my best to avoid notice.

"We'll go to Beijing," I heard Herr Schrader say, "to vacation for several weeks. Frau Beck's father has an estate there."

Herr Beck seemed as bored as I was. He said barely more than a few words in passing. His clear, dark brown eyes contrasted sharply with his chalky skin. Spectacles rested uncomfortably on his nose.

"As business partners, Herr Beck and I often travel to find new markets, but at this time, as I said, we will vacation."

"What kind of business are you in?" Paps asked.

Frau Beck was a mystery to me. She said nothing at all and it was difficult to see her face—the large brim of her hat drooped down over her forehead creating a shadow that lingered at her eyes. I managed to glimpse a rather soft jaw line, her face subtly v-shaped, her hair as black as pitch. It was incredible that her bracelets didn't slide off her thin, meagre wrists and off her long, thin fingers.

"Diamonds," Herr Schrader said.

That comment caused Mutsch to cough abruptly. There was a silence lasting several moments. Then the tedium of adult conversation continued.

"I see," Paps said.

"Frau Beck's father started the business. The three of us, her father, Herr Beck, and I, have done very well." Herr Schrader finished his drink and then signalled for our waiter. He again ordered cocktails and more mineral water for me.

Then the conversation turned to me.

"And you, Fraülein Völker, how has the voyage been?" Herr Schrader asked, "Have you seen a great deal? Have you learned a great deal?"

Frau Beck placed her elbow on the table, resting her chin in her hand. With her head tilted back, the shadow on her forehead disappeared. She was a very beautiful woman, strikingly so.

"It's been difficult at times," I said, "but we're fine here and look forward to our arrival in Japan."

I thought the less I said would be the better.

"Very well," he said. "And your thoughts on the customs and cultures you've witnessed?"

For the first time Herr Beck stopped eating and focused his gaze on me.

"I have a difficult time with the language barrier. We don't speak Russian nor do we speak Chinese and when we get to Japan . . ."

Suddenly Frau Beck perked up. She leaned back and then stared at me with her head titled even more.

"I do," she said.

It was then that I noticed the low bridge of her delicate nose and her dark, oval-shaped eyes.

Paps was surprised. "You speak Chinese?" he asked.

"Yes," she said, "my father, a government official in Beijing, is Chinese and my mother is French. I lived in China until my twentieth birthday."

Our meals arrived. Herr Schrader and Paps continued with their questions while Herr Beck ate in silence. I couldn't refrain from staring at Frau Beck. I dropped my gaze and tried to focus on my meal. After a while I found myself staring again. I couldn't help it. She noticed my infatuation.

"You have something to say to me?" she asked encouragingly.

"I'm embarrassed to say it but you seem like such an interesting person."

She threw her head back chuckling. "Well then, we'll have much to talk about," she said with a smile.

"Yes, Frau Beck," I said. "Yes, I'd like that very much."

The next morning we found ourselves at the border station. There was considerable movement on the platform. All but the young and infirm carried parcels and suitcases just as countless others had done at dozens of rail stations over the past month. It was as if everyone's belongings were physical extensions of themselves, grotesquely attached to and therefore inseparable from their hands.

I was alarmed when I saw the number of policemen at measured distances along the platform, idle yet watchful and vigilant. They were Russian, dressed in the same crisp uniforms as Katya and her charges had been.

We exited our car and proceeded into the station. The Schraders and the Becks were standing in the waiting room. They were fastidiously dressed and looked well-rested, as if they had just come from a leisurely stay in a hotel. We approached them and exchanged greetings.

"The railway employees have vacated our train for a search before we cross into China," Herr Schrader said. "We'll be here for a few hours.

When we board later we'll be scrutinized and so will our documents and papers."

Paps looked uncomfortable. "Will there be any trouble?" he asked.

"No. We're Germans," Herr Schrader said smugly. "Respect has preceded us all the way from Berlin." Then he smiled at me. "So in the meantime let's go have some tea or coffee."

The dining area was small, the few tables occupied. Other customers were standing, straddling their luggage. Smoke from cigarettes and cigars filled the air. "I prefer to wait for a table," Frau Schrader said. We all agreed. After a while one was vacated. It had five chairs. "For shame, I see there's not enough room," she said.

Mutsch quickly offered, "Please, seat yourselves. We'll wait for . . ."

"Nonsense," Frau Beck interrupted. "Darling," she addressed her husband, "you and the Schraders will sit along with them," meaning my parents, "while Fraülein Völker and I wander about." Her husband sat down immediately. The Schraders followed suit.

"Is that all right?" she asked Paps.

"Yes, of course," he replied, "as long as she won't be a bother."

"No, surely not," she said.

Frau Beck took my hand and ushered me out. We found a bench, sat down, and then quite unexpectedly she said, "When we're alone you'll call me by my given name. It is Li."

"Yes, Li," I said dutifully.

"And I'll call you . . ."

I caught myself just in time. "Erna," I said.

For the next hour Li and I chatted. "My family was poor," she told me, "living on an ancestral farm in the north of China. My mother gave birth to four daughters, my father inconsolably forlorn without a son. The convention then and in some places still was to drown the female babies since they never would be able to do their share of manual work. They'd be useless, only more mouths to feed."

I was horrified. "That can't be," I said, "no one would kill an infant!"

"It was so. But my father is a good man. He would not do this to his children. We left the farm and made our way to a desolate place where he found work in a mine. My mother, sisters, and I laboured alongside him until he earned enough respect to supervise the workings there. Eventually, because of the mine's overabundance of gems, he made a fortune and took us all to Beijing where his reputation and his wealth procured for us a beautiful home and, very soon, a respectable standing not only in the community but also in the government. I met my husband through my father's business dealings, he came to Beijing to buy precious stones. It seems you Germans are not happy without your," she wiggled her arm so her bracelets jangled, "jewellery." She laughed, and then she said, "Neither am I."

We saw my parents, the Schraders, and Herr Beck walking toward us.

"The next time we're together," she whispered placing her hand on mine, "you'll tell me all about you, won't you?"

"Yes, I will. Thank you for spending time with me."

She smiled. "You are most welcome."

We walked out of the station. We would board in forty minutes. The Schraders and the Becks decided to stroll along the platform where they stopped to talk with passengers, policemen, and anyone else who would listen. Paps, Mutsch, and I remained within view of our train. Finally, when the whistle sounded, Paps readied our documents and tickets and we proceeded to our car. A Russian policeman checked our papers and then motioned for us to go aboard.

Just as Herr Schrader had promised, there was no trouble.

As the train moved on I sat with my diary and my pad and coloured pencils beside me. I wrote down a few things about my fascination with Frau Beck as well as some of the recollections she had mentioned of her youth. Then I tried to capture her in a drawing. I reproduced fairly well her mysterious eyes but then lost my artistic way with the remainder of her enigmatic yet captivating facial features.

There was little fanfare when we crossed the border into Manchuria. The train's path raced by an outbuilding of demarcation surrounded by barbed wire fencing that stretched ten metres on each side before it inexplicably stopped. Those barriers wouldn't deter anyone from crossing.

Herr Schrader came by to inform us that as soon as we pulled into the first station we would need to disembark for as long as it took the Chinese authorities to search the train. "The entire staff will be changed," he added. "From here on all the attendants will be Chinese."

Later, the seven of us exited and proceeded to the waiting room in the station. Signs displayed both the Cyrillic alphabet of the Russian language and the ideograms of Chinese.

When we heard the whistle we readied to board. Our car only had two compartments so the seven of us were the sole passengers at the entrance doorway. There, a Chinese guard stood stiffly, his face wooden. Right away I saw the rifle strapped to his back. He looked more like a soldier than a policeman. As we approached he said something to our group. At once Paps handed him our documents, papers, and our Japanese visas. He reviewed them and then signalled for us to board.

As we were about to step onto the train the guard suddenly spewed out a venomous stream of Chinese. Paps, Mutsch, and I froze. I turned to see his face puffed, his cheeks red, the veins of his neck swollen. He was addressing Frau Beck. She looked outraged. She shouted something back at him, waving her hands, her bracelets swirling and clanking, yelling at him in a way I thought was so unlike her. He ranted and Frau Beck ranted back. Finally the guard yielded. Without reviewing the Beck's and the Schrader's documents he waved them to board. Frau Beck advanced toward me, pushing me gently onto the train. Her husband and the Schraders followed.

In the corridor, Mutsch asked, "What was that about, Frau Beck?"

"It's nothing," she said removing her hat and then raking her fingernails through her long black hair. "They think they can intimidate me."

Paps asked, "Is it because of us?"

Herr Schrader stepped toward Paps. "No, Herr Völker. Why would that be so?" He looked at Paps, his eyes searching my father's face. "Every time we come this way there is a bias or let's say an intolerance."

"What do you mean?" Mutsch asked.

Frau Beck returned her hat atop her head. "It's because of me. The provincials are upset that I have a German husband. They consider it treason. They wonder how I, a Chinese, can marry outside my kind."

"I see," Paps said. "We sympathize with you. I hope you consider our friendship some sort of comfort."

With that our companions retired to their compartment as we did to ours. Once inside I said to Paps, "There is bigotry everywhere."

The Schraders and the Becks were just finishing their meals when we entered the dining car for supper. I had brought my diary and a pencil. Already I had filled several pages with recollections, recording my experiences in great detail so I might relate them in letters to family and friends. Frau Beck looked up and pinched the brim of her hat as if in salute. It was so amusing. As the Schraders and the Becks rose from their table we ambled toward them. The adults exchanged greetings. A waiter was clearing plates and glasses. Herr Schrader asked, "May I remind our waiter to bring you a brick of caviar, Frau Völker?" Everyone laughed. I glanced at Frau Beck. She smiled and then winked at me. "When you have finished your supper may I have the honour of your company in the club car, Fraülein Völker?"

Without hesitation I asked Paps, "May I, father?"

"Yes," he said, "of course."

"In fact," I said, "I'm really not hungry. Can I go with Frau Beck now?"

"You must ask her, Lorechen, not me."

"Lorechen?" Frau Beck posed. She took my hand and led me from the table. "Lorechen!" she said again. "I'm curious to know how you've come to be called by that name."

In the club car I told Frau Beck, "They say it all the time except when they're angry with me. Then it's . . ." I almost said Ingelore.

She laughed. "Then they must never call you Erna!"

Frau Beck took my diary and drew an ideogram. "What does that signify?" I asked. She said with a smile, "Me! It's the character for "plum," for Li, for me!"

梅子

I began telling her about myself. My story brought her laughter, surprise, wonder, and at times tears to her eyes. She listened intently, cooing every now and then as I blabbered on.

At one point she asked, "Do you have siblings?"

"No, Li," I said. "Because of the way things were in Germany, I mean in Europe, my parents didn't want two youngsters to care for. Certainly an infant now would be quite a chore for them. One child is more than enough."

I might have blundered when I said Germany. Did I hint that we were Jews?

I was ashamed having to continue the charade of concealing my real name, my faith, and my true identity but I remembered Paps' admonitions—the wolves would always be chasing us.

"I see," she mused. "I have no children. None of my sisters have children. We all are barren. I've often thought that it is our punishment for escaping the fate of drowning. My husband wishes for sons. But as you know, to wish is not to receive."

"I'm sorry, Li."

"Well," she said, "we've been together for quite some time. Your parents are missing you by now."

We walked to our railcar holding hands the entire way. I had a deep liking and a great respect for Li. When I first saw her I imagined her to be arrogant and pretentious, pompous and overbearing. Again, my first impression deceived me. Herr Bayern, our landlord in Berlin, Herr Langer, who pretended I was his granddaughter on the trip to Amsterdam, Herr Zurinoff assisting Paps and me in Moscow. There were others too. I resolved, that in the future, I would not be so hasty in that regard.

After leaving the club car with Frau Beck and then returning to Paps and Mutsch, a curtain of malaise descended upon me. I was drowsy and achy. My nose leaked like a rusted faucet. My throat was sore. My fever caused me to have faces flash before my eyes. Mutsch immediately put me to bed. Paps placed a cold cloth at the back of my neck, Mutsch fluffed my pillow, and Frau Beck brought me soup.

I'm told that Mutsch and Frau Beck tended to me. I remember drifting in and out of sleep all the while thinking I could hear Gerta reading to me. I thought we were in the library in Wilmersdorf. But when I finally opened my eyes I saw that it was Frau Beck who was seated beside me, her long shapely legs crossed, her soft voice expressively recounting the story of *Rapunzel.*

Noticing her wrists were bare I asked her, "Where are your bracelets?"

"You're awake!" she chirped looking up from the book. "How are you feeling?"

"Better, thank you," I said. "But where are your bracelets?"

"Don't fret. We are stopped in Harbin. Your parents are in the station with my husband and the Schraders. I wanted to stay with you. The bracelets? Rather than chance to wake you with their clatter I removed them."

I smiled at her. "You're very kind, Frau Beck."

She reminded me. "When we're alone, I am Li."

"Yes, Li."

She placed her palms at my temples. "You're quite cool. No fever. That's good, isn't it? You'll be up and about in no time."

"Have I been a burden to my parents? To you?" I wondered.

"No," she said, "it's only that we are downcast because you've been sick. You do look better now. The colour has returned to your cheeks. You're as beautiful as before, as good as new!"

Just then Paps and Mutsch came in. The Schraders and Herr Beck were peeking in from the corridor.

Frau Beck stood up. "Her fever has passed. She seems much better."

Mutsch leaned down and put her lips to my forehead. "Yes, Lorechen, I think Frau Beck is right."

From the hallway Herr Schrader said, "It's time to eat. Shall we proceed to the dining car?" At that, he and Herr Beck were on their way.

"Can we interest you in some sweets?" Frau Beck said teasingly.

"As soon as I freshen up I'll be ready."

Mutsch applauded. Frau Beck kissed my brow asking, "We'll meet shortly then?"

On the way Paps said, "At the next station we'll linger for provisions and supplies to be brought aboard."

I was looking forward to wandering around somewhere, anywhere. I hoped Frau Beck would accompany me whenever there was an opportunity.

We were in the club car when the train slowed on its approach into the next station. My parents were thumbing through some newspapers. Written in Chinese, they offered no enlightenment but Mutsch said she enjoyed looking at the ideograms. "There are thousands of them, some different, some remarkably alike," she commented. "I can see the subtleties. It must take years to master the drawing of them."

Before long we were on our way again, this time to what Frau Beck said would be a quick stop in Mukden, an old Chinese city.

I could see that Paps' brow was tensed. Mutsch was wringing her hands. "What is it?" I asked.

"Lorechen," Mutsch said, "shortly we'll arrive at Mukden so it's time to pack. We will be changing trains."

"I understand," I said.

As my parents arranged their belongings, I placed my things in my rucksack, thinking again of Gerta. I double-checked to make sure I wasn't leaving anything behind.

The train arrived at the station. I saw throngs of people scampering about, the same view I had witnessed at countless other stations. I noticed that there were no carts readied on the platform for the dozens of pieces of baggage belonging to the Schraders and the Becks. That was odd, I thought. It would be quite a task to transfer all their things by hand.

We stepped onto the platform inching our way through the crowds to the place from where our next train would depart. Still, I didn't see the Schraders or the Becks or their belongings.

When we came to the train, my parents put down their suitcases. "We have about ten minutes before we leave."

"Where is Frau Beck?" I asked with sudden distress.

Mutsch and Paps looked to each other and then to me.

"I'm sorry, Lorechen," Mutsch said, "but the Schraders and the Becks aren't coming this way. They won't be on this train."

"Where is Frau Beck?" I demanded.

Paps said, "They've remained on our former train. Their travels will take them to Beijing."

I was overcome. With tears in my eyes, I screeched, "We didn't say goodbye!"

Mutsch embraced me. "She couldn't bear it, Lorechen."

I recoiled from her clutch. Paps said, "Frau Beck is immeasurably saddened. She refused to leave her compartment. She asked us to tell you that she feels tremendous loss and that your leaving will scar her heart forever."

I was about to collapse. Paps reached me just before my knees gave way. "I'm so tired," I said.

After a few moments, I recovered. I asked Paps if we could board our train as soon as possible so that I might sit down. He said we could. On our way to the train, Chinese and Japanese police officers were monitoring everyone's movements. Their vigilance was noticeable. I imagined we would be lost without Frau Beck and her ability to speak the language. Luckily, some of the officials spoke French. Paps offered our credentials to the guard. We boarded without any trouble.

The railcar was nothing like our previous one. There were no compartments, just bench seats. We plopped down. I leaned my head against the window.

"We're sorry, Lorechen," Mutsch said. "We'll miss her as well."

Even now, a decade later, I remember that day. I remember feeling so tired. I was exhausted from the life of a nomad and angered by the relentless hunt and chase that necessitated our journey and consequently resulted in the devastating partings from the few friends we did make. I was dejected by the loss of my relatives and friends in Berlin, dispirited by our wayward wandering, frustrated from having to hide behind our forged documents which didn't give due to our real names, so outraged that we couldn't go about as Jews for fear of reprisals and weary of continuing on. I could no longer recall a time when the wolves had not been at our shadows. I was so very tired of it all.

Mutsch handed me a small box. It was wrapped in a napkin from the club car on our previous train and secured with a blue ribbon, one I recognized had been tied around a section of Frau Beck's hair.

"In her misery," Mutsch said, "Frau Beck begged me to give this to you. It's a token of her friendship and enduring admiration."

I tugged on the ribbon and peeled back the folds of the napkin. I opened the box. Inside was one of Frau Beck's bracelets, a beautifully ornate yet tasteful band of attached silver squares. Inside each one was a polished piece of jade. It was magnificent. I slid my wrist through it. I could feel Frau Beck's presence. Paps and Mutsch were glowing. "It seems you've touched her in a very special way," Paps said.

At the bottom of the box there was a coiled piece of paper also secured with a blue ribbon. I untied the knot and unrolled a sheet of pure silk. On it was something written in Chinese characters and an address.

"That's where Frau Beck will be staying for the next month or so," Paps said, "she requests that you write to her at your first opportunity."

"But what's this marking?" I asked.

Mutsch said, "Frau Beck considers you her 'pearl' and asks you to practice writing the word in Chinese."

珍珠

I could not stop the tears that slid down my face. Mutsch handed me a tissue. Paps held my hand. I placed my head on Mutsch's shoulder. I fondled my bracelet, slowly gliding my fingertips over its smooth stones.

Within a few moments I was asleep.

The World of Garlic

June 1936

The jolting movement of the train woke us up. I thought the train had broken down because we were stopped in the middle of nowhere. I saw no town, only an old gray wooden building and some squalid huts nearby. When Mutsch peered out she pulled a face. "We're in the wilderness! Will we be able to get food here?" she wondered.

We got off the train. It was good to be walking on solid ground. The police and railway employees ushered us onto a narrow dirt road that led in the direction of the nondescript building.

On the inside of this unimpressive structure was a large elegant dining room. It reminded me of the Adlon, the fancy hotel in Berlin that my parents had taken me to a few times.

Sparkling chandeliers lit up the room and the burgundy-red drapes were drawn tight to shut out the sun. White damask cloths covered tables set with crystal glasses and gold-banded white plates each bearing a royal crown and an initial R. Ornate silver cutlery was etched with the same pattern. I was amazed to see the Russian influence on this place because there had been no sign of it at the past few railway stops.

"Look, Lorechen," Paps joked, "R for Rothschild!"

A bearded waiter came to our table. He was elegantly dressed in a tuxedo, his hair matted with pomade. He must have overheard Paps' remark. "The initial," he said in French, "stands for Romanoff."

"He looks like a Russian prince," I whispered.

The waiter's eyes met mine. "Many of my friends and my entire family have fled the Imperial Court just ahead of the Russian army, bringing only the possessions we could carry. Our pursuers relented at the Manchurian border."

His story sounded a lot like ours.

He went on. "We settled in Mukden, earning a living selling furs and jewels. Then my family and I came here to open this restaurant."

"Here?" asked Mutsch. "This seems so out of the way."

He continued to study my face.

Without looking to Mutsch he answered her. "It's not so far. We grow our own vegetables even though it's difficult with the weather and the less than ideal soil. We receive supplies and welcome diners that come by train. Overnight guests are accommodated upstairs." Then he withdrew a small pad and pencil from his jacket pocket. "May I take your order?"

Paps was intrigued. "Before you do, please tell us more about you."

The waiter blushed. "We were afraid of the army. Our flight was on horseback across the steppes. We endured the terribly cold winters when the snow blows across the barren land piling up in huge drifts. We've managed to avoid marauding bandits, most often the Mongols, who steal whatever they can. Sometimes they abduct people, even children."

I gasped.

"But," he said, "we've finally come to terms with them because we can offer them some business. They trade meat from their herds for other kinds of much needed supplies. They also bring news of Russia."

We ordered. There was caviar for Mutsch. We were served fresh fruits and vegetables, goat cheese with thick slabs of black bread, pastries and strong tea. The silver samovar set in the centre of the room was almost as tall as me. The meal was delicious.

When we finished, our waiter told us to exit the room, form a line outside, and only then return to the train. "You will not venture off the road. Do you understand?"

"Yes, of course," Paps said.

I asked Mutsch, "How can they live here? It must be boring and isolated."

"Just imagine," she said, "having lived among the rich of the Russian royal court and now to be living here. What a contrast! I don't know how they manage but I admire them for having made the best of a terrible situation."

We walked down the centre of the road to the train.

"This doesn't look very inviting, does it?" Paps asked.

The dusty rutted road disappeared into the gray world of the steppes. On either side sat meagre huts fabricated from scrap metal, flattened tin cans, rotted wooden boards, and cardboard boxes some still bearing the names of the items and manufacturers of the products they had once contained. Corrugated tin, rusted and bent, covered the roofs. There were no windows. Sacking hung over the doorways. Nothing softened the terrible drabness. There were no trees, no flowers, no grass, and no colour. The shacks looked inhospitable and utterly bleak.

We came to our railcar and returned to our seats. Before long we were on our way toward the Korean border.

"At our next stop," Paps said, "the authorities will review our documents before we're allowed to cross the border into Korea."

"It'll be the same then as so many times before?" Mutsch asked.

Paps cleared his throat. "Japanese, Chinese, and Korean personnel will verify who we are and where we're going. The examination may take time. There may even be a Russian presence or, for that matter, the Japanese and each may demand our papers."

"But we're in China. Why would they all be here?"

Just then we heard the screech of metal against metal. Paps looked out and saw we were approaching a station.

"Quickly," Paps said to me, "gather your rucksack and make sure you've got all your belongings."

When the train stopped Paps told us again we'd need to bring our things. "Compartment cars, a dining car, and a club car will be added to our train in preparation for the long route from here to Pusan at the southern tip of South Korea."

"We'll have a nice compartment again?" I asked.

"Yes, Lorechen, we'll be as comfortable as before." Katya and Frau Beck flashed before my eyes. I missed both of them so much.

We exited the train. We heard the clamour of languages, the vowel-rich, sing-song music of Chinese, Korean, and Japanese, the barking of Russian and German, then English, French, and countless others.

Meanwhile, Paps had his ears perked, listening to passengers travelling the same way we were. Soon, he led us to where four policemen were shouting orders in Japanese, Chinese, Korean, Russian, and French. Everyone opened their travel documents and presented them when bidden. After a long look at our papers one of the policemen pointed and said we could go, "*Vous pouvez aller au train.*"

Paps whispered, "Let's go right away." We sifted through the crowd. Before us was an observation car. A policeman checked our papers again and then signalled to enter. "Go!" Paps said, "we'll find our sleeper once we're aboard." Mutsch and I exhaled in unison and then hopped onto the train.

The car was decorated with plush upholstered swivel seats, low wooden tables, soft reading lamps, and expansive tinted-glass windows. I had an unobstructed view on both sides. On one side I saw a river splitting the city into two. From the other I saw lush rice paddies and farm animals. Nearby, fruit trees and mulberry bushes dotted the hills. The sky was a clear and beautiful soft blue with just a few scattered clouds.

There were several passengers in the club car, some reading books while others had their faces buried in newspapers. Children stared ahead blankly.

I heard a soft clicking sound. I looked back to see an elderly Asian man kneading his fingers, his fist closed, as if he were squeezing a lump of clay rhythmically. The sound intrigued me.

Suddenly a wooden bead rolled under my feet. Mutsch scooped it up. She handed it back to the man who smiled and then said something to her in Korean. Mutsch smiled back. The man had been rolling two beads together in his hand. I asked Mutsch, "What of that?" She brushed my brow. "It may have some religious significance or perhaps it just relaxes him."

Later, Paps asked if we were ready to go for supper. Mutsch and I said yes. "Before we do," he said, motioning to the bed, "we'll sit to say prayers. It's Friday so we should."

Mutsch was quick to add, "But let's whisper."

As we held hands Paps thanked God for our safety and the gift of family. He asked for continued fortune so that we would arrive in Japan in good health. "Freedom from oppression," he said, "is something we will never take for granted." Mutsch prayed for the well-being of our relatives. We had no knowledge of them but we did know that there was continued uncertainty and increasing upheaval in Europe. She wished everyone good health and sanctuary from the evils of bigotry.

"And you?" Paps asked me.

I cleared my throat. "I thank God for my parents without whom I'd be lost or perhaps even dead. I pledge my love and good wishes for my relatives and everyone who has helped us: Gerta, Herr Bayern, Herr Langer, Herr Zurinoff, and especially Katya and Frau Beck. Finally, I thank the Lord for watching over us as we continue on to Japan to begin our new life."

Paps ended our service. "Blessed be all who have crossed our paths, those of good will as well as the wicked. God will continue to favour the former and He must help the latter to see the error of their ways and to repent for their own sake and for the sake of mankind."

The first stop in Korea was Sinuiju. As soon as we arrived the odour of garlic permeated the air and invaded our railcar. On the platform adults and children were chewing cloves of it as we would chew gum! At first, the scent was delightfully pungent but soon it became overpowering to the point of bringing tears to my eyes.

"What an odour!" Paps said pinching his nose.

My nose ran. "Yes, it's so peppery and so spicy."

"I'm hungry," Mutsch said.

After more passengers boarded, we went to the dining car.

"Is there caviar on the menu?" Mutsch wanted to know.

Ever since we left Berlin I had the strangest sense of time and distance. When we began our trip in Merano, Italy, Japan seemed to be on the other side of the world, so far away that we might never reach it. The days were long, our progress insufferably slow, and the train rails stretching into the distance appeared as if they would never end. For so long our voyage took us simply to another station along the route. After we crossed the border into Korea from China, I welcomed the feeling that soon we might arrive at our destination. That our journey might someday come to an end.

It took perhaps twelve hours to transect Korea. I busied myself writing in my journal. I cherished my memories of Katya and her thoughtfulness. I fondled the bracelet given to me by Frau Beck, always recalling her kindness. I used my coloured pencils and drawing pad to illustrate the sights I had seen. Names and places found their way into my drawings. I packed and unpacked my rucksack a dozen times to be sure I would be ready when we detrained in Pusan where we would take a ferry to Japan. Each time I did so I thought of Gerta, remembering her love and devotion to my family.

During those twelve hours, my parents and I discussed tasks to be completed, accounted for our belongings, travel documents, and Japanese visas, and made lists of what each of us would do when we arrived in Kobe.

"I'll make sure we're settled in our new living quarters and then I'll go to the office and begin my work there." Paps said. "I will leave the domestic tasks and organization to you and Lorechen," he told Mutsch.

"Through all our trials," Paps reflected, "we've been blessed with good fortune."

Our train arrived at Pusan. Soon we would take our last steps away from oppression, away from the epidemic we saw sweeping toward our little place in Berlin and across all of Europe. We were eagerly anticipating freedom in Japan.

On our way from Sunuiju to Pusan, we had stopped in Seoul. I have a picture in my mind of a river traversed by several bridges, winding its way through that city. Paps told me that once the train departed we would be three hundred kilometres away from the port city of Pusan. "Once there," he said jokingly, "we'll board a ferry and we'll be only a hop, skip, and a jump away from Japan."

I was so excited! The only time I had been on a boat of any consequence was when I was nine or ten years old. We had cruised to Norderney, one of the Frisian Islands. We vacationed there for parts of three consecutive summers and during one of our stays the wonderful fresh air had cleared me of a bout of bronchitis just as the doctor had said it would.

I have vivid memories of that trip. In particular I remember how one afternoon as we lounged near the water's edge the life guards came running toward us. "Tidal wave approaching! Clear the beaches immediately!" they shouted.

"What's a tidal wave?" I asked, having never heard the word before.

We raced toward a cement bridge high above the boardwalk upon which the incoming tide crashed against its pilings. A strong wind sprang up, driving dark clouds ahead of it. Suddenly, someone screamed while pointing into the distance. A single wave rose high into the air, paused, and then with a tremendous roar raced toward us. It crashed furiously across the dunes, ripped apart a section of the boardwalk, and tossed vendors' stands and debris against the pilings.

I shrieked. "Will it wash us out to sea?"

"No, Lorechen," Paps said, "a tidal wave is only one wave."

Surveying the broken remains of the boardwalk and the hideously strewn carpet of personal items and downed branches, he gasped, "Look how much damage it's caused! All we can hope is that no one has been swept away."

Ingelore and her mother and father sailing on the North Sea to Norderney (East Frisian Islands), 1935.

We heard someone say that fifty years had passed since the last tidal wave had been seen in the North Sea.

Now, halfway across the world and several years later we were in pursuit of the land's end, where we would board a different boat of consequence to ferry across the Sea of Japan to the island of Honshu and then travel to our new home in Kobe.

We disembarked that morning in Pusan and trudged through the crowds, making haste to enter the station house. We needed to find the ferry terminal. Father thought it would be no more than a kilometre and so, carrying everything we owned in two small valises and one rucksack, we walked from the station. Once outside we felt the strong gusts and heard the angry howling of the wind swirling about. We pushed against its force making slow progress. Soon we located the ferry station.

To our great disappointment there was a typhoon alert in effect.

"How will we get to Japan?" I asked.

Paps looked exhausted. "We must wait and see," is all he could say.

PART THREE

Japan is on the Horizon

June 1936

By noon word came that the ferry captain felt it was safe to cross. Everyone waiting to board passed the message along. The news spread in a dozen different languages. The wind had died down and the sky was not as ominous as it had been a few hours before. Still, the day was dark and the air and water remained in turmoil.

Soon attendants began ushering everyone toward the ship. We did not move. We stood together, looking at each other, our faces showing a combination of hope and fear.

We walked the gangplank onto the massive ferry that rolled on the agitated waters. A Japanese officer in a gold-trimmed white uniform showed us to our cabin. On the way we passed a dining room, a lounge, a game room with tennis tables, and several smaller sitting rooms.

"It won't take long to cross," Paps said.

We surveyed our compartment. It was small with just a divan and a chair, a dresser with two shallow drawers, and a quaint lavatory consisting of a miniature toilet and sink.

Paps asked us if we wanted to go on deck to watch the ship's departure from the terminal.

"Is it safe to do so?" Mutsch wondered.

"Of course, darling," he said, "just don't stand too close to the railings."

"Oh, my!" Mutsch exclaimed.

Paps laughed and at once Mutsch and I could see he was joking. So off we went to the deck. As we mounted the stairs we heard the engines starting. Then we felt a slow, smooth movement beneath our feet as the ship left the pier.

"Next stop, Japan!" Paps said. "Doesn't that sound exciting?"

"Yes, father," I moaned as my stomach plunged and rose with the now more violent pitching of the ferry. I looked at Mutsch and saw she was experiencing the same queasiness I was. Without a word we rushed back to our cabin. I was grateful that we had a lavatory! Mutsch and I were so seasick!

Later, after the rough sea had quieted and our uneasiness had passed, Mutsch and I joined Paps on deck.

"Well," he greeted us, "hello my sleepyheads! You look much better now!" Then to me, "And you, Lorechen, you aren't as green as a frog anymore! How do you feel?"

"Better," my mother and I answered in unison. We laughed. Then Mutsch said, "We're starving. Can we get something to eat?"

"Yes, of course," Paps said, "some caviar?"

Mutsch, cringing at the thought, led me to the dining room.

Once seated we were joined by an unexpected guest.

Captain Shogawa was short and angular, his bearing suggesting a constant state of being at attention. Even his hair stood at attention, its straight black and gray bristles like spikes on a pineapple. His brow was weathered, his eyes clear.

"Welcome aboard!" he said in French.

"Thank you, Captain," Paps said. Then pointing to Mutsch and me, "My wife and daughter are now hungry after a bout with *le mal de mer*. Perhaps some tea and toast?"

"Forgive me," he said, "but earlier there was a huge demand for just those items and at present we have none left. It's too bad. Not only are most of my passengers seasick but even my crew are struggling!"

Mutsch and I looked at each other, our faces still pale with nausea. "It's the remnants of the storm," he continued, "the waters are rough, the waves strong, the motion unrelenting. Perhaps coffee? Or a cocktail? Crackers?"

"No, thank you," Mutsch responded, "but cold soda water, if it's not too much trouble."

With that the Captain snapped his fingers summoning a waiter to our table. He ordered in Japanese and the waiter hastily ran off to fulfill his request.

"You'll have your soda water very soon," he said. Then he walked out of the dining room.

After a while we went back on deck and found the sea much calmer, the wind gentle, the air crisp and clear. The setting sun gleamed with a calming afterglow, its light painting the crests of the gently swelling waves with golden flecks. Large white birds soared overhead, their feathers tinted pale pink in the shadows.

A man further along the deck was taking photographs. He came over to introduce himself. He spoke German and he and Paps began talking. Mutsch and I turned away to look at the views. "I must remember," I said, "to try to capture this seascape in a drawing."

She smiled. "Yes, Lorechen, you must try."

Paps turned to us. "Herr Gessler has asked if we'd like our pictures taken. Shall we?"

"Yes," I exclaimed.

Herr Gessler took several pictures of us before he ran out of film. Paps thanked him and then told us that Herr Gessler had promised to send the pictures to Paps' office in Kobe."

"How long will that take?" I wondered.

"I don't know, Lorechen," he said, "but no matter. At least we'll have a few pictures of our trip."

Several hours later there came a blast of static and then a man spoke in French over the loudspeaker. "Good evening. This is the captain speaking. We are approaching Honshu. You can see it on the horizon. We continue on to our landing at Shimonoseki."

Paps and Mutsch cheered. I exhaled with relief. Our long and eventful journey was drawing to a close.

As we approached, the island of Honshu swelled before us, its landmass slowly coming into view. We saw strange-looking boats in a harbour that Father called *junks*. They lolled gently in the still, dark water.

We docked. Customs officials came aboard to check visas and search baggage. One of them confronted Herr Gessler. The official bowed deeply and then in perfect English asked the man for his camera.

Herr Gessler replied, "I don't understand." His English was also good. "I merely was taking pictures of the sunset."

"You were observed taking photographs. This is strictly forbidden. I'm sorry but I must insist. If you do not comply it may be rather unfortunate for you."

Herr Gessler and the customs official stared into each other's eyes. Then the official held out his hand. Without a moment's hesitation, Herr Gessler handed him the camera and pouch. With remarkable efficiency, the official opened the camera and the pouch, removed the rolls of film, closed both, and handed the camera and now empty pouch back.

I whispered to Paps, "Why did he take the film? Officials must have seen him taking pictures before. Why did no one stop him then?"

"In these trying times," Paps said, "every country feels that it must keep secrets. Perhaps there were other ships on the water that the Japanese didn't want anyone to know about. I'm not sure." I thought of Katya and the detailed instructions she would give to ensure order. At that time it was to prevent us from wandering off or getting lost. But now it was this. What a crazy world!

I remember that evening clearly. It signified not only the conclusion of a long voyage that began in Wilmersdorf but also it was the last night that we were drifters, transients. Within a matter of hours we would have a home again and would begin a new life as German nationals in a country that would accept us for who we were.

After Captain Shogawa bid his passengers adieu, we went ashore. Paps led the way to the train. It was quite dark now and I could not make out much of our surroundings save for a few lights from some villages in the distance.

Once on the train, I dozed for a while. I woke with a start when the train arrived at a brightly lit station. I saw a sign with large Japanese characters under which was the word *KOBE*. My first thought was, how will I ever learn those strange symbols?

Even though it was late, the platform was crowded. What struck me was the curious custom of bowing. There were dozens of people doing it, their heads rising and falling like an undulating ocean. The women I saw were garbed in brightly coloured kimonos.

We exited the rail car and within a few steps I was swept off my feet into the arms of my Uncle Hans! Of course, Hans was not my real uncle, nor was his wife, Evchen, my real aunt, but both of them had always been two of my favourite people. I had known them all my life. How happy I was to see Hans, that tall giant with steel blue eyes and a gentle manner. He had arrived in Kobe with his wife, who we called Eva, several months before. He was working at the branch office of the same import-export business that Paps worked for in Berlin. Aunt Eva hugged us and wished us welcome. She was so regal-looking with her high forehead, classic Roman nose, clear gray eyes, soft slim hands, and voice that never failed to remind me of a lullaby. The five of us stood embracing and kissing each other.

"It's so good to see you," Uncle Hans said with his beautiful smile beaming. "You've made your way to Japan! We've been praying for your safe arrival."

Paps shook his hand so violently I thought both men would lose their balance. "Yes, yes," Paps said, "it's been a long and arduous trip but we're here now, we're safe, and we're with friends."

Uncle Hans pulled Aunt Eva to his side. "We have a wonderful surprise for you," he boasted, "one I hope won't be an inconvenience at this time."

"What is it?" I asked.

"Well," Aunt Eva said, "even though it's late, we've arranged with the staff to welcome you to the office. It's available now for your inspection."

"Now?" Mutsch asked in disbelief. I could see she was exhausted, her eyelids drooping, her usually perfect posture slightly rounded. "Now?" she asked again.

"Yes, now," Paps interjected. He looked more tired than Mutsch but this would be another example of his iron will and perseverance. He would overcome his exhaustion. "Let's go see the workplace. Thank you, Hans and Evchen, for your thoughtfulness."

Paps then addressed Mutsch. "As soon as we've seen it, Hans will escort us directly to our new residence." Paps always had a way of smoothing things over.

"Certainly," Hans said. "Let's go." With his arm extended he showed us the way. With Mutsch and me bringing up the rear, we followed Uncle Hans, Aunt Eva, and Paps. Outside the station there was the shiniest and longest automobile I had ever seen parked at the curb. It was idling, its trunk compartment open. As we came closer to it a young Japanese man in a chauffeur's uniform stepped out from the driver's seat, came around to the passenger side, bowed to all of us, opened the car doors, and then rushed to relieve us of our baggage. He took our things, placed them in the trunk, and then ushered us into the automobile.

The bench seats were enormous. There was plenty of room for the five of us. When we were ready, Uncle Hans gave the driver instructions in Japanese and we pulled away from the station.

I sat snugly in between Paps and Mutsch and to this day I still can feel the softness of that seat. Velvet is such an intoxicating fabric!

The office staff, some of whom Paps had known from the Berlin office, came out to greet us. My uncle made introductions in what sounded like a stream of mystical sounds, dozens of distinct vowels and tones. Whatever he said caused each of the employees to bow and smile. I bent over, too, though it felt strange to do so especially since I had noticed that the women bowed lower than the men. I later learned that the lower one's status, the lower one's bow.

Some spoke to my parents in halting English and, even though I considered myself competent in that regard, I understood only so much of their conversation. A few spoke German. I became anxious at the thought of learning Japanese and improving my English concurrently. I felt isolated and lonely—I wished my friends were here with me now.

Then we met Mr. Suzuki, Uncle Hans' assistant, and Mr. deCouto. Mr. Suzuki was short and stout but his face was pleasing. Arthur deCouto was different. He was the son of a Macao Portuguese. Arthur, fleeing his native country during a coup, had come to Japan and later married a Japanese woman. He was a slight young man with prominent cheekbones, a tawny complexion, and noticeably slanted eyes. His voice was pitched higher than any man's voice I'd ever heard. It was enchanting. He intrigued me. He told my parents that he spoke English, Japanese, and Portuguese fluently. Even though I felt shy in my new surroundings I wished he would talk only to me.

After an invitation to enjoy a spread of Japanese snacks and tea and a tour of the office, most people departed, bowing again. Uncle Hans took us outside and we got in his car with Aunt Evchen and Mr. deCouto. Mutsch grabbed my hand and whispered in my ear, "We're almost home, Lorechen."

"You'll like it there," I heard Aunt Eva say, "it's more of a home than a hotel, more like a country house or a villa

I remember the ride even though I was tired, hungry, and in need of a bath. As the chauffeur drove slowly through the streets of the city I saw men in dark trousers and jackets with towels around their heads pulling rickshaws whose passengers were half-hidden behind curtains. The car windows were open and I heard bells tinkling from all directions. There were women carrying packages wrapped in bright cloths, some had babies on their backs, the little ones clinging to the sleeves of their mothers' kimonos. Some children wore brightly coloured outfits while others wore dark skirts or pants with white shirts. I saw groups of girls playing hopscotch. As they went about their play, they sang, sometimes alone and sometimes in concert. Their songs sounded like poems or perhaps they were nursery rhymes.

Beside me in the back seat, mother followed my gaze, "Maybe those outfits are school uniforms? Though I'm puzzled why the children still would be wearing them this late at night."

As we rode along pungent odours from tiny cafés and eateries billowed into the car. Then the city thinned out, the buildings became smaller, the blocks less dense with development. We passed scrawny wooden houses with paper screens nestled in garden patches. Flowers were everywhere.

We arrived at the villa. Uncle Hans introduced us to the owners, Mr. and Mrs. Dimitriev, who had come to greet us. Mrs. Dimitriev was heavy-set. She was an ebullient woman of tremendous energy. Later, we learned that she and her husband were emigrants from Russia. She spoke quickly in English yet I could hear her distinct accent. I asked if she knew Katya.

"No, little one, I'm sorry but I don't know any person of that name," she said apologetically.

"Mother," I said, "Katya called me little one, too!"

Mrs. Dimitriev ran the villa, cooked gourmet meals, and professed that she would be ready to lend a helping hand at any time. Her husband was the caretaker, bookkeeper, and general manager. As we walked to the front door I marvelled at the beautiful grounds. There were sturdy trees and lovely flowers, some varieties that I had never seen before. The lawns were a lush green. The sprawling two-story villa was magnificent. It contrasted sharply with the much smaller Japanese homes I had seen along our drive. A wide veranda encircled the house.

Inside, the rooms were enormous. There were Persian carpets, soft lights, and plush couches and armchairs. Overhead fans purred to keep the rooms cool.

Mr. deCouto asked me if I would accompany him on a walk about the grounds. Paps overheard and immediately spoke on my behalf. "Yes, of course she'd love to."

I asked Arthur about the children I had seen. "Did you hear the children we passed on our way here? What were they singing?"

"They constantly study their characters and the sounds related to each one," Arthur explained. "They need to learn at least four thousand of them just to read a newspaper!"

I was astonished. "I guess I was lucky that I only had to learn the thirty letters of the German alphabet!"

Ingelore's first home in Japan, the villa in Kobe, 1936.

Suddenly, a large black cat ran through a puddle near the edge of the grounds. "Strange," I said, "I thought cats disliked water."

"That wasn't a cat, Ingelore," he said. "It was a rat! You'll see rats here so large that most cats are afraid of them!"

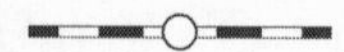

During our stay in Kobe I considered Hans Mendelsohn my favourite uncle. He and his wife had met in Berlin at the home of one of Hans' friends where Eva was the children's governess. They were married a week before they immigrated to Japan. Six months later, my family arrived in Kobe. The Mendelsohns helped us adjust to this strange new land. They introduced us to their friends, showed us around the city and its neighbourhoods, and secured the villa that was our home. I always admired Eva, her fun-loving personality and ready laugh delighted me.

"Come, Lorechen," Aunt Eva would say, "let me show you something." Then off we would go to the brook that ran behind her home. Sometimes we would wander around the grounds and inspect the wonderful trees. She introduced me to Okachan, or little granny, their faithful old cook.

Eva and Hans were childless and gradually they adopted me as their surrogate daughter. I spent plenty of time at their beautiful glass and stucco ranch house set among Kobe's rolling hills overlooking the Inland Sea. Cherry, almond, and apple tree blossoms spread a fabric of pink and white over large areas close to their property. In the summer I saw wild yellow, purple, and white orchids blooming among flaming red Japanese maples. Later in the year, huge purple and bronze chrysanthemums burst into flower among the graceful pines.

Midway up the long driveway to Eva and Hans's home rested a huge boulder. "An archeologist friend of ours says it was deposited here during the last ice age," Eva told me. At the base of the rock low-growing lacy bushes hugged the soil sending shoots over it in a web that almost completely covered the granite mass in sprays of tiny pink flowers.

Filled with treasures from all over the world, the interior of their home was as enchanting as their gardens. A family of carved ebony

The writing desk in the living room (above).
The view from the living room through the Japanese screen doors (below).

elephants marched across the fireplace mantle. Near the hearth were clusters of wooden statues of warriors and hunters. Intricately woven baskets were strewn there as well. An ancient silken scroll, what I later learned was called a *kakimono*, hung along one wall. It was hand-woven and embroidered, depicting Mount Fuji, its crown enveloped in clouds. An old Japanese man looked out dreamily on another scroll, his dark brown and black robe contrasting with the softly lit background. Of all their wondrous curios I was most interested in their metre-tall statue of Buddha, whose one hand rested on his knee, the other hand in front of the chest, fist clenched and index finger raised in a traditional pose. Peace, he seemed to be saying, looking so very wise and kind.

During our first days in Kobe, Mutsch and I tended to housekeeping duties even though Mrs. Dimitriev told us there were servants at our disposal. "We'll do the primary things ourselves," Mutsch said, "and after we've completed them, we may wish to avail ourselves of maids and domestics." I heard the guilt in her voice. Perhaps she considered the distinction of station another form of oppression, the very scourge we had been running from for so long.

Upon arrival, we immediately unpacked our luggage. After our long trip every article of clothing needed to be washed. In the afternoon we rearranged some of the furniture to make space in the centre of the room. We were finished with living in confinement, the rail cars and the compartments we inhabited for so long seemed so claustrophobic to us now. When Paps came home from work he inspected what Mutsch and I had done. He spoiled praise all about us!

Just then Mrs. Dimitriev stopped by to remind us to explore the rooftop of our villa.

"You can use it any time," she said, "to host parties or just relax or play table tennis."

Paps adjusted easily to our new home. He became absorbed in his work and looked forward to going to the office each morning. When he returned, he usually brought Mutsch a flower or a small article of jewellery, and for me a silk scarf or a handful of candy. When he found the time to garner such things I don't know.

Ingelore, Kurt, and Doris on the rooftop (above).
Kurt and Ingelore playing table tennis while the Mendelsohn's dog, Boya, lounges in the shade (below).

Sometimes I would go to Aunt Eva's home. First to greet me was Uncle Hans' black Siberian husky, Boya, who Uncle Hans said was ever so gentle with those he trusted but who could become ferocious when threatened. "Boya doesn't care for many people," Uncle Hans told me, "but it seems he's taken a liking to you. Perhaps he knows how much we love you!" During the rainy season Boya and I would sit for hours in the Mendelsohn's guest room. Its walls were lined with classics in English, German, French, and Portuguese. Books on the Orient, history, modern painters, and architecture were everywhere. Those days and that setting brought to mind warm and cherished memories of Gerta with me in the library in our home in Wilmersdorf.

Eva was a fine pianist. I loved watching her play the shiny grand piano, sitting erect she would play Chopin, Beethoven, and Mozart. Her fluid hands and fingers like streams of sunlight danced about the keys as Boya lolled nearby.

"You must come to hear Herr Waldstein," she said, "when we do our duets. He's a marvelously talented cellist with such powerful arms and yet such sensitive hands."

I remember those duets and times when Mr. Kaga, a colleague of Uncle Hans and Paps, would play his violin. During those recitals their home was crowded with guests. The music soared through the house, the melodies and harmonies so colourful and so magical I can still hear them today. When the stringed instruments reached a crescendo, Boya howled like a coyote.

I passed many hours with the Mendelsohns during the terrible war years. We fretted about what would happen if we were forced to leave Japan. The future looked so dim.

On one occasion Uncle Hans asked me, "You're terribly anxious about your father, aren't you, Lorechen?" This came after one of Paps' bad headaches when he had been confined to his darkened bedroom for an entire day.

"Yes, I am."

He consoled me. "The doctors will be able to help him. I'm sure of it."

I agreed but I could not stop thinking the worst.

The Earth Moves

Summer 1936

I could not understand why my father chose Mr. McKenzie for my English tutor.

"You've ten weeks to improve your overall language abilities," my father said, "in order to meet the strict entrance requirements for the Canadian Academy. It's the only private English language school in Kobe, so a tutor is necessary."

"Yes, father," I said.

Though Gerta did not speak English, the months and months of recitations with her when I was schooled at home in Wilmersdorf provided me with a rudimentary understanding of grammar and verb conjugation. I needed a more profound knowledge of the language before I'd be able to enroll at the academy. I wished Gerta and I could have resumed our lessons.

The CA, as we called it, was established several decades earlier by Canadian missionaries but was no longer affiliated with a church. It was staffed mostly by Europeans and I hoped I would be able to attach myself to someone who also could speak German.

On a hot, humid day in July, I walked to the McKenzie home for the first time. A maid ushered me into a dark vestibule smelling of stale tobacco and cats. The drapes were drawn tightly. Mr. McKenzie, seated in an armchair, looked up and spoke to me in English with a flurry of words I could not understand. He might as well have been speaking to me in Czech because his burr obscured his words.

"Good morning" he said condescendingly. He always spoke to me in that manner.

He stood up. His thinning reddish brown hair was combed back. His dark eyes protruded grotesquely from their sockets. He was overweight, his jowls limply hanging down from his jaw. His pipe was clenched between discoloured teeth too small for his mouth. From that moment on, and for all the years I knew him, Mr. McKenzie removed that brier only to refill it with tobacco. I still wonder whether he slept with it.

As we walked through his dark house I felt like I was back in Berlin, at one of its stately museums. The rooms were crowded with massive overstuffed chairs and sofas, embroidered pillows liberally strewn about. The thick carpets were covered with hair from Mr. McKenzie's ten cats. I felt some of the cats rubbing up against my ankles. Just then the maid dropped something in the kitchen. The sound startled the cats. Some jumped onto the furniture while others slinked into wicker baskets.

It was intolerably stuffy and hot inside the house.

I could not imagine Paps enduring an hour and a half each day in that stifling greenhouse. I whined about the darkness and dreariness to Paps. "Lorechen," he responded, "it's for your own good. You're lucky that Mr. McKenzie is on a break from his research and is available to tutor you before you start school." I never did find out what kind of research it was but secretly I fantasized that Mr. McKenzie was working as a spy for the British government.

In his dark study, Mr. McKenzie sat in an immense armchair behind an equally enormous cluttered desk. I tried not to squirm while I sat on a chair covered with fabric as rough as burlap. It made my bare legs itch incessantly. I soon came to realize there would be no formal lessons, no grammar, no vocabulary lists, just Mr. McKenzie talking about his childhood in Scotland, his family, and his cats. He even showed me his collection of pipes from around the world.

Each day Mrs. McKenzie served tea and crumpets halfway through my lesson. She looked older than her husband. Her hair, carelessly piled high on the top of her head, reminded me of a bird's messy nest. The McKenzies were the only people I knew who made no concession to the climate of Kobe. Regardless of the temperature, they always wore their tweed and woolen outfits.

Throughout the summer, our lessons continued in the tightly shut house. At times, it was unbearable. Nonetheless I gradually understood every word Mr. McKenzie said. One day he asked me about my life in Berlin. I began relating some of my most cherished memories of the people and places so dear to me.

He interrupted me after several minutes. "You know," he said with a supercilious tone, "you're speaking in nearly perfect English."

Suddenly I realized I had been! And, to my great surprise, without the McKenzie burr!

The next fall I started school. I came home those first few days crying like a child. "I'll never fit in," I sobbed, "I'm not used to regular school. Why can't I be tutored at home? I did so well with Gerta!"

"Nonsense," Paps said. He looked at me with a piercing stare. "You speak English fluently, don't you? You have met all your teachers, haven't you? You only need to allow for more time to adjust."

"But I hate school!" I said.

Mutsch raised her eyebrows. "I'll never hear those words from you again," she snapped. "Never," she emphasized, "do you hear?"

The next day, I met Joan, a pretty, blond classmate with big blue eyes. She noticed how frustrated and uncomfortable I was during our lessons.

"I'll be your helper," she offered.

I was surprised. Joan was popular. All the students knew her and everyone sought her acceptance and approval. Why did she want or need to help me?

Joan and I became friends. Many times on our way home from school we would talk about our hopes, dreams, and secrets. Whenever I needed help with pronunciation or vocabulary Joan was there to pronounce, define, and explain whatever words I was struggling with or searching for. I stopped worrying about what I believed was my shallow command of English and I rarely panicked when teachers called on me for answers or recitations.

I continued my lessons with Mr. McKenzie a while longer and still had tea and crumpets each time I visited. When Paps and my teachers at the Academy determined that I no longer needed a tutor I stopped going to Mr. McKenzie for lessons but would drop by occasionally to see them for we had become friends. A few years later, just prior to the invasion of Poland in 1939, they returned to Scotland and unhappily, as with so many others, we lost touch.

As 1936 drew to a close, we felt that the wave of Nazi terror in Europe would crest and savagely inundate nearly all its nations. Fascism seemed to be boiling across every border there.

Though I had grown up observing Chanukah rather than Christmas, that year our family and all whom we knew celebrated every occasion that helped us to forget, even for a little while, the tension and anxiety and the fear and dread of the times. We understood war was inevitable. Many of our friends and relatives were still stranded in Europe, many in hiding. Celebrations, parties, and get-togethers in our part of the world relieved our worries if only for a few hours.

On Christmas Eve, my parents went to a party at the home of some friends. I stayed at the villa with Kikuchan, our favourite maid, and Obachan, our cook. Mutsch had loosened her stance concerning the use of servants, although she still had some reservations. Mutsch settled on employing two. Paps had wanted more but Mutsch stood her ground.

Kikuchan was young, very slender and, at nineteen years old, not much taller than me. I don't know whether she was unusually short or if I was unusually tall for twelve and a half. She was so pretty with her dark eyes, beautiful olive-toned skin, and long shiny black hair that she often wore in a knot at the back of her head.

The two of us were fond of each other. She helped me with Japanese and I helped her with English. Though there was a language barrier between

Obachan at the dinner table and Kikuchan posing outside Ingelore's home in Kobe, circa 1936.

us most times we understood each other perfectly. Our relationship was uncommon because contact between Westerners and Japanese was defined and managed by class. I, as a German, was privileged and Kikuchan, as a native domestic, was not. Our interactions should not have gone beyond those distinctions. But we liked each other and decided to do away with those silly boundaries, confiding in one another and often giggling together.

I knew that Kikuchan was probably as lonely as I was. Like many of her contemporaries, she had left her home in the country to earn money in the big city to better her lot. And I imagine that working for foreigners in a Western-style home must have been a strange experience for her. She and Obachan lived in a separate wing of our villa that was separated by sliding rice-paper doors and furnished with the more traditional *tatamis*, a traditional Japanese rush-covered straw mat that covered the floors.

That Christmas Eve a messenger came by with a gift. I tore the outer wrapping to shreds in my haste, removing layer after layer of hand-painted tissue. Inside was a glass and wooden showcase containing an exquisite Japanese doll. I knew these dolls were art objects rather than toys. A small card read: *A little gift for Ingerorechan from your friends at Gerbers.* I smiled because I knew there was no letter *L* in the Japanese language hence the strange spelling. Paps and some of his colleagues must have arranged this! When I thanked Paps for the thoughtfulness he told me that the doll was handmade and dressed by the wives of several of the executives in his office.

I understood how much work had gone into dressing my doll. I was enchanted with this lovely gift. I was fascinated by the fact that all Japanese clothing was hand-sewn. Kikuchan had told me about traditional Japanese clothing. How the fabric was chosen for its colour and pattern and according to the age and gender of the wearer—the younger the person, the brighter the colours—a tradition that applied to doll clothing as well. She told me that ceremonial kimonos made of fine silk and exquisitely embroidered with gold and silver thread had family crests sewn into the back panel. Favourite motifs included dragons, birds, flowers, and trees and were chosen depending on the season. The fabric for kimonos was cut to the proper length for the wearer and would then be hand sewn with a tiny running stitch. Kikuchan told me that every seam was straight with the exception of children's sleeves which were rounded off at the lower edges. The sleeves served as pockets but all valuables were kept in an opening in the *obi* or sash. Before each washing, the seams would be taken apart and then yards upon yards of fabric would flutter from clotheslines supported by bamboo poles as they dried. Dry kimonos would be re-sewn by female members of the family, a skill taught to young girls early in life. In the winter, kimonos would be layered for warmth.

Together, Kikuchan and I opened the case. The doll's face was intricately painted. She was dressed in an apple-green silk kimono with tiny gold appliqués. Her brocade *obi* was interwoven with green and red silk yarn. The hair, courtesan-style, was piled in layers on top of her head. A bun sat low on her white neck. "White skin," Kikuchan said, "sign of great beauty!" Tiny silver combs and miniature bell-like, fluted bands were tucked into the layers of the doll's jet-black hair. Her kimono, open at the bottom, revealed a red embroidered lining. The outfit was complete with pure white *tabi*, socks that could accommodate the thick straw of the *zori* sandals around the big toe that also came with the doll.

Kikuchan and I admired the doll in the living room, a fire roaring in the coal-burning potbelly stove. We were playing *noh*, the Japanese equivalent of checkers, while munching on delicious rice cakes Obachan prepared earlier in the day.

Muschi, my cat, was sleeping in the space between the stove and sliding doors that separated the living room from my bedroom.

Several weeks earlier, Kikuchan had come into my bedroom with a package wrapped in Japanese cloth.

"Be careful," she said looking down at the floor.

Inside was a kitten! It looked like a little fur ball. Kikuchan said it was six weeks old. It had little black ears and a tail that formed a right angle to its body.

"She's beautiful, Kikuchan," I said. "May I keep her?"

Kikuchan beamed. "*Hai*! *Hai*!" Yes! Yes!

"But look," I said, "look at her tail! It's broken! The poor little thing must have caught it somewhere."

"*Nashi*!" No, she replied. "I did it."

I was incredulous. How could this young woman, so friendly and so warm, break a kitten's tail?

"It's good luck," she said.

I didn't tell her what I thought of this custom but the word *barbaric* came to mind.

Muschi was the first to know that something was wrong. Suddenly she jumped onto the couch and dug herself into the pillows behind my back. "Strange," I said, "I wonder what's the matter with her."

Kikuchan was standing up when suddenly she pitched backward and I was tossed off the couch! I saw my doll go sliding across the room! The stove lurched forward! Things were crashing throughout the house! Kikuchan, who according to custom had never touched me, grabbed me and pulled me into a doorframe just as Muschi started to mew frantically! In the kitchen, Obachan dove into the pantry.

This must be an earthquake! My heart was racing, my bones turning to jelly. I was terrified. Would the house collapse? The ground rumbled and swayed beneath my feet. The walls fissured, some of the windows shattered, dishes and pictures from shelves crashed to the floor, mirrors broke. I imagined the stove tipping over and starting a fire, the ceiling coming down around us, the wood rafters of the house splintering and crushing us to death. I felt numb with terror.

Kikuchan and I held on to each other yelling, "Stop! Stop!"

Suddenly everything became deadly quiet. We felt safe but we didn't move or release our embrace. Five minutes went by and then another tremor reverberated! Again my doll slid about the floor while Muschi screeched eerily.

Finally, it was over. Kikuchan and I held each other tight. We got up. Obachan came to us. I rushed to my doll, stepping over debris and displaced furniture. The case was resting against the couch, the doll lying precariously on her side.

It was a miracle! The case had protected her! Aside from dust and a few small pieces of plaster on her clothing she was in perfect condition.

Muschi was too!

The telephone rang.

"Thank God you're all right!" Mutsch burst into the receiver. "Just stay where you are. We'll be home as quickly as possible."

I hung up. I asked Kikuchan, "Where does she think I would go?"

Kikuchan and Obachan were visibly more shaken than I was. Perhaps they had experienced many earthquakes that were far more damaging than the one we just experienced and they feared the worst.

Kikuchan and I inched our way through the debris putting items away and picking up broken pieces of glass and pottery and slivers of plaster and splintered wood.

My parents arrived about a half an hour later. They had walked through streets full of rubble on their way home. Many trees lay uprooted, some wires were downed, and fallen branches and large pieces of roofs had crushed several cars.

They had been terrified for me. "You're our only child," Mutsch said with tears in her eyes, "and with you, Kikuchan, and Obachan here without us . . . well, we were worried something terrible would happen to all of you."

After a concerted effort to tidy up and countless trips to and from the trash, the five of us sat and talked into the early morning. Paps reminded everyone that Frank Lloyd Wright had designed the first earthquake-proof structure, the Imperial Hotel in Tokyo, ten years ago. Although it withstood every earthquake it eventually succumbed to the Allied bombing a few years hence.

The next day I learned that compared to some of the other houses and buildings, our home had sustained only minimal damage. I saw pictures in the newspapers of several places that had collapsed completely. It was very sad to see such ruin and destruction.

During the decade we lived in Japan we experienced numerous earthquakes, some more powerful and destructive than others but none terrified me as much as that first one on Christmas Eve.

In the New Year I returned home from school one day to find Kikuchan with a stack of mail on the dining room table. She smiled as she rifled through it. Shyly, she handed me one of the envelopes. It was addressed to me!

More than six months had passed since father had brought home stationery along with a dozen or so interesting Japanese postage stamps and had said, "It's time for you to write your letters to family and friends again, Lorechen."

Immediately, I sat down and wrote to Omi and Opa, Uncle Sieke, Uncle Hans, Aunt Jenny, and Aunt Irma and her stepdaughter Stella. I also wrote to Herr Bayern, Adah Metzger, and my cousin Ullie. I missed Gerta, Katya, and Frau Beck so much that I composed my longest scripts for them. My hand was nearly crippled when I finished. Paps mailed them the next day and I had forgotten all about them until Kikuchan handed me that envelope.

The envelope was made of some delicate but strong material. The lettering was impeccable and there was a slight hint of perfume about its seal. The stamp was from China. I opened it carefully.

Inside was a wafer-thin piece of rice paper. I unfolded it slowly and was pleasantly taken aback when I realized that it was from Frau Beck.

Dearest Erna, it began, *I was unaware that I was acquainted with someone named Ingelore.*

I gasped!

I had forgotten all about the ruse! The day after we arrived in Japan Paps secured proper papers for us through Herr Griesbach's connections in the immigration offices in Tokyo. Herr Griesbach has been our longtime benefactor. So, at the time of writing I had forgotten all about our masquerade.

My heart was racing as I read Frau Beck's next words, terribly ashamed now and frightened that she might be angry with me.

She continued. *I'm well, earnestly hoping you and your parents are, too, and I'm relieved and thankful that you arrived safely in Japan. It's occurred to me that you must have had your reasons to disguise yourself but it's no concern of mine. I'm as fond of you now as I was when last we were together.*

I was relieved that her words and tone suggested indifference, if not forgiveness. I wished I could explain all our trials and tribulations.

I love you for who you are not for your name.

I had told Kikuchan a great deal about Frau Beck. She was amazed when I showed her the bracelet she had given me. Kikuchan asked if I would read Frau Beck's letter aloud.

"But Frau Beck writes in German," I said.

"It doesn't matter. I'll listen to the words," she replied haltingly, her English still very much in need of improvement.

I told her, "I'll read it and you are more than welcome to listen to my native language."

It's been a long time since we were together. You may be interested to know that I gave birth to a precious little girl only five weeks ago. When we were in China I suspected that I was pregnant but I didn't wish to disclose that to anyone at the time, not even to my husband, for fear that the voicing of it would somehow affect me badly. I'm happy to say that I've been fortunate. Like you, my daughter is a treasured pearl.

I started crying. I remembered Frau Beck's guilt. How she felt she had been punished with barrenness for escaping the fate of drowning. I said to Kikuchan, "If anyone deserves good fortune, it's Frau Beck."

She went on. *Our vacation has been prolonged due to my condition and by some business concerns my husband and my father have needed to address but now we're about to return to Berlin. Before we do, I must go to the Records Hall to change the name of my daughter from Erna to Ingelore.*

I nearly fainted with happiness.

Please continue to write and to think of me often. Give your parents my warm regards.

She closed her letter with, *All my love and devotion, your friend, Li.* 梅

Nature's Violent Display

February 1937–April 1938

Kikuchan taught me the basics of Japanese flower arranging. It became a favourite hobby of mine. I have always been enamoured of plants and flowers, especially orchids.

The first hour of every Sunday afternoon was set aside for my drilling her in English, while the second hour was for my instruction in flower arranging.

Mutsch would purchase several different kinds of flowers and I would look for branches and twigs in the backyard and colourful pebbles and small rocks to use as accents.

I knew all about flowers and how to display them so I did not think that my first lesson in Japanese arrangements would be that difficult.

Kikuchan asked where my *tokonoma* would be. After she explained that a *tokonoma* represents the heart of the home I decided that I would designate a small area in a foyer just inside our front door as our *tokonoma*.

She wondered, "What are you going to put it in?"

"I'll use a vase," I said. She didn't know that word. "Watch me," I said all-knowingly.

Doris with Ingelore's first *ikebana* flower arrangement, 1937.

I selected a few stalks of gladiolus and irises and placed them in the vase, centering it on the table in the foyer. Mutsch came with a camera to take a photograph of my first attempt.

"I'll stand beside it," she said posing at the table.

I took the photograph.

"Well?" I asked Kikuchan, pointing to my display.

She bowed and then said, "It's not good. It's not art. It's very bad."

It was not until my third or fourth lesson that I grasped the complexity of Japanese flower arrangement. I learned that *ikebana* symbolizes the sky, man, and Earth and that they are expressed by three distinct heights.[27] The quintessence of any arrangement is simplicity, elegance, and creativity. Arrangements are situated in the *tokonoma*, which was originally the honoured place for Buddhist scrolls. The room with the *tokonoma* is the heart of the home, an area used to present precious art work, and as a symbol of respect for one's guests and their artistic pleasure.

Every well-educated Japanese girl like Kikuchan is trained in the art of flower arranging. The selection of flowers depended not only on the type of arrangement but also on the season. In the spring, branches of plum, cherry and pear trees were used. And while quince blossoms represent the sky, bright orange birds of paradise, daffodils, and azaleas represent man and pure white Shasta daisies, cyclamen, or tiny dianthus represent the Earth. A good arrangement is simple, clean and pleasing to the eye.

"Cut the branch like so," Kikuchan demonstrated. She made sure I could see the diagonal cut. Then she picked a particularly lovely flower, "Cut the flower straight. Never cut it like you would a branch! That is wrong, very wrong!"

After several weeks Kikuchan and I congratulated each other. My flower arranging abilities were satisfactory and her English had progressed as well.

---

27 *Ikebana* means "bring life to flowers." After fresh flowers are cut from the soil (the death of the flowers), they are given new life when they are arranged in a container or vessel. *Ikebana* is also called kado, which means "the way of mastering flower arrangement" in Japanese (Kubo, *Keiko's Ikebana: A Contemporary Approach to the Traditional Japanese Art of Flower Arranging*, 1).

"You're a wonderful teacher," I said.

She smiled, bowed and then without any hint of modesty said, "I am a good teacher for you!"

I still have my nightmare every so often. It is as frightening in Japan as it was the first time I dreamed it in Berlin. The only good that comes of it is that after I awake, catch my breath, and realize that I am safe, I can revisit its setting in my mind. How I would like to be back in our home in Wilmersdorf and, more importantly, spend hours with Gerta in the library.

On a Sunday morning that spring I woke to a soft breeze coming through my bedroom window. Birds chirped while tree branches scraped against the wall of our villa. But the serenity soon was disturbed when I heard Mutsch and Paps bantering back and forth in the kitchen.

It was very unusual for my parents to discuss something in loud voices. Although I have never heard them shout in anger, I do remember that on this particular occasion the discussion, while not heated, was considerably warmer than the level of tones I was accustomed to hearing.

"And this photograph from the office party?" Mutsch asked slowly and deliberately.

Paps answered, "Arthur was a little tipsy when he asked that we all group together. The parties provide food and drink and he had had his fill by then. These are the people I work with, darling. That is all."

Mutsch replied sarcastically, "I see that the party is not *at* the office and I see many of the people you work with wear makeup and kimonos."

Father exhaled in exasperation. "You know they are *geishas*. It's the custom in Japan. They are waitresses. When the photograph arrived in yesterday's mail I showed it to you right away, didn't I?"

"So Arthur felt it would be something for your eyes only? Is that why he sent it by mail rather than hand it to you? Was he afraid to do so in my presence?"

Paps' voice went up a notch. "He's on business in Europe. He must've sent it just before he left. There are no secrets here, darling, from you or from anyone else."

"Look at them!" Mutsch's voice was raised now, too. "They're so elegantly attired, their hair layered on their heads, their faces powdered. And I see they're the only women there! Where was I? Where was Arthur's wife? Where was George's wife? Where was—"

Paps must have been seated because just then I heard a chair scrape across the floor, presumably pushed back so he could stand. Interrupting her, he said, "—you will listen to me now. Every so often Herr Griesbach sponsors a get-together to build morale, afford time away from customers and business, and to provide an occasion for his subordinates to relax and enjoy food and conversation. That's all."

"Those women are nothing more than courtesans, Kurt, and you will not tell me otherwise."

He slammed his hand on the table. "No they're not! They're waitresses!"

I sneezed.

"Lorechen?" Mutsch asked.

I was discovered. Walking into the kitchen, I saw Paps, his face crimson. Mutsch's was similarly coloured, perhaps even more so.

I decided it was best to own up. "I heard you and Paps arguing," I told Mutsch, forcing a yawn.

Paps reached for me. I went to him and embraced him. "It's not an argument. Your mother and I are just discussing some things."

"Because of the photograph?" I asked.

Instantly I realized that I had let the proverbial cat out of the bag.

"How long have you been listening to us, young lady?" Mutsch demanded.

I went to Mutsch and embraced her. "I'm sorry but I find it upsetting when you and father are having a disagreement."

"Well, the proof is in the pudding," Mutsch said handing me the photograph. "What do you make of this, Lorechen?"

I looked at it. A group of shoeless gentlemen were seated on tatami mats in the background of the photo. Masks belonging to *kabuki* dancers hung on the walls of the restaurant

"It looks like a very nice restaurant," I said innocently.

"And what else?" Mutsch yelped.

Bowls of soup and platters laden with fish, meat, and vegetables, ceramic containers overflowing with rice, and porcelain cups filled with *sake* were everywhere. I tried to be as nonchalant as possible. "The cooks must have worked hard to prepare all that food."

With that my parents looked at each other and then simultaneously burst into laughter.

"Our precious daughter won't take sides!" Paps said.

Father explained again what I had already heard him try to explain to Mutsch. Then he said, "There's music, too. Some of the *geishas* sing while others strum an instrument called the *samisen*, something akin to a lute or a ukulele."

"So it's business, in a way," I said trying to bring the discussion to an end, hoping to placate Mutsch and release my father from the hook from which he was dangling.

"It's very strange," he said, "sitting on the floor while eating and being so graciously entertained." He quickly realized Mutsch might incorrectly interpret what he meant by "being entertained." I know I did. "What I mean to say," he offered, pointing to the photograph, "is that it's the custom not to stretch out one's legs. None of us Westerners manage to remain that way for long. We're always excusing ourselves to walk about to have the blood return to our lower extremities!"

Mutsch, with finality, said, "You must remind Mr. deCouto to leave his camera at home the next time Herr Griesbach summons everyone for a . . ." she hesitated, ". . . the next time he summons everyone for a business dinner."

Her sarcasm was muted though direct. I am sure Paps gathered her meaning.

Because Kikuchan was helping me learn Japanese, Mutsch reasoned that it was essential to keep employing her. She also was an excellent housekeeper. Obachan was indispensable because she prepared meals from ingredients that were relatively inexpensive and easy to procure and because she was older and more experienced Mutsch could rely on her to keep an eye on Kikuchan and me.

"We're helping them," my father explained to Mutsch. "The amount of money we spend on their salaries is small to us but large to them. Think of it as economic assistance. Either way, we won't be in Japan forever."

And Paps explained that our stay in Japan would depend on two things.

"It may be that when the business expands to the level Herr Griesbach demands we may need to consider relocating to America. There's a large company office in New York City."

"And the other?" Mutsch asked.

Paps drew in his breath, squeezing his temples between his fingers to try to ease the pain of another nagging headache. "Our company has seen a staggering increase in orders from the Japanese government for certain goods. Requisitions for some items have numbered in the tens of thousands. I'm certain the upswing is for the military. The Japanese are intent on overrunning China."[28]

"Do you mean . . ." Mutsch offered.

"Yes, Japan has dreams of the conquest of Asia. Also it may mean that they are stockpiling goods, gearing up for a defence of their islands from the fascists and communists. No one knows how far Hitler and Stalin and even Mussolini will go to . . ."

He did not finish his sentence. His words hung in the air, unfinished.

Mutsch changed the subject. "Well, luckily all of Lorechen's assessment reports from the Canadian School have been excellent. Perhaps you should begin to consider going to college in America."

"Yes, mother," I said.

Two weeks passed with no news about the future of our family in Japan.

One night at supper Paps announced, "Does anyone here know how to ski?" Mutsch and I laughed. "Next month we're going to the Japanese Alps for a short vacation and we'll learn to ski."

"Oh, I can't wait!" I said eagerly.

---

28 On 7 July 1937, Japanese troops engaged in a skirmish with Chinese soldiers in the vicinity of the Marco Polo Bridge just south of Beijing. Within a month, a full-scale war was underway (Gordon, *A Modern History of Japan: From Tokugawa Times to the Present*, 204).

"But," he said, "before we do that we need to do something else."

Mutsch tried to conceal a smile.

They were hiding something. "What's going on?" I asked.

"We're moving!" Paps exclaimed.

Over the next few days we packed and organized our things. For several afternoons Mutsch and I did some rigorous shopping looking for appropriate clothing for our ski trip.

As we readied ourselves to go the recurring cloud of regret settled upon us—it was difficult to say farewell to Mr. and Mrs. Dimitriev and our other neighbours and friends.

Fortunately, our goodbyes didn't need to extend to Kikuchan and Obachan since Paps had arranged for them to come to our new home with us.

Not only was our vacation in the Japanese Alps a welcomed change of routine but it was also an amazing adventure filled with exhilaration and discovery.

The mountains were deliciously imposing, their grand peaks covered in snow, the clouds about them singularly white and majestic, the underlying rock peeking through in pinto fashion where some of the snow had melted. The radiant sunshine was so intense it nearly burned my fair skin. The air was bitingly crisp and crystal clear, so very chilling yet refreshing. I believe we were near Matsumoto, an outpost surrounded by imposing summits.

The lodge was enormous, its masonry base made up of assorted rocks and boulders solidly supported the wooden upper stories of the building. The views from its many balconies were breathtaking.

After being outfitted with boots, skis, and poles the three of us ventured out into the snow. It was crunchy, a very thin layer of ice having formed on top of the powder from intermittent freezing and thawing. We struggled sideways, plopping our skis one by one and impaling our poles into the ground for support. We were attempting to get further away from the wooden terrace while trying to keep out of everyone's way. Many people were gliding past us as if we were standing still which for the most part is what we were doing. When we had flailed past the limits

The lodge near Matsumoto and the postcard from their travels that featured the view from the balcony.

of the terrace I turned to see Paps suddenly crouch, pierce the snow with his poles, push off, and then effortlessly glide down the decline away from us. Mutsch and I were flabbergasted.

"I didn't know you could ski!" I shouted after him.

Mutsch yelled, too. "I didn't either!" Then with an admiring glance, "That man never ceases to surprise me."

Me, too, I thought.

"Well?" Mutsch asked me, "Are we going to stand here all day . . ." Before she finished her sentence, she was off. A few seconds later, she was down. In between bursts of laughter I heard her shout, "Your turn, Lorechen!"

Skiing is an exercise in balance and equilibrium, neither of which came easily to me. I tried several times, warily progressing a metre here and a metre there only to have my body leaning, dipping, faltering, and then collapsing under the unforgiving force of gravity. Before long my mittens and leggings were soaked through as was the seat of my trousers. And although my back ached, all was well when we partook of the soothing warmth of the hot springs. It was the first time I was outside immersed in water when there was snow on the ground.

I reflect now both on those days and on that particular experience to discover that each underscores the broad scope of the Japanese lifestyle. Japan is a country so rich in culture and history that neither artist nor poet can adequately describe it. The landscapes are beautiful and its people kind. Yet at times we had difficulty because Asian and Western customs were often at odds with one another. In spite of these challenges, I'm proud to say that for more than a decade I was a Japanese citizen.

In the spring of 1938, the rainy season started and ended with a clap of thunder. At its onset the downpours were so unrelenting I believed there would be no end to the rain. For six weeks, two weeks longer than meteorologists had expected, angry clouds dumped torrents of water on the already saturated earth. The air was hot and humid. Thunderstorms were continuous. Each day seemed hotter and more oppressive than the day before.

Kurt and Doris preparing to ski (top left and right). Doris encountering difficulty (bottom left). Ingelore on the slopes (bottom right).

Indoors, everything smelled musty and dank. Nothing ever dried completely. Books and shoes would mildew before one's eyes. Furniture was damp and sticky. The sun never came out even when there were a few short breaks in the cloud cover. Everyone was irritable.

On clear days the view from our hilltop home was beautiful. Kobe, surrounded by gently sloping hills, is situated around a natural harbour formed by the Inland Sea. When the weather allowed, we would stare into the distance at the shimmering white cherry blossoms and pink azaleas thriving everywhere. Our first summer in Japan, I was astounded by the profusion of orchids of all sizes and shades, from delicate cream to dark mauve, competing for space among the small wild roses that grew in abundance throughout the tended gardens.

But in the spring of 1938, the view was shrouded in grey—drab and dreary. The azaleas in front of our home slouched, drowning in puddles of water. The tops of the low-growing junipers were barely visible above the pools that engulfed them. The white river stones that had been raked around the base of the plants had already washed down the hillside.

More and more of the soft soil was eroding, carving ruts into the hills behind our home. The roots of trees and bushes were exposed where the unremitting rain had washed away the earth.

Mutsch and I, together with Kikuchan and Obachan, were standing at the kitchen watching the muddy waters stream down the hill.

"I wish it would stop raining," I complained.

A few moments later we sensed that something was about to happen. Outside on the balcony, Mutsch pointed down. "See the stones? See how they're swept down the hill? Do you hear them banging against the retaining wall?"

Then, I saw a much larger rock loosen and I watched in disbelief as it surged its way down the hillside. The force of impact cracked the retaining wall. Mutsch had seen it, too. She grabbed the three of us and led us to the front of the house. We heard snapping noises, then a rushing of water. Part of the retaining wall had given way.

"Everyone! Everyone out of the house! Now! Now!" Mutsch screamed. Kikuchan screeched and bellowed, "*Dete ike*! Get out!"

Ingelore's second home in Kobe with the prominent retaining wall.

We fled outside into the rain. A second later, an uprooted pine tree went crashing through my bedroom window. Part of its trunk and several large branches rested halfway through the sliding doors that led from there into the living room.

We huddled near the corner of the house that, for the moment, seemed safe. Everywhere there were masses of mud, stones, and broken tree trunks. Then we felt a gentle rumbling beneath our feet. To our horror a mass of earth broke free and slid away, rushing downhill toward the houses below. The staccato of the banging and cracking of rocks and trees echoing below was deafening. And there was that odour, the acrid, pungent smell of rotting vegetation and decomposition.

"We must go down the hill!" Mutsch yelled.

Holding on to one another, trembling with fear, we stumbled along, sometimes stepping, other times sliding uncontrollably while desperately trying to maintain our balance. Below we saw neighbours cowering against fallen trees. Everyone was stunned, frightened, and rushing toward hardened ground.

At the bottom of the hill, heads were counted. Our neighbours, their children, and our servants all were accounted for.

A man came running down the hill, yelling in Japanese. I understood most of the words but could not make out the meaning. One of our neighbours, a man from America, interpreted for us. "He says the mud slide is rushing toward the harbour and business district."

"Where's father?" I asked Mutsch. "When's he coming home?" I started crying. Then some of the children with us began crying, too. Mutsch tried to comfort everyone but it was obvious that she was preoccupied with concern for Paps' safety.

We were in trouble. The road that descended the hill was blocked by mud and debris so there was no way for us to get down. But we did not know whether our house would hold onto its footings or collapse and then slide down on top of us. Mud oozed and slunk its way down the hill. Our small outcrop of safety was shrinking. We were soaked, our clothes caked with mud, and our shoes stuck in the gluey quicksand of the pasty soil.

In an instant a light shone brightly. "Look!" I yelled, "The sun is out!" Then there was a loud clap of thunder. In the chaos, we hadn't noticed that the rain had stopped. We cheered as the sun broke through the clouds. Above us the mud had stopped moving. It appeared as if the long storm had passed.

We stayed where we were until Paps came home. Despite the terrible confusion he had managed to find us. He had waded through water and mud above his knees. We hugged.

Most roads were impassable, blocked by sludge, uprooted trees, automobiles that had been swept along, and even sections of houses. Thankfully, neither our home nor the houses nearby had been carried away. The water in the harbour, usually crystal clear, was an ugly, dirty yellow and full of debris. Much of the city was covered in mire. Bodies of animals and even some humans were seen floating by. The stench was so strong we could almost taste it.

But we were safe and together again. "Were you frightened?" Paps asked.

"Yes, we were terrified. Especially when the tree went through the house," I whispered.

With stoic resignation in his voice, he said, "That's how nature can be. Usually it's beautiful. At other times it can be very destructive. Nature is just like people. Most often they are good but other times they are evil."

I understood. Before that day, I had never thought of the peculiar parallel between nature and human nature. Not until the earth turned to soup did I see the connection.

The mudslides had stopped. After a cursory inspection of our home by emergency workers a short time later, it was decided that we could return to our home if we avoided my bedroom and the kitchen. Paps was encouraged to procure restoration estimates as soon as possible. He said he would do so in the morning.

"I'll arrange for repairs," he told Mutsch, "and while I'm doing so, you and Lorechen will go to Kamakura, if the trains are running."

"Why?" Mutsch wondered.

"I want both of you out of Kobe and away from any danger. There could be an outbreak of disease. I promise I'll join you there as soon as our home is rebuilt, cleaned, and refurbished."

The following morning on our way to the railroad station, Mutsch and I saw the devastation caused by the mudslides. The ruts of drying and dried mud were everywhere. The swath of disaster had mercilessly drowned the once-pristine city of Kobe. It was tragic to see many small fragile wooden houses, some of which had been pulled off their foundations, crumpled as if they had been crushed by a giant's footsteps. Beautifully tended gardens had been turned to swamp. Rocks and fallen trees blocked many of the roads. Here and there people were beginning to dig through the slimy mess for their belongings. The smell was overpowering.

After a long train ride, Mutsch and I arrived in Kamakura, still stunned by the horror of the past twenty-four hours. We had lived through the worst mudslides and flooding that Kobe had experienced in many years. Kamakura felt like a world away.

We checked in to the hotel. The lobby was magnificently appointed with gleaming tiles, polished hardwoods and brass, colourful *ikebana* displays and varied assortments of flowers. Our room was similarly tastefully decorated.

Ingelore on one of the Hotel Kawana's balconies.

The day after we arrived, Mutsch and I walked among the lush greenery at the limits of the golf course abutting the hotel, enjoying the spectacular views. Not too far in the distance we saw gentle waves striking against the craggy rocks along the shoreline of the Inland Sea. Sunshine danced on the water. Feather-like clouds floated by. All was peaceful.

On the third day, during breakfast, a Japanese police officer came in. He clapped his hands to get everyone's attention. First in English, then in French, and then in Japanese he told everyone to be cautious because of an approaching typhoon!

Were storms pursuing us?

We finished our meal and then went outside. The wind had picked up. All at once the sky turned black and the rain started.

"Not again!" I moaned. "We won't be able to take our golf lesson!"

The rain increased in intensity. Mutsch and I, along with several other guests, ran into the lobby and through the French doors into the enormous ballroom. The cathedral ceiling was three stories high. Shimmering crystal chandeliers were suspended from honey-stained wooden beams. Against one of the walls, opposite the doors, stood an immense fruitwood bar with hundreds of liquor bottles displayed on mirrored shelving, rows of glasses on each end.

We could see sheets of rain were blowing against the glass and metal frames of the French doors. Over the sound of the torrents we heard waves crashing against the rocks along the shoreline only thirty metres away. The wind howled and hissed, tossing lawn chairs and tables about.

A group of convalescing Japanese army officers in snow-white hospital kimonos huddled in one corner of the room. Mutsch and I had met some of them the day before. In very broken English they said they had been wounded in the war and were on a few days' leave from a nearby military hospital.[29]

Off by themselves, in a small recessed area, a young European couple on their honeymoon who only had eyes for each other were oblivious to what was going on outside. By the bar, a group of middle-aged Japanese men still in their golf garb guzzled their drinks and waited impatiently to resume their game. Other guests were gathered in small groups about the ballroom. Many of them were whispering in English.

We stood near the doors, entranced by nature's violent display.

A slender young man in a hotel uniform approached. "It would be better to stand away from the windows," he cautioned in English. "One never knows what—"

29 The second Sino-Japanese War occurred between 1937 and 1945.

He never finished his sentence. We heard a horrifying sucking noise followed by a deafening crash. The French doors had been blown into the ballroom! Shards of broken glass danced in the air. The heavy metal doorframes, bent and twisted, the doors hanging from their broken hinges were banging back and forth. High above our heads the chandeliers swayed menacingly. People screamed. Some ran toward the back of the ballroom trying to get out into the hallway. The manager and a young assistant stopped them.

"Please! Stay calm," he pleaded in perfect English. As he spoke his assistant translated into Japanese. "At the moment this room, especially the back area, is the safest place in the hotel." He held up his hands. "Please do not return to your rooms. The windows to the balconies could shatter. We are doing everything in our power to keep you as safe as possible."

Several hotel employees came running. The manager shouted orders "Board up those doors at once!"

My heart was pounding. "Mutsch," I panted, "this is no better than being in Kobe. I'm just as scared as I was a few days ago." I felt a spray of water hit my face. The wind picked papers and napkins and blew them about the room.

She was calm. "This is not the same, dear. You heard the manager. We'll be fine," she said reassuringly.

The typhoon continued to scream and whistle. In our alcove, a small window above our heads had been spared. Through it we could see the sky had taken on a strange yellow-green tint. Workmen barricaded the French doors with heavy wooden planks and while we watched them struggle against the wind the lights went out, plunging us into near-total darkness! Several women screamed. Not a minute later, more employees arrived with oil lanterns. The glow of the lanterns reflected off the mirrors and glass to provide adequate light.

Suddenly I heard Mutsch gasp! I turned to her and saw a rolling, moving carpet of black! Terrified rats, pursued by large cats, raced about, over shelves, around the bar, and in between chairs and tables. Round and round they went, the rats screeching eerily, the cats darting after them. We heard more glasses and bottles crash to the floor. Some guests became hysterical: screaming, flailing their arms, and running in circles. The rats ran in wider circles. Flushed out by the typhoon they raced through the ballroom looking for an escape. Employees and bartenders wielding bottles and kitchen utensils chased after them. At once the cats and rats engaged, tearing at each other, biting and scratching. Fur was flying!

Eventually, the cats and the employees won the battle! I had been clinging to Mutsch, too afraid to watch, but now I released my grip and cautiously peeked around. The cats paraded triumphantly out of the ballroom through the back doors, their broken tails held high.

The noise of the wind and rain slowly subsided. The manager proclaimed, "All clear! All clear!" His employees seemed unfazed. They continued with their efforts to clean up.

"What could possibly happen next?" I asked Mutsch. She smiled. "Well, Lorechen, I think we've had enough excitement for a while. Let's hope that's the end of it."

We were permitted to return to our room which miraculously had not been damaged. Exhausted by the day's events, we soon fell asleep.

In the middle of the night we awoke to a loud knock at our door. Mutsch answered. A hotel employee told us that once again we were in the storm's path and that we must leave our room immediately. Mutsch and I hastened out into the hallway, where we were told to sit on the carpet with our backs against the wall. We could hear the typhoon race over us. We sat there for almost two hours. Finally, the storm had spent its fury. Mutsch and I returned to our room and collapsed on our beds.

In the morning, the air was crisp and cool. The sky was a wondrous shade of azure. The Inland Sea was calm. By the afternoon, gardeners had cleared away the debris.

Oddly, the turf was dry enough for our golf lesson!

Two weeks later Paps arrived. I recounted to him much of what Mutsch and I had experienced especially the details of the awful cat and rat chase.

"It's hard to believe how violent nature has been these past several weeks," Paps said. Then, pointing to a copse of pines he added, "Those

Kurt and Ingelore standing at the shoreline of the Inland Sea (above). Kurt, Doris, and Ingelore posing with the group of convalescing Japanese soldiers.

old trees over there have withstood many storms and the constant pounding of the surf. They survive because the sun shines on them." He looked toward the sky shielding his eyes with his hand. "The storms bring the rain without which nothing can survive." Turning his gaze on me, "As for the rats? Well, I don't care for them either, Lorechen. But they have a purpose, too. They provide food for larger animals. It's nature's way."

Then he became glum. "Lorechen, during the cleaning and rebuilding of our home, the workers found your diary and your drawing pad. I'm sorry to say they were ruined. I placed them in the sun for an entire day but the ink and coloured pencil had run together. I'm so sorry."

I was despondent. All my writings, all my drawings were gone.

Mutsch ached for me. "Please, Lorechen, try not to be sad. You still have your memories. I am certain that you'll return again one day to the recording of your adventures."

"Yes, mother," I said half-heartedly. "I'll try."

Paps kissed my forehead. "Very good, my angel. And now I need to tell you both that there have been developments in Europe."

Mutsch and I were silent.

"There will be war. Six months ago Hitler and Mussolini met. The Italian leader was celebrated and nearly dragged across Germany to be shown the strength and might of the Nazi regime. He was trying to impress Mussolini and to show that they wanted the same thing, that they had the same goals. There will be war."

Mutsch was visibly shaken. "What of our relatives? What of our friends still in Germany?"

"I do not know," Paps said. Then haltingly, "A month ago, Austria fell."

Mutsch couldn't catch her breath. "What's next? Poland?"

Paps reached for her hand. "I'm not sure. Perhaps within a matter of weeks it will be Czechoslovakia."

"Are we safe here?" I asked.

His brow was furrowed. "Yes, Lorechen, we are. The turmoil is half a world away." Then he mused, "Try to remember what nature recently taught us. There is a balance to everything. In its agony, some of the world will surrender but much of it, in its strength, will become more resolute in the face of evil. Though we've endured many trials, I fear you, too, may have some troubling moments in your life that are yet to come. Like a typhoon, I hope they'll be brief." As was his habit, he kissed my forehead. "Always look up, my angel, and try to capture the sun!"

The War is Coming

Autumn was a wonderful time of the year. The hills pulsed with red and bronze maples and chrysanthemums. The daytime temperatures were pleasant and at night a slight chill required us to don our sweaters.

My instruction in English and Japanese was going very well and the reports from my teachers at the Canadian Academy continued to note my sterling progress. At home, Paps, Mutsch, and I conversed solely in English. Kikuchan augmented my education with lessons of both the *katakana* and *hiragana* systems of syllabic writing. Even though I was fourteen, Kikuchan decided to use the same teaching method applied to Japanese first graders! Soon I was able to read signs in store windows, bits and pieces of newspaper articles, and most of the time I understood basic sentences when spoken slowly. Sadly, I have forgotten most of what I learned.

Mutsch and I had begun to do a great deal of gardening along the gentle slope that stretched from our home down toward the retaining wall. We both perspired profusely as we worked and our hands were caked with dirt. Once back inside, we would take turns freshening up.

On one particular day after we came inside and changed our clothes, Mutsch was slumping and rubbing the small of her back. "I'm so sore," she complained.

Kikuchan put down the laundry she was sorting and said, "I can help you."

"What do you mean?" Mutsch asked her.

Without hesitation Kikuchan led us to the living room and stood in front of the convertible sofa, one of the items Paps had managed to save after the mudslide many months ago. Kikuchan pulled out the concealed mattress and said, "Lay down."

Mutsch was dubious. But with Kikuchan's insistence, and not-so-subtle hand gestures, Mutsch reclined face down on the mattress. Kikuchan then straddled her and began massaging Mutsch's shoulders. A chorus of *oohs* and *aahs* filled the air as Kikuchan's fingertips glided across Mutsch's back, her palms pressed, her knuckles kneaded and her thumbs found their way into every aching and knotted muscle on Mutsch's back.

Both Mutsch and Kikuchan seemed to be entranced by the massage—Kikuchan hummed while Mutsch moaned, their eyes closed.

After twenty minutes Kikuchan said to me, "Your turn."

I lay down next to Mutsch. Kikuchan knelt astride me and started massaging me. It was heaven! Her hands located and quickly relieved whatever tensions I had. Mutsch sat up. "Isn't that wonderful, Lorechen?" she asked. I was too much in a daze to answer. I was so relaxed.

September 3, 1939 is forever branded into my memory. That Sunday morning the sun shone brilliantly in a cloudless sky and a gentle breeze blew. Obachan and I were returning from an outing. I often accompanied Obachan when she went shopping for fruits and vegetables. Sometimes she would take me to farm stands and I would watch her barter for chestnuts, pears, persimmon, and kumquats. But most often we would stop by private homes where she knew the cooks. The cooks would trade vegetables and herbs they had grown on the grounds of their employer's homes for Obachan's needlework and sewing. Our arms were laden with bags of radish, cucumber, mung beans, bamboo shoots, onions and cabbage as we walked up the hill to my home. We had been gone for most of the morning and it was well past lunchtime.

Several steps from the front door I happened to look up. I saw the curtains drawn in my parents' bedroom. That's odd, I thought. Perhaps Kikuchan was cleaning and she wanted to stop the bright sun from getting in her eyes or heating up the room.

In the kitchen, Obachan and I unpacked and put the foodstuffs away. Mutsch entered, looking haggard.

"How did you fare?" she wondered.

Ignoring her, I asked, "Mother, what's wrong?"

She plopped down at the kitchen table.

"Mother?" I repeated.

"Your father has a terrible headache. He's in bed resting. I put an ice-pack on his forehead. He needs darkness and quiet."

I cringed with worry.

"Your father insisted on going to the office this morning even though he could barely stand up, something about a meeting with prospective buyers. I urged him to stay in bed but he wouldn't listen. He told me he'd be fine and I wasn't to worry." She leaned back in the chair. "So, do you know what I did?" she asked.

"Tell me," I said.

"After an hour or so, I went to his office."

I can only recall a few other times when Mutsch has behaved so brazenly or countered what Paps had said or done.

"I strolled in," she said proudly, "and the men who were busily working at the tables looked up. Your father's chin dropped into his lap. After a brief welcome, he ushered me into an office sputtering incoherently. His face was agog. He was incredulous."

"What did you say to him?" I asked.

"I told him I'd spoken to Uncle Hans and he was kind enough to arrange for your father and me to see his personal physician immediately."

"On Sunday?" I was amazed.

"Yes, Lorechen," she exhaled. "Hans and the doctor are golfing partners. They had already finished their game by the time I contacted him. Hans told me that the doctor would be more than happy to interview and examine your father." She went on. "Your father was reluctant to leave his office. But I convinced him."

"What did you say?"

"I said, 'Kurt, you will regret bearing witness to the scene I'm about to create right here and right now in front of your friends and associates if you refuse to go.'"

Kurt? I wondered what had happened to *darling*, *dear*, and *honey*? She must have been very angry to use his given name.

"And?" I asked hesitantly.

"He tidied his desk, made his apologies to his colleagues, and then we left."

Mutsch told me that the doctor they had seen was a general practitioner possessing subsidiary specializations in osteopathy and acupuncture. After a long examination, some skeletal manipulations, and an agonizing session with hundreds of needles being pressed into a dozen areas of Paps' head and neck, Paps was cleared to return home. The doctor prescribed rest and relaxation and gave him medicines—some of which were pharmacological while others were herbal mixtures to be used in teas and soups.

"He's resting now," she said dejectedly. "All that and then there was the news of . . ." She caught herself.

"What news, mother?"

"Hitler invaded Poland a few days ago. I am so worried for my sister and Stella."

Every one of our letters to family sent from Japan had gone unanswered. We had had no word from any of Paps' and Mutsch's families. We did not know where they were or if they were safe.

Two days later I received three letters, one from my cousin Ullie, one from my childhood friend Inga, and another from Frau Beck.

Frau Beck's news was tragic. Her daughter Ingelore, my namesake, had died from complications of pneumonia. She was not yet three years old.

Clutching the bracelet Frau Beck had given me, I cried into the night.

Six months later I met Paul Sernau, the handsomest man I had ever seen. He had dark skin, thick, prematurely graying hair, and piercing black eyes.

"How do you do, Ingelore?" He bowed deeply as he shook my hand.

How elegant, I thought. I hoped he would kiss my hand as he had my mother's a few moments before. His wife stood next to him. She was also attractive. With her wavy auburn hair, smooth white skin, and gleaming teeth she resembled a famous film actress, Garbo or Dietrich.

We were at Lake Biwa, a beautifully serene body of water not far from Kyoto. Paps and his colleagues, with Herr Griesbach's blessing, had organized an out-of-the-office party to celebrate a recent sales accomplishment. Paps invited Kikuchan and with the rest of the staff from the office, their families and their domestics, our group numbered about three dozen. I remember that day because Mutsch, Paps, and I had hiked through the dense woods, walking among the white and red azaleas and wild purple orchids. The lake shimmered in the sunshine.

For lunch, we were given a pristine white box that contained fresh vegetables and rice wrapped in seaweed, delectable pieces of sweet and sour fish, and a luscious pastry. It was so artfully arranged that each box resembled a beautiful painting.

In the afternoon, just after our picnic-style lunch, several of the men played baseball while others dressed up in their wives' kimonos, powdering their faces white in the tradition of geishas and securing to their heads elaborate wigs decorated with silver ornaments. A few maids provided music on samisens.

Whenever my mother remembered that outing, she would laugh and smile. But I recall that she had refused to go unless father assured her no geishas would attend as she could not bear their presence.

I remember the crack of a bat and a ball soaring into the sky. I saw Paps running in from the outfield screaming, "I can get it! I can get it!" He raised his glove only to see the ball fly over his head toward the limits of a fence near where he was originally positioned.

Later, Paps would field a ball to throw a runner out at home base. He threw the ball so hard that it went way over the metal cage behind home base and the runner scored. Paps took off his glove, threw it on the ground and kicked it.

"It looks like your father is having a tough day!" Mutsch said.

I have vivid memories of Kobe in the fall. The hills surrounding the city were animated with the swaying movements of deciduous trees, their leaves blazing red and orange in the wind, as alive as fire. The Japanese maples are especially brilliant. The darkness of the muted yet radiant pine trees contrasted with the bright vibrant colours everywhere.

One night Paps arrived home from work looking particularly fatigued. For several weeks he had been at the office for what seemed like twenty hours a day, even on Sundays. "Business has been nonstop," he said, "the Japanese military is our most demanding customer and we're having trouble filling all of their orders."

At supper, Mutsch persisted in diverting us away from conversations about business. We talked about the gardens, Obachan's facility in acquiring fruits and vegetables, Kikuchan's interest in learning more English, and other such trivialities. Paps was aware of her efforts. "Still, we must monitor more closely what's happening in the world," he insisted. "Look and listen for any news that may affect us."

Mutsch and I gathered news from a variety of sources. Kikuchan would read the Japanese newspapers and then translate them into English as best she could. She didn't know what news I might be interested in so as part of her lessons I would tell her which key words to look for. Sometimes I would draw pictures to help her understand. My list and scribbles included Hitler, Stalin, Mussolini, America, China, and war. Herr Schnee, our next-door neighbour, an elderly widower born in Austria but who had lived in Japan all of his adult life was also a good source of information. Often Aunt Eva and Mutsch would share information over coffee or tea.

At the office, Uncle Hans and Arthur deCouto discussed the news with Paps. Father kept his ears open while listening to conversations among his colleagues and to the short wave operators broadcasting from a radio situated near his desk. I can clearly picture his eyeballs moving from side to side as he listened.

Between the three of us, we knew, more or less, what was going on in Japan, Asia, and Europe.

The news was not good.

By this time, Hitler's armies already had invaded Denmark, Norway, Belgium, Luxembourg, and Romania. France had fallen. Britain was under siege. London was being bombed. The Soviet armies had rolled into Finland, the Baltic States, Lithuania, Latvia, and Estonia. Italy had crushed Egypt and Greece. The continent was in an avalanche of conquest.

Whenever we would talk about the goings-on, Kikuchan would sit quietly on a tatami mat in the corner of our living room busying herself with embroidery or practicing her English lettering.

"The war on the Asian mainland is raging. China is trying to defend itself. The Japanese won't relent until their interests in Manchuria are satisfied. Korea is in shambles," Paps said.

Mutsch wondered, "Will the Japanese Minister and the Emperor continue with this senselessness?"

Kikuchan dropped her needle.

"I don't know," Paps said. "But it seems the Japanese didn't anticipate how much resistance the Chinese would offer. What a nuisance it is that they resist oppression. It doesn't appear that the American embargo has had much effect on the aggressive Japanese."[30]

Kikuchan stood up and left the room, a sneer on her face.

I excused myself and went to find her. In the kitchen, she was leaning against the counter, her arms folded tightly across her chest with her head bowed, staring intently at the floor.

"What's wrong?" I asked her.

She slowly raised her head. "You and your family are against us and you are against my Emperor. You are silly to favour the Chinese."

It was then that I realized Kikuchan's English wasn't so broken after all.

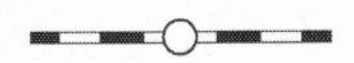

30 In July 1939, Roosevelt broke off the Japanese-American commercial treaty to deter Japanese expansion. Later, when Japan moved into Indochina, the Americans countered with an expanded export embargo (Gordon, *A Modern History of Japan*, 208).

Nearly a year later, I arrived home from school one day and was surprised to hear Paps' voice in the kitchen. I immediately assumed that he was sick again. His crushing headaches had returned and I worried that his disregard of the doctor's advice to slow down and make concerted efforts to control and lessen the stress he was under at work finally had come home to roost. He looked awful.

"Paps," I shrieked, running toward him. "Are you all right? What's wrong? Why are you home?" Mutsch threw her arms around me just as I was about to crash into him. "Your father is fine, Lorechen. There have been some developments in the world which—"

"—What's wrong?" I insisted.

"I'm fine," Paps assured me. "I'm home because there's been terrible news circulating at the office."

"Oh no," I blurted out, "did you lose your job? Did the company fail? What will we do?"

Kikuchan was sitting in her usual spot in the corner of the room, working on some embroidery.

"Yesterday," Paps said in exasperation, "the Japanese attacked Pearl Harbor, a United States military installation on the island of Oahu in Hawaii. Ships were sunk. Countless American servicemen and many civilians died. A terrible tragedy."

I looked at Kikuchan. I could tell she was listening but I didn't know whether she could understand everything Paps was saying in English. I worried that he might say something inappropriate.

"This will mean war for certain and we—"

I interrupted him. "—*Erzählen Sie mir in Deutsch*!"

He looked at me, puzzled. I nodded my head in Kikuchan's direction. He quickly understood and continued in German. After just a few words, Kikuchan snorted, stood up, and left the room.

He went on. "I'm astonished that you didn't hear of this at the Academy but maybe they wanted to spare you the worry and anxiety. The news is everywhere, on the radio, in the newspapers. It is the topic of conversation at every street corner. Most Japanese feel that the action was provoked by the Americans."

I was amazed. "I didn't hear anything!" Then I asked, "What do you mean? What provocation?"

Paps drew in his breath. "Japan won't withdraw from China and it won't forgo its agreements with Hitler and Mussolini. The Americans will not lift the embargo and continue to be ever watchful of Japan's expanding influence in the Pacific and Asia. But this horrible event ensures there's no stalemate anymore. There will be war."

His words saturated the air, making it hard to breathe.

Mutsch held my hand. "This changes our situation and we may need to discuss how we should react to this news. But not until later, Lorechen.

"Yes, mother," I said, "and only among the three of us."

In the spring of 1942, Mutsch and I had decided to exercise more often. We were just coming home after a brisk walk on a gorgeous, though crisp, spring day when I heard a droning low-pitched sputtering sound in the distance. Shielding my eyes from the bright sun, I saw a single plane off in the distance, it was gliding in ever widening circles. It seemed to be floating in the cloudless sky, its speed so slow I feared that at any moment it would fall to the earth.

"Mutsch," I said pointing, "I wonder if there's something wrong with that plane. It sounds so different from the ones we usually hear."

She looked up. "You may be right. Look at how low it's flying."

The plane circled once more and then it banked sharply, levelled off, and turned toward the Inland Sea. Moments before it disappeared I thought I could see an American flag on its wings.

I said, "Could that be a . . ."

Suddenly, we heard sirens wailing. Mutsch hurried me into the house.

At the supper table, I told Paps what we had seen.

"Yes, Lorechen," he said, "a few men at the office also heard and saw that aircraft and then shortly after the air raid sirens blared. Some say that it's the first American plane to fly over the Japanese mainland since the outbreak of the war. It's assumed it was some sort of reconnaissance flight, most likely unarmed, testing the Japanese defence systems."

"Who would do such a dangerous thing?" I asked.

Paps exhaled. "Some are speculating that it was the famous Doolittle on a solo mission. He has a reputation for being bold."

That night, talking about the plane incident we discussed how much more complicated our lives might become. We tried to anticipate what would happen during American bombing attacks. Naturally, we identified with the Allies and we wanted desperately for the Axis powers to be defeated but we felt no animosity toward the Japanese. However, our feelings changed when we learned of the brutality and horrors perpetrated by the Japanese armies in China and the Philippines.

We were fortunate to have made it to Japan. Although Japan was one of the few countries that had given Jews a haven, we still were cautious because we knew we couldn't hide our Western identity. Even in crowds we stood out, literally, each of us at least a head taller than the majority of the Japanese citizenry. Nor could we excuse ourselves from any conversations about or observations of German immigrants because the suspicion that we might be Jews was always near. We didn't openly profess or betray our heritage and religion for fear of reprisals.

A few years ago, my father told me that Hitler had requested that the Japanese government extradite all German Jews. Incredibly, the Japanese steadfastly refused the request from their fascist ally. From that moment on my admiration for and gratitude toward the Japanese increased. Both the people of Japan and the government had been fair, hospitable, and decent to us even though it was rather obvious that we were aligned, at least in ideology, with their enemy, the United States. Despite our differences we were treated humanely and with respect. The only limitation imposed on us was that our movement was confined to a twenty-five kilometre radius from our home and from Paps' place of business. This wasn't a hardship for us. We managed.

There is so much grief and sorrow in the world: in Austria, Czechoslovakia, Poland, Norway, Denmark, Holland, Belgium, Luxembourg, France, Great Britain, Greece, Yugoslavia, the Balkans, China, Korea,

Malaysia, Thailand, and the Philippines. So few nations avoided invasion, war, casualties, destruction, domination, and oppression at the hands of the Nazis, the Russians, the Italians, and the Japanese.

I remember telling Paps, "The struggles and hostilities of the rest of the world are so far away."

In his wisdom, he responded, "That won't last for long, Lorechen."

During the conflict we felt safe in Kobe, as safe as one could feel during wartime. Paps thought that it was rather unlikely that the United States military would invade the Japanese islands. He believed that the might of American air power would rain down upon us sooner or later. On the one hand, he welcomed it because he thought it would shorten the war not only in Asia but also, hopefully, everywhere else. On the other, he knew we would be caught in the horror of it.

We felt deeply conflicted. Paps and Mutsch were thankful that we had been graciously and unconditionally provided refuge in such a beautiful country. But in order for the barbarity to end, my parents wanted our adoptive nation to be defeated. I'm as sure now as I was then that the Japanese knew where our allegiance lay. Yet, we weren't persecuted.

In preparation for the air attacks, barrels of all sorts were filled with water and then lined up on the shoulders of roads in cities and in towns and villages and along lanes in the countryside. Soon they rusted, the water inside them turning reddish brown. Bamboo tubs from the markets that had held tofu, delectable soybean cakes, and other foodstuffs were also used. When the air strikes began I saw people jump into them to escape the tremendous heat of their burning homes and properties and when they themselves were on fire. For many, the barrels proved to be lifesavers.

Many buildings, in whole or in part, were reinforced and converted into air raid shelters. But it was not enough. The majority of the homes made of wood were destroyed by the incendiary bombs.

We had first believed the Japanese to be stoic but soon came to realize that tragedy is a great equalizer. The response to the loss of a father, a mother, or a child is the same regardless of race, faith, origin, or upbringing.

Paps said, "Mourning has no nationality."

The Americans Strike

I graduated from the Canadian Academy in the spring of 1942. My reports were sterling and my parents were bursting with pride. My English was much improved, my Japanese satisfactory, and my grades and accomplishments noteworthy. The ceremony was understated and brief because of the tense political climate. Paps and Mutsch shared with me their hopes that I would attend college in the United States.

Paps said in earnest, "Whatever the cost it's of no concern for you. You'll go to school in America at any university you choose. We want the best for you."

Later that summer, I remember Paps and Uncle Hans rushing in the door one evening. They were late for supper, very late. Mutsch and I had set the table hours ago. For the past half an hour Obachan already had been trying to keep the vegetables warm and the rice from coagulating into a solid ball. Kikuchan had been distractedly dusting and sweeping even though everything had been neat and tidy since late afternoon.

"Where have you two been?" Mutsch asked as Paps strode toward her and kissed her forehead.

Uncle Hans set his briefcase on a chair. "Sit! Sit! There's news!"

We rushed to our places at the dining room table. Obachan placed the food in front of us and Kikuchan poured sake for the adults. Once we were seated, the four of us joined hands, lowered our heads, and sat in silence for a few moments. For some time now we had been offering thanks and prayer without speaking. Obachan returned to the kitchen. Kikuchan sat on her tatami mat.

"Tell us what's happened!" Mutsch said excitedly.

I looked over at Kikuchan. She was mending a pair of silk stockings.

Paps blurted out, "There's been an attack. Around noontime a small squadron of American planes bombed Tokyo!"

There was unadulterated glee among us!

"Will this be the beginning of the end of the war?" Mutsch wondered.

"I don't know," Uncle Hans said. "We were sitting at our desks, everyone in the office as busy as bees when we heard the chatter from the short wave radio."

Paps rushed to say, "Perhaps this will convince the Diet and the Emperor that further aggression and the continuation of war are now futile." At the mere mention of the Emperor I noticed Kikuchan twitch. She understands us perfectly I thought.

I interrupted him, whispering, "*Es ist am besten wir sprechen Deutsch jetzt.*"[31]

As the words came out of my mouth I saw Mutsch glance over at Kikuchan. My mother understood my meaning but my father seemed perplexed.

Mutsch said, "That would be rude, Lorechen." But then she said, "Kikuchan, please go and help in kitchen."

The little mouse on her mat in the corner looked up, smiled, stood, bowed, and then left the dining room.

"What was that all about?" Paps asked.

Mutsch grabbed his wrist. "It makes Kikuchan uncomfortable when we speak ill of her Emperor."

"I see," Paps mulled.

Uncle Hans continued, "It's a tremendous feat, so brazen and one accomplished with such authority!"

---

31 *It is best we now speak German.*

We understood the meaning of the raid. While it was true that it had caused comparatively little damage, it made the Japanese border look permeable.

Uncle Hans said, "The Japanese government is embarrassed. The Japanese people are astonished such a thing has been accomplished against what they believed was the impregnability of their homeland."

"And," Paps added, "the daring feat will be a tremendous morale booster for the Americans."

The shadows of frustration and fear soon descended upon us again. Rationing took hold. The prices of groceries and household items tripled and quadrupled. Several months later, the items became scarce and prices increased as much as ten-fold. Paps had to consider dismissing Kikuchan and Obachan. He chose not to dismiss Kikuchan because he felt Mutsch still needed help with the daily tasks and upkeep of our home. I wasn't so convinced. I was beginning to be suspicious of Kikuchan. Nothing specific came to mind but I couldn't help myself.

"We must keep Obachan, too," he said, "she can make the limited food we have edible."

Our daily meals invariably were scant, we were always hungry. Mutsch had begun to store extra foodstuffs and supplies in a closet in advance of the rationing and we were fortunate to have them. The canned goods were stacked like bricks—I vowed to never eat another can of salmon as long as I lived. When our stock eventually ran out I came to know the idiom "be careful what you wish for."

There was a flourishing black market especially out in the country where farmers would offer produce and eggs at outrageous prices. We rarely partook in these covert transactions because we were frightened the Japanese authorities would catch us. Once we emptied Mutsch's larder, our dietary staple was rice. Unscrupulous merchants would short weight our purchases by adding pebbles to the burlap bags of rice.

I saw Kikuchan eating insects to stave off the hunger. This was repulsive to me. I couldn't bring myself to do it.

Then the Japanese government devised evacuation plans for all the major cities. Everyone was encouraged to flee.

Uncle Hans often would come to our home after his workday. He and Aunt Eva lived several kilometres down the road so whenever he had time he would stop in for a visit. Usually Paps would already be home and we would have eaten our paltry supper of rice. Hans would refuse Mutsch's offers of food because he was well aware of the near-famine conditions. Like us, he and Aunt Eva had very little. He would stay to drink a glass or two of sake, tell a joke, squeeze my cheek, say his goodbyes, and continue on home. During his visits he would relate to us what he had heard during the day, not only from his colleagues but also on the short wave radio. Paps' duties had kept him out of the office lately so he, too, was eager to learn the latest news. Uncle Hans' opinion of the mindset of the Japanese military, the war-bent political aspirations of the Axis, and even of the Emperor himself were ungenerous, to put it mildly.

Holding his glass high for emphasis, he said, "The Japanese soldiers are savages. The reports of the atrocities committed by them in China, Korea, and on the islands in the Pacific are horrendous."

Mutsch and I cringed.

"Doesn't the government understand the hopelessness of war with the Americans?" he asked in disbelief. "Soon they'll see their sacred islands overrun."

More sake. His face now beet red, anger and frustration visible on his tensed body. His eyes opened wide. "And the Emperor," he shouted, "what's to understand? He's oblivious to everything. His advisors must be denying him the reality of the ardent Americans, their might and resolve. He's a puppet at best." More sake. "He's divine, all right," he belched, "with his imperial head in the clouds."

A few days later Uncle Hans was arrested and interned. We were terrified.

"Don't worry," the authorities told a frantic Aunt Eva, "soon your husband will be released." This was no small comfort to us. We didn't know what *soon* meant. In confidence, Paps said, "Perhaps it's just the typically polite response of the Japanese to someone's anxiety."

Every day Aunt Eva went to see Hans where he was being held at a compound not far from the outskirts of Kobe. She brought him small amounts of food and some clothing and books. She told us that he was comfortable and well-treated but for the time being he wasn't allowed to leave.

"Hans seems fine," Aunt Eva told us. "He exercises, can shave and bathe, and he reads his books."

Herr Griesbach and Paps appealed to dozens of government officials for Hans' release. For weeks Paps didn't receive any explanation for Hans' internment. Many of the Japanese office managers where Hans and Paps worked pulled every string they could but they, too, were stonewalled with polite smiles and bows.

"If it's because he's German," Paps reasoned, "or if it's that he's a Jew then why haven't I suffered the same fate? There must be another reason."

It was Kikuchan.

Our little mouse had overheard Hans' ranting and railing. Although he often spoke in German, the effects of the sake inexplicably caused him to shout in English much of the time. I knew how much Kikuchan understood. At the Canadian Academy I was considered a quick learner for my rapid grasp of both English and Japanese. Kikuchan learned swiftly as well.

We found out later that she had reported Hans to the local police. She was most offended by what she felt were his unforgiving and offensive remarks concerning the Emperor. The authorities questioned her repeatedly and, based on her testimony, they decided to investigate him and his business.

Several Japanese officials arrived at the office. They questioned some of Hans' and Paps' colleagues. No one said anything disparaging about him. Demanding to see the company's books they encountered an annoyed Arthur deCouto, the company's accountant. "I had no choice but to submit to their request to review the ledgers. Not that it mattered of course since there was nothing to hide." The police used this inquiry as the basis to arrest Hans as a matter of municipal security. Kikuchan had convinced the authorities that Hans' anger and hatred would manifest itself in some sort of action against the Emperor. This accusation was completely unfounded and untrue. Uncle Hans had difficulty disciplining his dog.

Six weeks later he was released. He told us he had been questioned about the company. As Gerber was a major supplier of goods needed by the Japanese army this tactic was a dead end for them. He said he had been treated well, never threatened.

From that day on I worried that Paps would be interned since he was the company manager. But neither he nor any of the other administrators and lower-level employees at Gerber were ever accosted or taken into custody.

Kikuchan was dismissed summarily. We were not sorry to see her go.

It was only a few days later that we heard the thrilling and exhilarating news of the Allied invasion of France at Normandy. This eerily coincided with the bombing of Japanese cities on Kyushu. Would our island Honshu be spared? We didn't think so. The Americans and their bombers seemed to be everywhere.

In November of that year I recall approaching our home after a morning-long visit at a friend's to find the curtains drawn in my parents' bedroom. I dropped the spray of wildflowers I was holding and rushed into the house.

Mutsch was hunched over on the couch. There were soiled hankies on the floor. She looked up at me and I saw the overwhelming concern in her eyes. "Your father," she said slowly wiping the tears from her face, "had to be escorted to the hospital by Uncle Hans and me. His headache was paralyzing him."

I gasped. I rushed to her side. Frantically I asked, "Is he all right now?"

"He's resting," Mutsch whispered.

There was something else. I knew it. "Tell me, mother," I begged.

She tucked a hankie into the end of her shirtsleeve. With a serious look on her face, she reached over to touch my shoulder. "Your father is very sick. After examinations and consultations with several doctors and specialists the preliminary diagnosis is a brain tumour."

My breathing instantly became rapid. Chills burrowed up my spine. I nearly fainted. "What can we do?" I was pleading.

"Nothing now. There's no room at any of the hospitals. There are too many wounded Japanese soldiers. All the beds are taken. Many suffer on mats on the floors and in the hallways. The doctors tend only to them."

We didn't say anything for quite some time. Then I asked, "Is there medicine or other remedies?"

"No," she wailed, "your father is very ill!"

On 9 March 1945, almost five months later, we heard the welcome news that three hundred Allied bombers had pummelled Tokyo. Several other major cities were hit the following day: Nagoya, Yokohama, and Osaka. We knew it wouldn't be long before Kobe was hit.

And so it was.

As the first bombs fell on Kobe on 16 March, Muschi disappeared. No calling, no promise of her favourite food, no shaking of her favourite toys, absolutely nothing would lure my adored cat from her hiding place, wherever it was. I was terrified that she might be injured. We turned all of her usual hideouts upside down. She had vanished.

Our home wasn't damaged. We were on the outskirts of the city, far enough away from the manufacturing and industrial areas. Yet, the whistling of the bombs as they fell sounded as if they would land in our backyard. At times I could feel the ground trembling. In the city, fires raged everywhere.

Paps and Mutsch, along with many of our neighbours, realized our hilltop homes were no longer safe. It was decided that we would move to Bunkamura, a small village a two-hour train ride from Kobe. We were to run for our lives, again.

While my parents packed as many of our belongings as was practical, I kept on looking for Muschi. What will happen to her? Will she starve? Will she be hit by a bomb and die?

"Lorechen," Paps said the day before we were to go, "we have to get out of here. Once you and Mutsch are safely settled, I promise I'll come back to find Muschi."

"But how will you do that?" I asked.

We hugged. "Leave it to me."

When we arrived at our tiny Japanese-style house in Bunkamura we were relieved to find that it had running water and a gas stove.

"It'll only be a matter of time before our utilities are reduced or terminated," Mutsch said dejectedly.

She was right. Within a few days the water was cut off completely and then restored for one hour each day. When it was available we would scramble to fill every empty vessel. Soon the gas was discontinued. After that, we cooked whatever food we had on a hibachi. When the charcoal disappeared from the stores we used wood gathered from the surrounding forests.

As food became scarcer, Bunkamura proved to be an island of hope because it was flanked by farms. Sometimes we would barter for eggs, fruit, and vegetables and on very rare occasions we would obtain a chicken. There were figs there, too, and I couldn't resist pulling them off the heavily laden trees. However, most of our meagre food supplies came from ration centres set up by the government.

Aunt Eva and Uncle Hans were steadfast in their desire to remain in their home. I remember Hans saying to Paps, "Your decision to leave is premature and unfounded." Soon after, our home in Kobe, not far from his, was hit and destroyed. Miraculously, Hans' home was spared.

One night Paps tried to sneak into our house in Bunkamura just before Mutsch and I were about to help Obachan present some rice and vegetables to the table. We saw him tiptoeing in. He was carrying a sack.

"Is that food?" Mutsch asked. Suddenly, we saw the burlap bag in his hands moving of its own accord!

True to his word, Paps had travelled back to what was left of our home in Kobe. He found Muschi cowering in a hollow formed by the upended roots of a fallen tree. She was dirty and thin but her eyes were bright. I didn't know who to hug first, Paps or Muschi! I was so appreciative that my father had come to the rescue, again.

"Your father took a tremendous chance," Mutsch said, petting the cat.

Muschi was with us for the remainder of our stay in Japan. She was happier in Bunkamura than in Kobe because there were plenty of field mice to catch and bring to us as an offering. When we refused to have her bring her gifts in the house she sulked. Eventually she knew what to do with her captives. She would find a shady spot outside and then indulge herself. She never went hungry.

After our beautiful hillside home in Kobe was destroyed I realized how difficult life had been for Mutsch. When we left Berlin I was an adolescent, as resilient and as naïve as any other, Mutsch was in her mid-thirties more or less set in her ways. She had run from the Nazi wolves, she had kept me safe while she watched out for a husband who suffered from debilitating headaches, and she had dragged our baggage and me across half the world for months on end, only to arrive in an alien society. It must have been incredibly taxing. What was even more traumatic was that she had had to leave her in-laws, her siblings, and her friends behind each time.

As the homemaker, no matter where she was–in Charlottenburg, Wilmersdorf, in Kobe in our villa or in our hillside second house there and now in Bunkamura–she was expected to organize, maintain, and supervise the living conditions. But those tasks never overwhelmed her. Even though Mutsch always had been uncomfortable with change her strength enabled her to persevere.

My father was more fortunate. Because he remained in the employ of the Gerber Company most of his days in Japan were similar to his days in the Berlin office. He travelled a great deal, but when he was home with us he only needed to check in at the office in Kobe once or twice a week.

I knew that he was constantly worried about the safety and well-being of Mutsch and me.

We lost touch with Mr. and Mrs. Dimitriev, our former landlords; with Herr Waldstein, the accomplished cello player; and, with my tutor and his wife, Mr. and Mrs. McKenzie. Kikuchan was gone. Because of the daily threat of bombing Aunt Eva rarely left her home so we didn't see her for months at a time. Uncle Hans visited our humble house in Bunkamura on occasion since sometimes his duties and Paps' overlapped and they would travel together. Hans would stop by briefly before returning to Aunt Eva in Kobe. To my displeasure, I seldom saw the handsome and intriguing Arthur deCouto anymore.

May of 1945 was a particularly worrisome month. The Allies were intent on ending the war posthaste. They persisted in their efforts to bring the Japanese people to their knees. The bombing went on and on, in Nagoya, in Tokyo, and in many other coastal cities. Every night, the glow from fires lit up the night and the ground shook. Amid the explosions we heard horrid screams of suffering. Much of the still air was smoky. It reeked of destruction and death.

We didn't learn of the long-awaited news until 10 May 1945. Our hearts were lightened. Our hopes and dreams were rekindled. Nazi Germany had surrendered. The war in Europe was over.

My parents and I returned to Uncle Hans' home in Kobe. It had managed to remain unscathed from all the bombing. The structure stood incongruously amid the flattened rubble of nearly every other building within a two or three kilometre radius. Aunt Eva was convinced that God had placed His hand over it.

A few of Uncle Hans' friends, our family, and some colleagues from the Gerber office gathered together to celebrate. Uncle Hans' servants prepared a wondrous buffet. From where they were able to acquire the abundance and variety of the foodstuffs presented I don't know. There were small candles lighted everywhere. Flowers adorned the tables.

Everyone was in a joyous yet cautious mood. For the first time in many weeks I heard laughter. Even Boya, Uncle Hans' dog, was content, busily munching on a bone.

"Lorechen," Uncle Hans asked me, "would you be interesting in helping my friend Per Bjorstedt care for his children? His wife died a few months ago giving birth to their youngest. The little one is just an infant. There are three little girls. Per is desperate."

I was stunned. My mind raced as nearly every memory I had of Gerta taking care of me flashed before my eyes.

He went on. "He needs to continue with his duties as Swedish Consul. He has a wonderful staff in his home at present but he wants someone he can thoroughly trust and who can help educate his little ones."

I remembered all that Gerta had taught me. I also thought of how Gerta would reprimand Hansi for singing too loudly during my lessons.

He reached for my hand. "I recommended you highly to him. Think about it. It's a big responsibility, but a rewarding one. You'll need to discuss it with your parents."

I smiled. "I'm certain they'll allow me to."

"Well," he cautioned, "remember you would be living closer to Kobe than you do now. Everyone's aware that the air raids are becoming more and more frequent."

Over the next few days I discussed the proposal with my parents. They reasoned it would be good for me as well as good for the children. "It's an opportunity for you to do what's been done for you," Mutsch said.

Paps was troubled. "The Americans will continue to bomb Kobe and your mother and I would never forgive ourselves if we put you in harm's way. Without you . . ." his voice trembled, ". . . without you we'd be lost."

Mutsch was stoic. "When we can we must try to make the world a better place."

"Maybe it's something I was meant to do," I said.

The next day, arrangements were made for me to go to Kobe to be in the employ of the Swedish Consul. I would live with Per and his children. Paps had mixed feelings about the plan. He cried as we embraced. "You're my angel," he said over and over.

Paps escorted me to Per's home. My introduction was quick because Per was on his way to work. He was an extraordinarily handsome man. His children were three of the most gorgeous little girls I had ever seen.

Paps and I said our goodbyes, both of us crying. Per led me inside. My enormous bedroom was on the second floor of his majestic home. I was expected to watch over the children, do some limited housekeeping tasks while supervising the Japanese servants, and devise and implement a rigorous course of general studies for his two older children, ages seven and five. He insisted that I always speak to them in English. I was to oversee the care of the baby as well.

Little did I know that my responsibilities would also include many nights spent dragging the children and the household staff to air raid shelters.

What my parents wanted for me was to mature, to become an adult much the way Gerta had during the years she was my governess. Few jobs could have done that better or more rapidly. I found it difficult to cope with the anxiety and assume the responsibility of my appointment. Indeed, I had to show Per I was worthy, responsible, and capable.

After a few weeks I found myself becoming more and more enamoured of their father. He was tall and athletic-looking, his dark blond hair wispy and always clean. I would stare at his face, studying its proportions; his dimpled chin below his soft slightly ripened lips a lithe punctuation mark between his lovely cheeks; his nose straight and thin; and, his eyes so strikingly crisp and clear. The whiteness of his perfect teeth was stunning. I noted his strong hands and artistic fingers, often the subject of my thoughts as I dreamed of him placing his hands in mine.

Each weekend I would go home to my parents in Bunkamura. At times it was a harrowing experience. On several occasions the train would stop suddenly and everyone would be instructed to jump off and dive into the ditches as American planes soared overhead. Another time the train I was on was shunted to a sidetrack to allow for a train full of Allied prisoners of war to pass. I remember hearing their voices through the open windows. I saw their exhausted eyes. They were dirty. Some had bandages about their heads, a few still blood-stained. They looked hungry. And yet there were smiles. Many were waving their hands, brandishing the V sign.

"Lorechen," Paps said when I told him that I had returned the V sign to the soldiers, "I thought you had more sense. We're sympathetic to the Americans' plight and we empathize as best we can with their condition but you must watch for Japanese soldiers. If they had seen you, you might have been arrested. Please," he begged me, "you must be more careful."

"No one saw me," I assured him, "but I'll be more careful in the future."

For weeks I worried that the police were coming for me.

On 6 August 1945, I awoke to a very quiet house. I believe it was around 9:30 or so. I was fully rested and refreshed but surprised to find that I had been left to sleep so late. Immediately I snapped to. Where were the children? Who was watching them? I put on my robe and hastened downstairs.

The two older children were seated at the table eating breakfast. The infant was asleep in a cradle nearby. Per's cook and the housekeeper were attending to them.

I spoke in Japanese. "Why did no one wake me?"

The cook bowed and then whispered, "We were told to let you sleep."

I surveyed the two youngsters at the table. They were shoving spoonfuls of cooked eggs and pats of butter into their mouths while the baby slept. "Very well," I said.

Per knew what a task it had been to care for his children these past few months. The infant was a constant drain. Even though I felt a strong bond with her, she was fussy and unappeased when I wouldn't immediately attend to her. The older girls were the same, relentlessly vying for my care and assistance. But my tutoring sessions with them provided me with opportunities to rest while they worked on activities.

Just then the front door was pushed open with such force a painting mounted on the wall in the entryway crashed to the floor. Per burst through the door looking distraught.

"Is everyone safe?" he demanded.

"Yes, yes," I said pointing to the children. "What's wrong? Are you all right?"

He went to the girls at the table. Although happy to see their father they kept on wolfing down their food. He placed his palms on their heads. "Thank heavens," he murmured. He looked to the baby and then exhaled loudly.

Next, he came to me. He embraced me, his large hands pressing against my back, forcing my chest into his. "I'm grateful you're safe, too."

I felt my heart flutter. "But why are you home?" I stammered, looking up into his chestnut-brown eyes.

He released me, stepped back, and then drew his hand across his forehead. "About an hour ago there was a tremendous explosion at Hiroshima. The initial reports are of total destruction. The city has been levelled. Tens of thousands of people are dead."

"Was it the American bombers?" I asked.

Per stared at me. "No," he said, "there are no reports of a phalanx of planes. It is supposed that it was a single plane but that most certainly cannot be so because no one bomber could have caused such destruction." He drew in his breath. He was pensive. "I'll direct my servants to watch the children while I escort you to the train station. You'll return to Bunkamura. If your parents haven't heard the news yet they soon will. They will be beside themselves with worry."

Quickly, I dressed, packed my rucksack, said goodbye to Per's staff, and then hugged and kissed the children. "I hope to be back soon," I said.

Grabbing my hand, Per dragged me through the house, out the front door, and into the back seat of a large chauffeur-driven black automobile.

He ordered the driver, "Proceed immediately to the train station."

In the back seat, even with the large space between us, I could smell tobacco on Per's shirt. The odour was pleasing, a bit acrid yet woodsy, an aroma I relished as I inhaled deeply.

The driver sped through the streets, the tires squealing as he negotiated the turns. At one intersection the car veered to the left and I slid a few centimetres into the chasm between us. He responded by extending his hand, palm up. I placed my hand in his. He then rested his other hand on top.

"I'm so grateful for what you've done for me," he said with warm sincerity. "I don't know what I would have done without you all these months." My heart raced. "When you came to me I thought it was the best decision for my children but now I see that it was best for me as well."

His eyes were searching mine.

"Thank you, Per," I said.

He pressed my hand between his palms. "Ever since my wife died I have been in want. It's been so difficult," he said.

The blood was rushing through my veins. My pulse was churning like the wheels of a locomotive.

Suddenly the car stopped. Per and I were thrown forward, we released hands to brace ourselves against the front seat. The driver yelled a stream of obscenities and then stomped on the accelerator. We were pushed back into our seats.

"Per," I said, placing my hand on his knee, "I feel the same way. You have been special to me."

He looked as if he were about to cry. "Thank you, Ingelore. I've been lonely, depressed at times. I have felt without purpose since my wife passed away and I have been looking for something to fill a hole. I must say—"

"—Yes," I interrupted him, "yes, I've been lonely, too."

"—your presence in our home and the way my children have taken to you, the work you've done with them and the way you cared for them while I was away from them has renewed in me the need to go on. But not alone. And so . . ."

I waited impatiently for the words, his pledge of eternal love and everlasting devotion to me and then the notice of his intent to ask Paps for my hand. Please, I screamed inside my head, please let this be so!

He coughed. ". . . and so I have decided to return to Sweden. Their grandparents miss them immeasurably. But we will be so sad to leave you."

My heart sank, my hopes deflating by the second. I heard the broken pieces of my heart crash at my feet.

"Parting is difficult because, in a way, we are family. I will always cherish my memories of you. And my children will as well." He looked at me quizzically, alarmed by what he saw. "Are you feeling ill?"

I inhaled deeply. To calm my nerves and to prevent my blood from boiling, I exhaled as slowly as I could.

"I'm fine," I said dizzy with melancholy. "I'm fine."

The car arrived at the station. Per extended his hand to help me out. When I grasped it I realized my palm was moist with perspiration. My fingers almost slid away of their own accord. After handing me my bag, he placed both his hands on my shoulders. He looked down at me, studied my face for a few seconds, and then leaned toward me, his eyes closed. I closed mine, tilted my head up, and pursed my lips. Chills of frustration ran through me as I felt his kiss upon my forehead.

"Travel safely to your parents," he said.

"Yes, I will," I mumbled.

My hopes were dashed. When I boarded the train I realized that my life had been changed again and for the first time my heart, my tender and giving heart, had been broken.

The Emperor Speaks

August 1945

There was Mutsch, standing at the doorway of our meagre house, her hands clasped so tightly as if she were trying to wring all the worry and fear from her body.

When she saw me approach she ran to meet me. "Are you all right, Lorechen?" she spat out. "The news! I was so worried for you and your father."

"I'm fine, mother," I said in my most reassuring voice. My heart was shattered but I couldn't let on why. "Where's Paps?"

She kissed my cheeks. "He'll be here shortly."

A half hour later Paps came home, tripping as he ran into our house to see if Mutsch and I were safe. "Are you alright?" he said. "There's been a terrible catastrophe."

"Yes," Mutsch said. "What have you heard?"

We sat at the table. We found ourselves holding each other's hands in a ring just as we had when we had prayed in our train compartment long ago.

"I heard the news on the short wave radio," Paps said. "Operators from all over the world were reporting what they'd heard. Much, if not all, of

Hiroshima is destroyed. The Americans have wreaked their revenge on the Japanese. Herr Griesbach ordered us all to flee Kobe and return to our families. The business is closed indefinitely."

Mutsch was shaking. "We can't stay in this country any longer! Soon there'll be war on the ground. We must go to America as soon as possible."

Paps smiled. "That's just as I was thinking, dear. I've discussed this with Herr Griesbach and he's finally agreed to honour my request for a transfer to the office in New York. We can now begin planning our trip to America."

For the past nine years we had found lasting peace in a peaceful land. But there was no way there could be such a thing for us now in Japan.

Mutsch nearly fainted with relief. "Yes, darling. And when we get there we will find you the best doctors and hospitals so that you can find relief from your headaches. Perhaps Lorechen could go to college. Either way, we will be safe. And that is all that matters."

"Yes," Paps said. Then he paused. "I can hardly even imagine the suffering in Hiroshima. It is beyond belief. What in the world will happen next?"

The attack on Hiroshima made it more difficult to understand the logic of the Americans. Why would they kill tens of thousands of civilians? We knew that it would be the might of the United Sates military that would eventually end the war but to do so in such a manner? The Japanese had been good to us, they had provided us a haven even when they were bidden to extradite German Jews. Their collective national moral conscience had not allowed them to. The Japanese are a wonderful people. Is this how the world repaid their kindness?

As Paps said so many years ago, there's so much good in so many.

Paps took charge. "We'll pack our things and return to Kobe so that I can keep watch over the both of you. Then, as soon as the office reopens, I'll tidy my affairs and we'll go to America."

Over the next few days the three of us did as we had done in Wilmersdorf. We made lists of tasks and then assigned them in an orderly fashion. We didn't have many belongings but we arranged them with dispatch. We were getting ready for another voyage that would take us halfway across the world. But before we were able to set in motion the last and perhaps the most intricate of our plans, another explosion blinded and obliterated the Japanese city of Nagasaki on 9 August 1945.

The catastrophes of the past week had forced the Japanese people into submission and the war, if not officially over, was for all intents and purposes ended with two crescendos of unimaginable horror and overwhelming destruction. The events of the last week had taken an incalculable toll on the country. Both Hiroshima and Nagasaki had been levelled and hundreds of thousands of civilians had been killed.

Everywhere we looked we saw hunger, suffering, and fear. A once proud people would cower whenever a foreigner was in view.

We moved back from Bunkamura to Kobe. Obachan came with us. Uncle Hans found us a decent apartment in a small building that had been spared. Herr Griesbach reopened the office. There was no business to speak of but he did so to restore some sense of normalcy for his employees, to renew their camaraderie, and to have everyone return to the payroll.

On 14 August, we gathered in Paps' office near the radio, waiting for what was presumed would be a moment of tremendous historical significance. One of Paps' colleagues clapped his hands to hush us. We heard intermittent static and then a voice. I distinctly remember looking at the clock. The hands, one atop the other, were pointing up as if toward the heavens.

It was Hirohito.

For the first time, the Emperor spoke directly to the Japanese people. No longer was he an isolated god in a secluded and protected palace. He was everywhere.

I don't recall much of his speech because I was too overcome with a sense of relief. My mind raced with thoughts. I imagined Paps, Mutsch, and I sailing across the ocean to America. I had visions of Paps in a hospital receiving treatment for his headaches.

When the radio transmission ended, Herr Griesbach proclaimed, "The war's over! We are at peace!"

Everyone bowed and embraced each other. There was consummate glee. As Paps and Mutsch chatted, someone tapped me on my shoulder. It was Arthur deCouto. I was awestruck by his smile. He looked so happy. He offered his hands and then extended his arms signalling me to embrace him. I did so without reservation.

"It's been a while," he said stepping back to eye me up and down. "And look at you! Such a beautiful young woman!" His stare lingered on my legs.

My mouth was full of cotton. "Arthur," I managed to slur.

"You're such a vision. We must renew our friendship."

"Yes," I stuttered. "I'd like that very much."

Warmth oozed its way throughout my entire body. If there was anyone who could heal my broken heart it was Arthur deCouto.

The Americans arrived and set up headquarters in hotels and airfields in dozens of cities. They commandeered every large building still standing. General MacArthur was in charge.

"Will the American soldiers be here long?" I wanted to know.

"It'll depend on many things, Lorechen," Paps explained. "There's much work to be done. So far the Japanese people have welcomed the Americans so perhaps whatever needs to be done will be done quickly."

"What will become of the Emperor?" Mutsch asked.

Paps mused. "There's some ambivalence. Should he remain as the spiritual and national leader? Or should he be punished for his role in a conflict that caused so much suffering and destruction?" The Emperor always had been an integral part of the Japanese people's religion and patriotism.

Paps looked on the bright side. "We'll do well with the reconstruction. Our company is providing materials and supplies not only to the

Japanese people but also to the American soldiers."

Suddenly Paps became sombre. "There is something to be cautious about though, Lorechen," he said gravely. "Throughout the country the sick vastly outnumber the well. All kinds of diseases are being contracted by those left with inadequate water. Be careful when you're near other people. Make sure you wash your hands every chance you get."[32]

At home, Obachan did her best to acquire whatever food she could and to prepare it well. Every meal, no matter how meagre, began with silence just as all our others had. But for the past few months Paps had been taking longer to offer thanks. There were many more recipients of his gratitude. First and foremost were his words of appreciation and indebtedness to God for our safety and for the gift of family, then to the Japanese people for their almost decade-long shelter of us, to the Americans for ending the war, to Herr Griesbach for his kindness and largesse regarding Paps' employment, and to our friends who not only had weathered the same storms we had but who also had helped us when we were in need. Almost in tears, he would close his remarks with a special devotion for Mutsch and me.

One evening, Obachan brought to the table rice sweetened with beet rinds. It was the best dessert she could offer. She couldn't understand how such an ordinary thing was so special to us. I look back now and appreciate all she did. As I helped Mutsch clear the table that night, Obachan bowed and told us she would be retiring for the night. Then she apologized for the supper she had prepared.

"You will say no such thing!" Mutsch said hugging her. "Now go to bed and sleep well."

We went for a short walk after dinner. The night was cloudless, the stars radiant. After about fifteen minutes Paps stopped. "It's ironic that the Americans are helping the Japanese now, after so much conflict and confrontation. I'm sure the people here don't know how to respond.

32 Between 1945 and 1948, some 650,000 people contracted cholera, dysentery, typhoid fever, diphtheria, epidemic meningitis, polio, and other communicable diseases (McClain, *Japan*, 531).

Should they be grateful? Suspicious? Some cooperate with the hope that things will be better, others go along with them out of fear."

Obachan also wondered what would happen. Many of the first American soldiers to hit the Japanese shores were the same ones who had fought their way through the jungle islands in the Pacific. They had been isolated, far from civilization and civility for months. Most of them wanted nothing more than to go home and start life anew. Many Japanese expected callousness from them, contempt, perhaps even revenge.

Occupation

1945

I was particularly fond of a group of Signal Corps officers whose duty it was to defuse bombs that had been dropped but had not detonated. Major Jay was my favourite. He was a handsome young man with eyes as black as coal, very curly dark hair with tiny ringlets that draped his forehead like grapes dangling from a vine. He seemed always to be smiling. I loved looking at him and his pronounced dimples.

One time I said to him, "I'm worried about your dangerous assignments."

As usual, he grinned. "Don't worry about me, Ingi," he joked. "I've made it this far and I don't intend to go home in a box at this late date!"

This was hardly reassuring to me.

I learned that Major Jay could play the piano as well as a professional. The tune "I'm Dreaming of a White Christmas" was popular at the time and he played it beautifully. At someone's urging he began to sing. Whenever I heard that song I pictured him playing it for me and me alone even though there were always dozens of people huddled around.

There were parties every night at the Officers' Club located in a British colonial mansion that had survived the bombing. It had been used for receptions and balls when foreign dignitaries arrived in Kobe. My parents had taken me there for a reception in 1938 or 1939, our second or third year in Japan. At the reception we attended there was an endless procession of people shaking hands with a lady in a funny hat wearing white gloves. We were in line. I curtsied. Later, while people stood around chatting, champagne flutes in hand, I wandered about. The rooms with high ceilings were full of antique furniture and old paintings. Outside, gardens were surrounded by velvety-smooth lawns and rose beds. If you walked across the pebble path there was a waist-high cement wall that overlooked the Inland Sea. I imagined English masons built it to prevent their countrymen who had imbibed too much from plunging over it into the water.

After the British consular staff had gone home at the start of the war in Europe the mansion was not empty for long. It housed a high-level German delegation and accommodated visiting Nazi officials still exploring diplomatic channels, trying to convince the Japanese government to extradite German Jews back to Berlin. The irony of this history wasn't lost on me now.

Many years later all that remained of those wonderful gardens were unkempt and weed-infested lawns. The Germans had neglected the pristine landscaping. Evidently, the art of English gardening didn't appeal to the Nazi mind.

At the mansion, I was introduced to rum and coke. The strongest beverage I had drunk before was wine which was permitted only on special occasions and even then only under my parents' supervision and unrelenting surveillance.

The parties with the Americans were wonderful. We danced and talked all night. Jay and his officer friends wanted to know about my life in Japan before the war. They were amazed to learn how kind the Japanese had been to me. I asked them about their experiences, especially about the fighting on the islands in the Pacific, and I was surprised to hear few complaints. "Sure it was hard," one would say, "hot and tedious and the snipers were everywhere." Another would join in, "The mosquitoes were as big as the birds back home!" Jay said that the worst thing were the snakes that fell onto his shoulders from overhanging branches. Conspicuous by their absence were stories about their buddies being killed. If the conversation became too serious, Jay would lighten the mood by shouting, "We're here now and we're having such a good time!"

It felt good to laugh again. Our lives had changed dramatically since the end of the war. There were no more air raids and frantic trips to shelters. For the first time in years we had all the food we wanted. We could travel wherever and whenever we chose. But what I loved most of all was dressing up for the endless rounds of parties hosted by the soldiers at the Club. Before the war all my clothes had been hand-tailored, some locally and some brought back from Shanghai or Hong Kong by my father. But during the war we salvaged whatever we could, altering dated items into something more current. Shoes however, were our biggest problem. None were available and no amount of repair and polishing could restore the ones we had. And oh how I had missed wearing silk stockings. I remember Kikuchan sitting on her tatami mat in the corner of our dining room spending hours at a time with tiny hooks meticulously repairing the endless runs in our old pairs. When she was finished with them they looked brand new.

The music from the Officers' Club was soothing and soft. They would play the new Benny Goodman recordings that were so popular in the States. But part of me still preferred the old-fashioned waltzes, the kind Paps had taught me to dance to before the war.

I noticed that although there were dozens of gorgeous Japanese girls both willing and able to entertain their American overseers, several of my Caucasian girlfriends and I were able to pick and choose at will from nearly all the officers and the huge flocks of enlisted men—each one of them as eager to have fun as we were.

Many of my soldier friends frequently came to my house. Most often their arms were laden with cartons of food of the kind my parents and I hadn't seen in years. Obachan became adept at preparing fabulous meals with the new and unique foodstuffs. Within a few weeks half the army must have learned of Mutsch's reputation as a gracious hostess and of Obachan's mastery and magic in the kitchen.

“They must think of you as a surrogate mother,” I said to Mutsch, “as a symbol for what they long for back home, that’s why they always drop by.”

“No, Lorechen, they come here to see you,” she teased.

Our humble home became a meeting place. Meal times echoed with laughter and good conversation. Being alive was fun again! We were euphoric! We wanted to make up for all those years of deprivation, fear, and hunger. This was not only true for us but also for the young American soldiers who had lived through the horrors of a war they hadn’t created but were unable to avoid.

The good company and good times were one thing but too much good food was something else altogether. My digestive system rebelled. I came down with hepatitis. The army doctor explained that my liver was not able to digest fats after such a long period of deprivation. I had a high fever. I turned yellow all over. My sclera were no longer white. I stayed in bed for weeks while linens, towels, and everything else I came in contact with were washed daily to rid the fabrics of the yellow hue. But there was no keeping me down. Life was too full of fun to waste time. Soon I was back with my soldier friends on condition that I adhere to a strict diet of foods that were crushed, mashed, or puréed! Another irony, I thought, after years of being hungry.

Much too soon for me but not for them, many of my soldiers were called back to the United States for discharge. Farewells, as they always had been, were very difficult for me. I had finally found a group of friends, marvellous young men who were strong, good-looking, and full of life and now they were leaving and I would be alone again. Some were returning to wives and children, others to families and friends. Their loved ones surely must have missed them. My only consolation was that since my parents and I were going to America we might see each other again.

The replacement troops that came in relief to continue with the Occupation had spent most of the war years in America. Many of them resented being sent overseas after the war. There was no glory to be had in peacetime. And since many hadn’t endured the hardships of war they were immature and sought recognition by acting like conquerors. Some were rude and uncivilized. They took advantage of the Japanese girls, treating them like slaves, having their way with them against their wishes, thus perpetuating the cliché of the ugly American. I recall the commanding officer in Kobe, an Army Colonel. After a few drinks, his sport was to roll down the lawn in the front of the Officers' Club while clutching any Japanese girl he could catch. It was revolting and embarrassing, not only for the girls but also for many of the men on his staff.

The Time of My Life

Spring 1946

I first met Harold Grossinger at the Officers' Club. He had been sent to Kobe with the Occupation forces and assigned to the motor pool even though he had been trained for and did intelligence work in France during the war. He told me several times that from the moment he came ashore he'd fallen in love with Japan and when his tour of duty ended he wanted to stay on as a civilian employee attached to the Army. I liked him right away. He was very good looking, so much so that all the girls considered him to be the epitome of what was meant by the words tall, dark, and handsome.

The third or fourth night I saw him at the Club, he rushed in and walked rapidly in my direction, as though pushing against a storm. He handed me a drink and then hurriedly pulled me into the dining room. The liquid in my glass was splashing all around as I ran to keep up with him!

"Harold, what is it?" I said smiling as I looked up into his seductive sky blue eyes.

"The Colonel's asked me to open the first Post Exchange on the base in Osaka," he said finding it difficult to contain his excitement. "We went to see the building earlier this morning. It's an enormous old warehouse, one of the few that wasn't bombed."

His energy was contagious. "I'm so happy for you!" I beamed.

"Well, get this, Ingi," he breathed into my ear, "I'm supposed to open in two months and I want you to be my personnel manager!"

"Who, me?" I was shocked.

He spurted his words. "Yes, you! You speak Japanese so you can hire all the people we need!" Then, putting two of his fingers under my chin to tilt my head upward, he said, "Please say you'll take the job!"

He was breathless. And so was I. God, what a handsome man he was with his curly black hair and classic facial features! It all sounded so exciting to me. But there was one person whose permission I needed. My father would have to be sold on the idea and for some reason I didn't think he would be. So rather than have Harold think of me as a girl who was still under my parents' protection, I said, "You have my heartfelt congratulations, Harold! I'm sure you'll make it a tremendous success. But you know I'm supposed to leave shortly for the United States. How can I accept your offer?"

He leaned forward for a kiss. I willingly obliged him.

"You know how the bureaucrats work! Who knows when your visas will come through!"

I kissed him again. "Harold, I'd love to but . . ."

A smile burst across his face. "But nothing! You'll do it! I know you will! Remember, we only have two months so we'll have to get started in the morning. It'll be fun working together!"

He led me outside onto the veranda overlooking the Inland Sea. It was a balmy, clear night.

"What a beautiful spot," Harold said softly. "I don't think I'll ever leave this country. And I know I'll miss you terribly when you finally get your visa and go to America. But right now I'm too excited about this new job and working with you to even think about that."

At breakfast the next morning Paps, Mutsch, and I discussed Harold's idea. I was pleasantly surprised when my father offered no resistance. He said, "Yes, Lorechen, it's a good opportunity for you. You'll be safe with all the soldiers around but more importantly you'll be able to put your many skills to use."

Harold picked me up around lunchtime. We drove to the warehouse chatting and laughing the entire way. When we arrived, he escorted me in, squeezing my hand almost to the point of discomfort. I could just imagine the enormous building stocked with food and clothing, soldiers walking the aisles full of goods. But it was filled with mouldy cardboard boxes and scattered with office files and broken furniture. Cobwebs hung like Spanish moss from windows and doorframes. There was trash and discarded personal items littered everywhere.

"Achoo!" I sneezed. "This place smells terrible and look at the mess!"

He was quick to comfort me. "Don't worry Ingi, the Colonel promised to send some GIs from the bucket brigade. You know, custodians. They'll be here shortly to clean this place up, as good as new. In the meantime, let's see if we can lay out an office for you." He was so happy to have me with him. "The Colonel found a couple of soldiers with carpentry experience! They'll also be along soon to figure out what supplies we'll need for renovations."

"This is incredible, Harold," I said. "There are so many Japanese who would give their all for lumber and cement and tools and plaster to rebuild their houses! Where will these things come from?"

Harold smiled. "Don't you worry about a thing! The Army and I have our ways! Next problem?"

"Well," I asked, "after the boys clean up, how about a table and some chairs?"

He kissed me. "You'll see!"

By evening, after the Army custodial help had gone through the place like a tempest, the warehouse was relatively clean. Using chalk on the concrete floor, Harold and I completed the task of outlining a reception area, an office, spaces for showcases, and storage locations.

"The GI carpenters and a half-dozen Japanese labourers working for the Army will arrive tomorrow," he promised.

The next day workers were waiting when we arrived at the warehouse. A delivery had already been made! In the alley there were large bundles of framing lumber, buckets of nails, pails filled with plaster, and crates brimming with hammers, saws, and other tools.

Inside, the soldiers and some local Japanese men were quick to understand what Harold and I wanted them to do. I clarified the chalk markings on the floor with them. I found out that one of the Japanese workers was an accountant before the war, another a chef at a posh hotel in Osaka, and two others had worked in management positions for the railroad. And here they were, now common labourers.

After they understood the plans, they went right to work. They measured, sawed, studded out the rooms, closets, and counters, lathed and plastered, and built showcases, shelving, and storage units.

Harold commented, "I can't believe how quickly the Japanese learn and how quickly they work. Look at them! And they're so pleasant. It's just amazing."

I wasn't surprised. Having lived in Japan for a decade I had witnessed, countless times, the resolve and determination of the Japanese people.

We decided to run a single advertisement for sales help, stock boys, and cleaning positions in the local Osaka *Mainichi Shimbun* newspaper. We included an application form in the copy so whoever was interested could come with their information in hand.

When we arrived at the warehouse the day after the notice was published a long line of people snaked around the building with hundreds of hopefuls patiently waiting.

"What have we done?" I asked Harold as he ushered me in the rear door. "How will I interview all those people?"

Harold melted me with his magnetic smile. "You'll do just fine, Ingi."

He snapped his fingers to get everyone's attention. There was complete silence. "You're up, Ingi," he said playfully patting my buttocks. Then he disappeared into the stock room.

"*Kon'nichiwa*! *Yoi asa*!" I said smiling, greeting and wishing them good morning. The sad sea of faces stared back at me as if they were drowning and I was the sole proprietor of a life raft. I thanked them for coming but made it clear that I would only be hiring two dozen people at this time. There were murmurs. I could see disappointment settling over them like a dark cloud. I knew that many factories and retail establishments were not yet back in business after having been destroyed in the bombings. Many of the Japanese were hungry and frightened and in need of work. I felt great sympathy for them.

One by one the applicants filed inside for interviews. The assortment of candidates was unbelievable. I talked to Japanese women with babies on their backs, men and women too old to work but who obviously needed to do so, a young man on crutches, another with a missing limb, several girls who appeared so young I found it difficult to believe they were in their teens. Widows pleaded with me for employment. Widowers cried for a chance. Orphans begged for any kind of work. It was heartbreaking. The interviewing process was slow because of the written applications. I only read *katakana*, a simple form of script used mainly by children. But I was lucky. The fifth applicant, a young girl in a colourful kimono, spoke some English. She was so pretty with broad cheekbones, a pleasant smile, and the blackest, straightest waist-length hair I had ever seen. I hired her on the spot as my assistant. Yaniko was so happy yet she hid her smile behind her hand in the traditional Japanese way, bowed, and then sharply drew in her breath between her teeth to show her pleasure.

We worked out a system. I did the interviewing and she read the written information. By the end of the day we had talked to about half of the applicants. We promised to see the others the following day.

Within a week, Harold, Yaniko, and I hired thirty people. Seven were assigned as stock clerks. One of them, Imo, the young man on crutches, was the most agile of the six. We employed fourteen sales girls and nine women and men as custodial staff. One of the sales girls had been a teacher whose job had evaporated when a particularly intense B-29 bombing raid hit the school where she worked. Two of the cleaning women had never worked outside their homes before but their husbands had been killed in the war and they were now living with their parents and they needed to support their own children. I felt for them.

By the second week, the warehouse had taken on the look of a department store. Harold and I were amazed. Display cases, shelving, and storage closets were almost complete. To the sound of sawing and hammering, Yaniko and I continued to train our personnel. It was easy since everyone was eager to work. And then our first shipment from the air base arrived. We received linens, towels, blankets, Army surplus clothing, and canned goods. Yaniko said that she had never seen such bounty, she was moved to tears to see so many items in one place at one time.

Each morning, Harold and I checked the progress of the construction. He suggested we paint the walls and ceilings white to get away from the drab olive colours of the Army material. I suggested our sales girls should wear kimonos. Harold agreed. "Yes, that's a great idea! They're much more colourful and interesting to look at than the washed out skirts and tops they usually wear."

Several days before the opening, one of the sales girls sent a note by way of another that she would be absent for two days because of her grandmother's death. But when she used the same excuse twice more that month I confronted her. "Fumichan," I asked, "how many grandmothers do you have?" She looked at me with apprehension and burst out crying. "Please forgive me. My baby's sick and I need to stay home. My mother is too old to care for a sick baby."

The Japanese would tell a lie rather than hurt someone's feelings but why she thought I would be angry if she stayed home with her sick baby I didn't know. I explained that staying home to care for a child was reason enough to be absent. I didn't want to commit the ultimate insult of shaming her in front of the others. Surely, if I had, Fumichan would have had no choice but to resign. So I asked Yaniko to inform the others discreetly about how I felt regarding absences. She did so and soon after I sensed a high degree of respect from my employees.

The time flew by. There were only three days left until our opening. Except for a few mouldings not yet attached to doors and storage units and the delivery of glass pieces for some of the display cases, construction was complete. The custodial staff cleaned, re-cleaned, and polished everything. Our makeshift department store sparkled like freshly fallen snow. It was a pleasure to see how much pride the Japanese took in their work.

Twenty hours before the opening, three massive Army trucks arrived. The GIs dragged in carton after carton of blankets, sheets, pillowcases, and towels. Cases of canned olives, pickles, tuna, and salmon were brought in. There were even two small cases of liver pâté! More packages were rolled in on hand trucks. Boxes of coffee, hot chocolate, Spam, and canned beans were stacked along the walls. The last arrival took the combined efforts of several GIs. They wheeled in a Coca-Cola vending machine and three cigarette machines! It was incredible! Many of the soldiers bringing the supplies and linens were the same ones who had brought the building materials at the outset. They marvelled at the place, wondering aloud if they could have completed construction, remodeling, and all the other finishing touches in so short a time. Harold winked at me. Of course they couldn't have, his look told me.

The big day arrived. At 9:00 a.m. on a clear spring day, Imo opened the polished corrugated doors, proudly stepping aside to allow in a crowd of GIs. Many came with their Japanese girlfriends. The sales people bowed low, their obis pressing flat against their backs. Their brightly coloured kimonos reflected off the glass cases. The soldiers pressed forward, sometimes shoving to get closer to the showcases. Yaniko quickly signalled the girls to take to their stations. I was amazed at how professional they all were while keeping pace with the demands of our customers. Harold browsed around, watching the soldiers. On a few occasions he had to remind them that they were in the presence of women. Some of the GIs were rude and overbearing. Harold kept them in line.

Fumichan looked confused when one of Harold's friends, a burly, soft-spoken soldier from Alabama, approached her. He wanted to know whether we carried molasses. We didn't. She told me later she didn't believe he was speaking English!

At another counter, one of the girls was in trouble. Yaniko was there before me. Harold was yelling at a GI, appearing just in time to stop the soldier from pulling the Japanese girl into the back room. This second wave of Army guys were so different from the first wave of GIs who had arrived from the Pacific Islands where they had already encountered a different culture and suffered the trials of war. Even though the first GIs hadn't been with women for more than a year, most behaved like perfect gentlemen. There is something to be said for the courage, bravery, and fortitude gained in battle.

Other than a few incidents, the day was a tremendous success. By evening, we were exhausted but exhilarated. When the last customer left, Harold and I called the staff together to tell them what a fine job they had done. They hid their beaming faces as they bowed and thanked us. Then Harold told me to tell them, "Now, everyone go home! Enjoy your evening! Come in an hour earlier tomorrow to clean and restock." There was no reaction. Then he told me to add, "Of course you'll be paid overtime!" Giggling and chattering like a flock of magpies, they left the warehouse. After all the hustling, jostling, and confusion of the day the store was now eerily silent.

"We did it! We did it!" Harold sang, dancing me around the floor. I held on to him tightly. "Do you realize how successful this day has been?" He had already tallied the receipts, but I didn't need to see the figures. I saw how quickly the merchandise disappeared from the shelves.

"And now young lady," he said kissing my forehead, "it's time for us to celebrate. Let's go to the Officers' Club to see what excitement we can find there!"

When we arrived, the lobby was strangely quiet. The dining table where our friends usually waited was unoccupied. Damn it, I thought, Harold will be disappointed. Why couldn't they be here on the one night we want to celebrate?

Suddenly the back door opened and our friends rushed in with a bouquet of red roses for me and an enormous wooden board painted as a medal of honour for Harold! Harold was very touched. I was speechless. "How did you know that our day was such a success?" I asked them.

"That's the Army! A salute to Grossinger and to Ingi!" is all they said.

And celebrate we did! The men had arranged for the band to play. We danced until the early morning, laughing and reminiscing and listening to stories of home from the GIs. I shared with them my haunting encounter with the trainloads of American prisoners of war and what it was like during the bombing attacks.

As dawn broke, Harold and I walked along the grounds, arm in arm. The sunrise was spectacular. I felt so happy and yet a sadness fell upon me as I realized all this would soon end.

"Strange, isn't it," I said to Harold, "that for so long I've been waiting to go to the States and now that the time is near I'm not sure I want to leave here. These last few weeks have been so exciting, especially with you, and I guess there's a large part of me hoping that my visa doesn't come too soon."

He hugged me tightly. "I know," he said earnestly, "I'll miss you terribly. But your dad needs medical care and I know he and your mom won't leave Japan without you. Maybe I'll tire of Japan and eventually I'll come to the States and we'll see each other often. But for now, I want to stay here, for as long as possible. So let's enjoy the time we have. No more sadness, okay?"

He unlocked his eyes from mine. "Look! It's light already! It's five a.m.!" I gasped. I knew my parents would be flaming with worry. "I'll take you home now," he said, "and we'll have just enough time to shower and change our clothes before we leave for work!"

What transpired when I arrived home that morning is better left unsaid.

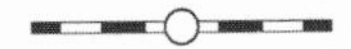

The Post Exchange warehouse turned out to be a very profitable undertaking. The Colonel was pleased with our sales volume. When the *Stars and Stripes* ran an article about it the store was flooded with GIs from a neighbouring base, resulting in a rapid depletion of our inventory. Due to Harold's connections, we were able to restock immediately. Every soldier must owe him a favour, I thought.

We did have some problems. Absenteeism plagued us. Part of the problem was the terrible condition of public transportation. Yaniko told me a thirty-minute train ride could take as long as two hours on some mornings. Japanese trains were famous for their punctuality but that all changed after the bombings. Some of our employees lived in cramped houses with dozens of elderly relatives who often needed their attention. Regrettably, the more attractive Japanese girls soon learned that they could make more money faster by entertaining GIs in certain ways that perpetuated the stark contrast between overlords and minions. There were some who decided to escape the city and return to the country where there were opportunities on recently revitalized farms. One of those was Yakochan, our best sales girl, who moved back to Bunkamura where her family was trying farming again. Yakochan's husband had been a kamikaze pilot who had kept his solemn pledge, piloting his plane into one of the American battleships near Okinawa. Then she lost everything in an air raid that mercilessly bombed her home. For a while, the job had given her purpose and she worked harder than most others.

"I am sorry," she said, "you were so good to me. I will miss you. I will never forget you."

I enjoyed every moment at the warehouse and wished that life would just continue on as it was. Then word came from the American Consul that our visas were being processed and that Paps would have them in hand within the month.

Fate Intervenes

July 1946

If only I had listened to Mutsch that morning.

She intercepted me as I was preparing to leave the house. "Please, Lorechen," she begged, "please stay home today. I have this dreadful foreboding."

"What is it?" I asked distractedly as I approached the front door. "By the way, do you like these white linen slacks I'm wearing? The tailor delivered them yesterday. They look so good on me!"

She held my arm. "Yes, dear, they're wonderful. But I've been sleepless these past few nights and last night I had a terrible dream."

I was standing on the porch. "Don't fret, Mutsch," I said, kissing her on the cheek, "I'll be fine. You don't have to worry about me!"

I was off to meet Jack. A man I had met at the warehouse a few weeks ago. We hit it off after a few days of flirting and repartee. He would come in, smile at me, and then ask for something he presumed wouldn't be immediately available.

"Maybe you can help me," he would say winking at me, staring me up and down. "I'm looking for some, well, I don't know what the English word is but in Japanese it is *aijō*."

"Oh, yes, soldier! I'll see what I can do!" I would respond coyly to his request for "affection."

I walked to the end of our narrow dirt road where it intersected a main thoroughfare. We decided we would meet there as we had several times before.

A relationship between us slowly developed. Jack was a handsome, very muscular member of the military police assigned to the Officers' Club. He had stopped by my house to meet Paps and Mutsch. They weren't particularly impressed with him. "He's nice," Paps said, "but not too bright! You've dated so many intelligent fellows!" Jack seemed dull to them. He was born and raised on a farm in Ohio and until he had been drafted he had never been anywhere else.

"Wow!" he once said, "I didn't know the world was so big and so full of people!" Secretly I agreed with my parents' evaluation of him but it was his innocence and naïveté that made him so attractive to me.

And to top it off, because he was an MP, he had access to a jeep!

Jack rumbled up in his jeep to our meeting point. I hopped in, kissed him twice on the lips, and then shouted, "We're off!"

We drove out of the city on a road that wound its way up into the mountains. Signs in English and Japanese were posted to alert drivers that railings around its serpentine curves were not yet installed. Last night's rain had washed the air crisp and clear and the sun shone brightly. We drove by slender trunks of bamboo glistening as though streaked with honey. I pushed aside Mutsch's nagging intuition, how could anything go wrong on a day like this?

"So," he asked as we made our way around a particularly sharp curve, "shall we continue with your lessons?"

"Yes, sir!" I saluted.

Jack stopped the jeep. He and I switched places. We knew this was in strict violation of Army regulations. Civilians weren't permitted to drive military vehicles under any circumstances but we reasoned that no one would see us. Jack had promised to be a good teacher. And true to his word he was. I felt confident as I engaged the gears and slowly accelerated.

Some of the bamboo already had been harvested. The sloping terrain looked like a checkerboard of fence posts. I took one hand off the steering wheel and said, "See how many have been cut? What's left looks like random spikes coming up from the ground!" I kept babbling on. "Have you ever seen a circus performer's bed of nails? Look! There!" I pointed. "The entire hillside looks like one!"

He grabbed my thigh. "Yes, that's so interesting. But let's go a little slower right here, Ingi."

The spear-pointed stumps of the bamboo fascinated me.

"Are you paying attention?" Jack asked.

I leaned over and kissed him. "Of course I am, silly."

I refocused just in time. Suddenly, the road felt soft underneath the tires. I squeezed the steering wheel to maintain control. When I stepped on the brake I didn't feel much of a response. The jeep had a mind of its own. I turned to avoid another curve but it was too late. In an instant we were rolling down an embankment.

When I regained consciousness I was lying under the jeep. Jack was bent over me, as white as a sheet. Relief showed clearly on his face when he saw my eyes open and heard me speak. I asked him if he'd been hurt.

"No, no," he said. "I'm fine. Are you all right? Are any of your bones broken? Are you bleeding?

"Jack," I said matter-of-factly, "I'm perfectly fine." Then I swooned. When I came to, Jack took charge.

"I have to lift the jeep so you can slide out. Do you understand? Can you do that? As soon as I say go, try to move quickly," he yelled.

With superhuman strength he raised the jeep a few inches. I was about to close my eyes and fall asleep but I remembered his words. Somehow I crept out from under the overturned jeep. We had rolled into one of the checkerboard patches. I was supine on broken glass. Fatefully, neither of us had been impaled on the bamboo spikes. The sickening odour of gasoline engulfed us. With Jack's help I tried to stand up. It was then that I realized I was totally numb below the waist. My white slacks were drenched with blood. Just before fading into a dream I heard Jack shouting for help. Three Japanese farmers heard his cries. They came sliding down the embankment. They cleared away some of the glass, offering to take Jack and me down the mountain on their oxcart. But first they had to get me back up to the road. They put together a makeshift stretcher from the discarded bamboo branches. When they lifted me up I screamed in agony. Eventually, they succeeded in moving me. I was falling in and out of awareness when I realized that I was nestled on some straw in a wagon. One of the farmers threw some rags over me when he saw that I was shaking. Even though the sun was blazing I was freezing. When the cart started moving, Jack was next to me, holding my hand, trying to prevent me from rolling from side to side. The ride was harrowing.

"Don't worry, Ingi," Jack said, "you'll be fine. We're on our way now."

My mind was wandering. I was scared and in tremendous pain. What will my parents say? I was freezing. How will I thank these farmers for helping me? What will happen once we get down the mountain? I thought of Jack. Will he be court-martialled? I blacked out.

Then I felt a familiar motion, and heard a familiar chugging. I was on a train. I opened my eyes to see dozens of eyes staring back at me. I recognized Jack and felt him holding me. I shut my eyes again. It was dark. Then it was silent.

The next thing I remember is the wail of a siren. Is that from an ambulance? Was I in it?

More darkness, then light, then the sound of cloth being ripped. I suddenly felt aware. I was on a gurney. I heard a woman's voice. "You're at the Army hospital. You're going to be fine." The nurse was cutting off my slacks. Then she said, "We need to see if your bladder has been punctured. I'll insert a catheter. Hold still."

"I want to go home," I told her. I must have been sedated because the words dribbled out of my mouth. "My parents will be worried."

"Not today, sweetie," she answered. "A doctor will be with you shortly. Try to relax." I nodded off.

When I came to, Jack was with me. "Hello, baby," he said softly. "Don't worry. Your parents will be here shortly. The docs have done their best and you'll be fine." Then he whispered, "No one will ever know you were driving, understand? I was, you remember now, don't you?" I was much too groggy to comprehend the implications of what he was saying. "Why can't I go home?" I wanted to know. "What's happened to me?"

Before he could answer I drifted off again.

Later, when the pain woke me, my parents were there. Jack was almost incoherent when he had called them.

"I'm so sorry. I'm sorry. I should've listened to you, Mutsch."

They were relieved to see me. At that moment I don't think they had any idea of how seriously I'd been hurt. I didn't either.

"Just rest, Lorechen," Paps said. "Everything will be all right."

I woke several times during the night, hearing voices and moans and although I sensed movement in my room I didn't know for sure if anyone was with me.

The next morning I was taken to the operating room and placed on a cold hard table with a hole cut out of its centre. An Army doctor came in.

"I'll need to drain the blood and fluid from the edema on your side. It's the size of a watermelon, young lady. Only then can we put you in a cast."

"A cast?" I asked in astonishment. "But why?"

He explained. "We took x-rays during the night when you were incapacitated from a massive dose of sedatives. Your pelvic bone is broken in three places. In order for it to heal properly you must be rendered immobile."

I fainted.

When I awoke, Mutsch told me, "The doctor drained your edema several times. He's ready to form the cast."

I was in agony. My broken pelvis was suspended over the hole in the table. The doctor was preparing the plaster. "I hope you realize how lucky you are," he said. "I'm sure you understand that things could've been far worse."

He wound the cold wet strips of plaster around my midsection. The table allowed the doctor to apply the cast without moving me. After what seemed like hours, I was wrapped in cold plaster from the top of my rib cage to the end of my coccyx bone. Then I was wheeled back to a room where heat lamps hastened the hardening process. I felt like a roast in an oven!

A week later I went home by ambulance. The driver and Jack carried me inside.

"We moved your bed closer to the window, Lorechen, so you can look outside. Perhaps the scenery will help cheer you in some way."

"Thank you, mother," I said. "That was so thoughtful."

I was immobile for weeks. Whenever I tried to move the pain was excruciating. Mutsch became my nurse, toiling without rest, tending to my every need. Obachan prepared my favourite foods. I could eat very little because whatever I did ingest wedged itself above the cast. As a result I lost weight. Soon, I realized the cast was too big, sliding up and down a few millimetres, adding to my discomfort.

Many of the army boys came to see me along with some of my girlfriends who hadn't yet left Japan. Jack was the most loyal and most attentive. He told me that several days after our accident there had been three other crashes on the same road, one occurring at the exact spot where we had gone off the road. The sandstone over which the roadway had been laid eroded during the rainy season. Consequently, the weight of the automobiles caused the road to give way.

No one in the Army investigated our accident and to our great relief the question of who was driving was never posed. Everyone assumed Jack had been. It was our secret.

To this day I regret pressuring Jack to teach me to drive. I caused a great deal of trouble for Jack, for the Japanese farmers who had helped me up to the road, for the medical staff at the hospital, and of course for Mutsch and Paps.

I didn't know it at the time but my carelessness on that day delayed our departure from Japan by almost three months. My convalescence was slow and gruelling. All the while I remained disgusted with myself. Because of me Paps would have to wait even longer for the specialized neurological care and treatment he needed to diminish his suffering.

My routine during those weeks was simple. Most days Paps had already left for work when I awoke. He would leave a note telling me that he had kissed my forehead, how much he loved me, and that he hoped I would have a good day. Then Mutsch would look in on me when she heard me stir. After a cheerful greeting, she would wash my face and hands and the parts of my body that weren't encased in plaster with cloths soaked in warm water. Obachan would bring breakfast into my room, a broad smile on her face and a tray of food always sporting a vase with an orchid—she knew it was my favourite flower. After eating I usually dozed for an hour or two. Then Mutsch would return, fluff my pillows, and ask if she could do anything for me. Most of the time we would just chat, reminiscing about our travels and envisioning what lay ahead for us in America.

Sometimes I would stare out my window at the farmers stopping with their wagons of fruits and vegetables. Obachan would be out front and centre, trading her handmade kimonos. Because of her we were never without beans, rice, herbs, carrots, and the like.

"Your father has received our visas. We'll leave Japan shortly!" Mutsch said excitedly one day.

"When will that be?" I asked.

"The Army doctor thinks that you'll be able to travel in fifteen to twenty days. So," she emphasized, "you must continue to rest."

Two weeks later I was startled awake by what I thought was the sound of thunder, a deep earth-shaking continuous rumbling. Then I heard the screech of brakes, doors opening and slamming shut, and voices. I looked outside. It was the Army. In front of our house were four jeeps, a half-track and an armoured personnel carrier. Dozens of soldiers were milling around. I saw Jack. He was talking to a Colonel.

I was terrified. They'd come for me! The secret was out! Everyone knew that I had been driving the jeep in violation of Army regulations. Jack will be court-martialled! I'll be imprisoned!

Mutsch came into my room.

"Mother, I'm so sorry," I moaned. "Now when they take me away I'll no longer be a nuisance to you."

She laughed. "What are you talking about?"

I stuttered. "The soldiers. The Colonel. They're here for me."

Mutsch's eyes opened wide, her mouth agape. "How did you know? Did Obachan tell you?"

Just then Jack burst into my room carrying a bouquet of roses.

"Jack, Jack," I begged, "forgive me. I . . ."

He was smiling. "Hey there, Ingi! It's good to see you. These are for you." It was one of the few times in my life that I was speechless. Jack handed me the flowers. Mutsch left the room. Then Paps came in.

"Father, you're missing work!" I cried even louder. "All because of me!"

He held my hand for a moment, kissed my forehead, and then walked out of my room.

"Stay right there," Jack said blowing me a kiss, "I'll be right back." He left.

Herr Griesbach and Arthur deCouto entered. They wished me well. Everything was happening so fast. They smiled and then turned away.

Uncle Hans and Aunt Eva tripped in. They brought me candies. They were talking to me but I couldn't focus on what they were saying. My mind was whirling, spinning like a propeller. They left the room.

I thought this was *mein Abschied*, my *au revoir*, my goodbye, and my *sayonara* just moments before I would be shackled, carried out of my house by the soldiers, like a broken piano, and then escorted to an Army penitentiary for the rest of my life.

Three of my girlfriends with whom I had spent many wonderful nights at the Officers' Club fumbled their way to the side of my bed. They were crying. I started crying. Then they went to the kitchen.

Mutsch and Paps returned. "Are you ready, Lorechen?" Mutsch asked.

I composed myself and breathed my last breath of freedom. "Yes, mother," I said stoically.

Then the party started.

And what a party it was!

Evidently, the Army doctor had told my parents that I was released from his care and permitted to travel. Paps had received our visas. I vaguely remember overhearing Paps tell Mutsch that Herr Griesbach had purchased tickets for travel on a ship called the *Marine Falcon*. While I was napping, Mutsch and Obachan would be busily packing, trying to be as quiet as mice. Everything was set. By the end of the month we would be on our way. We would sail across the Pacific to America, where we would arrive at a city called Seattle.

All the preparations for our departure had been done in secret so that I could rest and heal. So when the Army vehicles, the soldiers, my relatives, and my friends arrived all I could think was that it was time for me to atone for what I had done.

My *bon voyage* party lasted all afternoon. Jack arranged the extravaganza in concert with Paps, Mutsch, and our Army buddies. The soldiers brought a wealth of food and drink from the Post Exchange warehouse. A radio operator somehow set up his walkie-talkie so we could hear the music of Benny Goodman and Glenn Miller. Most of my former boyfriends, numerous male acquaintances, and other men I had danced with at the Officers' Club came by. Because I was bedridden only three or four people could comfortably arrange themselves around me. Everyone took turns. For most of the day I felt a bit like a living museum piece with curious visitors stopping by to observe. It was wonderful nonetheless.

Uncle Hans, Aunt Eva, Herr Griesbach, and Arthur deCouto left with tears in their eyes. Then came a procession of soldiers. Each one kissed me. I lost count of how many there were.

Jack was the last in line. He held my hand gently and stared into my eyes. "I can't ever forget you, Ingi," he said.

I was sad. "I won't ever forget you," I breathed. He kissed me on the lips. Then he was gone.

Paps, Mutsch, and Obachan came in. "Well," Mutsch asked, "have you had enough excitement for one day?"

I was comforted to the point of tears. "Yes, mother, I'm so grateful."

Paps said, "You've made a mark on the hearts of so many, Lorechen."

An hour went by. I had almost fallen asleep when I heard the rumbling of more Army vehicles. Mutsch yelled, "Oh my, the jeeps again!"

Yaniko had come to see me. She bowed and waved her hands several times as if to push away formality. She kissed me. When Fumichan arrived she did the same. She told me that she and some others from the warehouse had come to say their farewells. A few of the custodial staff peeked in, other sales people, then Imo.

When they stepped aside, Harold Grossinger was in my doorway.

"It's been a while," he said.

The last time I had seen Harold was the day before the accident. After a few days in the hospital and once I had regained a clear head, I was crestfallen when I realized that he hadn't come to see me. Initially, I was angry with him. When I was discharged from the hospital I expected him to come see me at home. When he didn't come I became worried. Did something happen to him? Why was he ignoring me? I alternated between feelings of exasperation and anxiety. Where is he?

"Yes," I replied, "a very long while."

Harold sat on the edge of my bed. We looked at each other for what seemed an eternity. Obachan came in to offer him tea, but he declined.

"I want to say something." His voice was tinged with regret. "I must explain why I haven't, why I wasn't . . ." He blew out his breath. "Look, Ingi, when I heard about what happened I was overwhelmed with worry. Word came that you were in a serious accident. A private told me that you had been run over by a jeep. I was about to rush to the hospital when I found out who you were with and my worry changed to . . ." He was near tears. ". . . I'm ashamed to say it. But I was hurt. It burned me up."

We were holding hands now. "I'm sorry, Harold," I said earnestly, "it was just a day out to drive around the countryside, nothing more."

"I had no right," he pronounced, "but I couldn't get the idea out of my head that you were with another man."

Even when contrite he was handsome.

"It was just a bit of fun," I said. "He was a boy with a jeep." I remembered the first time I had met Harold. Even then I knew in my heart that he would be a part of my life. I often thought that maybe there was a chance for us to be together as partners or at the very least lifelong friends. "Please, you don't have to defend yourself," I said.

He smiled. "I'm used to having my way with . . ." He stopped. "What I mean is I've been lucky with women. And then you came along. We had so much fun. We are so good together."

"Yes," I agreed, "we are. But we both know I'm leaving for the States soon. You're going to stay here. We'll be a world apart. More than anything I hope that we'll see each other again."

He stood up. "I'll go now, but remember this. In many ways I'll be with you always and you'll always be with me. Goodbye, darling."

I closed my eyes. He pressed his soft lips to mine. My heart was beating fast, blood rapidly coursing through my body. I nearly swooned.

When I opened my eyes he was gone.

Another Story Begins

October 1946

When I awoke the next morning Paps, Mutsch, and Obachan were in my room. I knew what was coming. I was about to lose another small piece of my heart.

"Repeat for Obachan everything I say now," Paps told me. "She must hear it in her own language so that she fully understands."

Mutsch held Obachan's hand as Paps spoke. I translated. "You've been our most faithful and loyal . . ." He stopped. He didn't want to use the word servant, she had been so much more to us. ". . . our most faithful and loyal friend. We're sad to leave you." He handed Obachan an envelope. "Take this as a small token of our appreciation that you remained with us during the times of trouble and that you shared times of joy and happiness with us. We'll miss you so very much."

The old woman looked inside. Paps had enclosed a thick wad of yen banknotes tied with string. Obachan froze when she saw how many there were. She burst into tears.

"This," she stammered, "this is not–."

Paps interrupted her. I spoke his words. "–That's the least we can do. There is enough money there for you to return to your family and relatives, to make life somewhat more comfortable for yourself and also for them if you choose to do so."

Mutsch handed her a basket. Inside was Muschi. "Please take good care of Lorechen's cat?" Obachan promised she would. She bowed to each of us and then stood tiptoe to kiss Paps on his chin. Mutsch embraced her. I put my fingertips to my lips and then tossed my hand aside. She knew what I meant. Then she did the same to me.

"I will not forget you," she said, "You are wonderful. I will remember you forever." She left my room.

Obachan picked up a rice sack that contained all her belongings: a few pieces of clothing and dozens of needles and countless spools of thread. They were the only things of value that she possessed. Then she bowed again and left our house, crying uncontrollably.

Paps' travel-weary valise bulged with the additional clothing he had acquired during our stay in Japan. Mutsch's torn suitcase was full. My tattered rucksack was plump. After a decade I still had something of Gerta's with me. I had wrapped Frau Beck's bracelet in its rice paper and tied it with its blue ribbon before placing it in my bag.

In the early afternoon, Paps brought a tray of food to me that Obachan had prepared earlier that day. It was filled with plates of tasty vegetables and rice and of course a small vase with an orchid in it. Obachan never forgot. We readied for our last meal in Kobe. Paps said prayers and Mutsch and I held hands.

Later, a large black car and an Army ambulance drove up to our house, clouds of dust billowing behind them. Herr Griesbach exited from the rear passenger compartment of the car. Two soldiers and the Army doctor who had cared for me got out of the ambulance.

They all crowded into my bedroom: Herr Griesbach, the Army doctor, Paps, Mutsch, and the two soldiers. "I'll give you a sedative," the doctor said. "It'll make travelling a little easier for you. The drive to Yokohama may be uncomfortable. For the most part the roads are bumpy. This will help." He rummaged through his bag. Everyone else went into the living room.

I began to feel drowsy. The last thing I remember is the soldiers carefully picking me up and placing me on a gurney and wheeling me out to the ambulance. Mutsch climbed in beside me as the soldiers placed our baggage in the car. Paps must have ridden with the soldiers and Herr Griesbach. From then on everything was foggy.

I don't remember how long it took to drive from Kobe to Yokohama. Mutsch held my hand the entire way. When we arrived, the ambulance stopped and the doctor and the soldier got out.

Then I fell asleep again. When I came to I was in a hospital bed, frightened to find myself there. Paps calmed me. "Everything's okay, Lorechen. We're on board the ship, in the infirmary. Mutsch, the Army doctor, and the ship's doctor are discussing what's required for your care before we leave. Are you all right?"

"Yes, father," I said.

I felt the ship tremble and then I heard the engines come to life. A whistle blew. I sensed movement. We were on our way. Mutsch came to my bed. Then I dozed off again.

Still sleepy, I heard Paps talking to Mutsch. "Dr. Hoke is the ship's physician. He'll be here shortly to meet Lorechen and talk to her about her care." I found myself impatiently wondering when someone would remove this dreaded cast!

"My dear, Lorechen," Mutsch said, "while you were napping your father and I were on deck. The sunset behind us was magnificent. The ship has left the harbour and we're sailing on the open ocean. We're on our way to America."

The news from Dr. Hoke was disappointing. He told me my cast wouldn't be removed until I was released from his care in Seattle. There he would make arrangements for a stateside colleague of his to do the procedure in an office not far from the harbour.

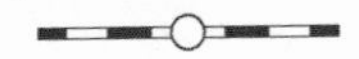

The three of us had been pursued by wolves for so long, our faith and our heritage a shadow that stretched across the world. Our voyage had always taken us east, toward a sunrise, toward the hope and promise of a new day. And so we followed the sun one more time.

Epilogue

Ingelore arrived in the United States on 28 October 1946. Reminiscing many decades later, she related that her voyage from Japan to America aboard the *Marine Falcon* was memorable. At the outset she relished the excitement of finally "going home" and she remembered sailing across the Pacific toward a vivid sunrise every day.

The trip was dampened by the fact she was confined to the infirmary. While convalescing there she forged a close camaraderie with the ship's Navy nurse, a woman named Pat, who had taken very good care of her. A few hours after the *Falcon* put into port in Seattle a physician, who was a colleague of Dr. Hoke, removed her cast. Ingelore recalled that the doctor's office was in a tall building that overlooked the beautiful Seattle harbour. While there her father quickly fell in love with the city and he vowed to return for a visit someday and perhaps to settle in the area. This was not to be.

After the cast was removed Ingelore was given a pair of crutches with strict instructions not to walk without them. She was still in a great deal of pain. And even with her crutches she could not walk! She was very weak and for quite some time she suffered from lightheadedness and vertigo as well as nausea whenever she stood—the result of having been bedridden for so long.

From Seattle, Kurt, Doris, and Ingelore travelled east across the United States by train, arriving in New York City five days later. The trip was

Clockwise from top left: Harold (front, centre) with his flight crew in Corsica, 1944; Ingelore, on her wedding day, with Doris and a bridesmaid, 19 October 1947; Ingelore in front of the Brandenburg Gates, 1989; Harold, Ingelore, Doris, and Kurt at Ingelore's wedding, two years before Kurt's death.

taxing for Ingelore, both physically and emotionally. She found it difficult and uncomfortable to sit on the swaying train and standing with crutches was too painful and precarious. For most of the trip, Paps and Mutsch took turns describing the landscapes to her. Eventually, she adapted to the crutches and the pain subsided. She bragged that after a while she was able to run with her crutches! After seeing some of the scenery for herself, she promised to explore the entirety of America someday, from north to south and from east to west. Many years later, travelling extensively with her husband after retirement, she did.

Once they reached New York City Ingelore's greatest concern was for her father's condition. His headaches, once intermittent, now were constant and much more severe. They settled in Flushing, Queens, New York, and soon after Mutsch made arrangements for her husband to undergo tests at a New York City hospital. The diagnosis presented earlier in Japan was confirmed. Kurt had a cancerous brain tumour. The prognosis was grim.

Ingelore never forgave herself for the jeep accident. She believed that her three-month convalescence in Japan not only had delayed Kurt's medical treatment but also had allowed the tumour time to grow. The doctors assured her that her father's cancer most likely began to develop when he was a teenager and that the slight delay in their travel was not related to the seriousness of his present condition. Nevertheless feelings of guilt tortured her for most of her life. "Had it not been for my foolhardiness," she often would lament, "then perhaps something could have been done sooner to save my father's life."

An operation was scheduled to remove Kurt's tumour. By a strange coincidence, one of the attendants on the hospital floor was the *Falcon*'s nurse, Pat. She had been discharged from the Navy and had gone to live with relatives in Manhattan. Ingelore called Pat an "angel incarnate" since she had taken care of her on the *Falcon* and now was tending to Kurt in the hospital. As Kurt had told his young daughter a long time ago, there is so much good in so many people.

Kurt's operation left him partially paralyzed and unable to speak and think clearly. After months of physical therapy and with the aid of a leg brace, he was able to walk slowly but not without great pain. Ingelore was amazed at her father's almost superhuman determination. Despite his challenges, he taught himself to use his left hand to write and do other daily tasks.

From the moment Kurt left the hospital, Doris devoted herself to helping her husband live as normal a life as possible. Every day, no matter what the weather, she succeeded in getting him down a flight of stairs and out for a walk, at first in a wheelchair and later with the aid of a cane. Doris exercised his limbs, massaged his sore legs, fed him the most nourishing meals she could concoct, and supported him in his quest to get well. Nothing was too much for her.

When he was unable to squeeze a little rubber ball with his right hand, an exercise prescribed by his therapist, or when he had trouble recalling a word, he would often lose his temper. But Doris always remained calm. Ingelore recalled an incident when in the grips of frustration, her father lost control. He tried to throw a chair at Doris but Ingelore wrested it away from him at the last moment. When he calmed down, he burst into tears. Ingelore heard him say, "I don't know what's happening to me." Doris, caressing his wrist, replied, "It's all right, dearest, you'll soon be better."

Of the many people who helped the Rothschilds prepare to leave Berlin until their arrival in America, George Griesbach certainly was their most committed benefactor. As one of the three founders of the J. Gerber Company, George had hired a young Kurt at the Berlin office, Kurt's first meaningful employment. Later, Griesbach's connections and his altruism provided Kurt and his family not only the opportunity to leave Germany safely but also a new position in the Kobe office in Japan. According to the *Marine Falcon*'s manifest, Griesbach paid for the family's transport. Once in America, Kurt again worked for the company in New York City.

After Kurt's operation, even though he was never the same, Griesbach provided employment, keeping a place for Kurt at the office for those days when he felt well enough to work.

Not long after the surgery, Kurt suffered a debilitating stroke and his ability to continue in his position was irreversibly compromised. Yet again Griesbach came to his aid, giving Kurt a monthly salary. This went on for years. And when Kurt died in December 1949, it was George who continued to help support Mutsch.

From the time she left Japan, Ingelore and Harold Grossinger never lost touch, managing to maintain contact via letters. Although his dream was to remain in Japan, Grossinger returned to America sometime after his discharge and settled in the New York City area. They rekindled their friendship. Eventually, Harold Grossinger did marry, and he and his wife Faye would often visit Ingelore and her family in Ossining.

Ironically, the love of Ingelore's life was named Harold but it was not Harold Grossinger. Harold Stahl was a friend of Grossinger's and a veteran as well so both had much in common. Harold Stahl served in Europe with the 1st Emergency Rescue Squadron. Its mission was to patrol the seas and rescue downed Allied pilots. Based in Ajaccio, Corsica, he flew more than a dozen missions over the Ligurian Sea off the coast of Genoa, Italy, which at the time remained occupied by the Nazis.

The encounter between Ingelore, a twenty-two-year-old German immigrant, and Harold, a US Army Air Force veteran, was casual but auspicious. Something clicked and Ingelore Rothschild and Harold Stahl were married on 19 October 1947.

Word never came from Berlin. After Ingelore reluctantly accepted that many of her relatives and friends had been corralled by the Nazis or had perished during the Allied bombing raids of her birth city, she silently grieved for many years. She never learned that her paternal grandparents, Leopold and Hedwig Rothschild, died at Auschwitz. She felt a tremendous sense of loss for the friends and acquaintances of whom she was most fond, notably Gerta Klaus, Katya, Frau Beck, Herr Bayern, Inga Goldman, and Adah Metzger—their whereabouts unknown.

From the moment Ingelore arrived in Japan in 1936, at the age of twelve, she swore she never again would set foot on German soil. She kept that vow for over half a century. But in 1989, she and Harold went to Berlin to celebrate the ninetieth birthday of her Uncle Hans, Kurt's brother. She cherished her reunion with him for the rest of her life.

While living in Flushing, Harold Stahl worked in New York City in the garment industry. He was very successful. In November 1949 they were blessed with a daughter. The family moved to Bayside where a son was born in April 1953. The family moved again in 1957 to Lee Avenue in Ossining, in Westchester County, New York.

Uncle Sieke often visited his niece and her family at their Lee Avenue home. Ingelore's daughter, Darilyn, vividly recalls one visit in particular. She remembers Sieke seated across from her in the backyard of her childhood home on a warm summer's day, his short-sleeved shirt revealing to the young girl, for the first time, the blue numbers tattooed on his forearm. It was a startling symbol of his suffering and a reminder of the persecution the family had faced not so long ago.

Ingelore and Harold would often visit Uncle Hans and Aunt Evchen, the Mendelsohns. They lived in a beautiful home in Peekskill, New York. Their yard displayed magnificent gardens in the Japanese style complete with an assortment of orchids and a waterfall. The Mendelsohns never did have children and their affection for Ingelore never waned.

Many years later the Stahl family relocated to an area in Ossining called Stillwater Lake. Their home was also decorated in the Japanese style.

Harold Stahl died on Wednesday 1 June 2006 of an intestinal aneurysm. He and Ingelore had been married fifty-eight years.

Ingelore Erna Rothschild Stahl, failing to thrive, died precisely thirteen weeks to the day after her husband on Wednesday 31 August 2006. She was eighty-two years old.

Bibliography

Benz, Wolfgang. *A Concise History of the Third Reich*. Berkeley: University of California Press, 2006.

Bracher, Karl Dietrich. *The German Dictatorship: The Origins, Structure, and Effects of National Socialism*. Translated by Jean Steinberg. New York: Praeger Publishers, 1971.

Burden, Hamilton T. *The Nuremberg Party Rallies 1923–1939*. New York: Praeger, 1968.

Crozier, Brian. *The Rise and Fall of the Soviet Empire*. Rocklin: Prima Publishing, 1999.

Feinstein, Elaine. *Pushkin: A Biography*. Hopewell: Ecco Press, 1998.

Fischer, Klaus P. *Nazi Germany: A New History*. New York: Continuum, 1995.

Fowler, Glenn. "Joachim Prinz, Leader in Protests For Civil-Rights Causes, Dies at 86," *New York Times*, 1 October 1988.

Friedrich, Otto. *Before the Deluge: A Portrait of Berlin in the 1920s*. New York: Avon Books, 1972.

Gordon, Andrew. *A Modern History of Japan: From Tokugawa Times to the Present*. New York: Oxford University Press, 2003.

Kubo, Keiko. *Keiko's Ikebana: A Contemporary Approach to the Traditional Japanese Art of Flower Arranging*. North Clarendon: Tuttle Publishing, 2006.

Lewis, Martin W. "Why Russian Jews Are Not Russian." *GeoCurrents*. January 21, 2011. http://www.geocurrents.info/cultural-geography/why-russian-jews-are-not-russian.

Mahlendorf, Ursula. *The Shame of Survival: Working Through a Nazi Childhood*. University Park: Pennsylvania State University Press, 2009.

McClain, James L. *Japan: A Modern History*. New York: W.W. Norton, 2002.

Medvedev, Roy. *Let History Judge: The Origins and Consequences of Stalin*. New York: Columbia University Press, 1989.

Shirer, William. *The Rise and Fall of the Third Reich: A History of Nazi Germany*. New York: Simon and Schuster, 1960.

Shlapentokh, Vladimir. "Putin's Jewish Anomaly Comes as a Surprise." *The Moscow Times*. 6 February 2008.

Vogt, Hannah. *The Burden of Guilt: A Short History of Germany 1914–1945*. Translated by Herbert Strauss. New York: Oxford University Press, 1965.

Washburn, Katharine, and John S. Major, eds. *World Poetry: An Anthology of Verse from Antiquity to Our Time*. Selection translated by John Frederick Nims. New York: W. W. Norton, 1997.